# HealthCare Lean

## The Team Guide to
## Continuous Improvement

How to Create
The Exceptional Client Experience &
Magnet Organization through Lean Teams

By
Lawrence M. Miller

Copyright, Lawrence M. Miller, 2012
Annapolis, Maryland, 21401
www.ManagementMeditations.com
LMMiller@lmmiller.com

All rights reserved. No part of this book may be reproduced or transmitted in any form or by any means, electronic or mechanical, including photocopying, recording, or by any information storage and retrieval system, without permission in writing from the author or publisher.

Published by
Miller Management Press, LLC
ISBN Number: 978-0-578-10778-3

# Table of Contents

Forward — 5
Introduction — 7
    Chapter 1: Revolution or Evolution — 13
    Chapter 2: Action Learning: How We Change Habits — 21

Part One: Getting Organized
    Chapter 3: What is Lean? Principles and Purpose — 31
    Chapter 4: Writing Your Team's Charter — 45
    Chapter 5: Organizing Your Team — 57
    Chapter 6: Stages of team development — 73
    Chapter 7: Clarifying Decision Styles — 79
    Chapter 8: Standard Work — 85
    Chapter 9: Customer & Client Requirements — 93
    Chapter 10: Your Team Scorecard — 105

Part Two: Improving Performance
    Chapter 11: Solving Problems — 119
    Chapter 12: Motivation and Human Performance — 143
    Chapter 13: Mapping Your Value Stream — 163
    Chapter 14: Analyze Variances — 181
    Chapter 15: Eliminate Waste — 193

Part Three: Improving Teamwork
    Chapter 16: Leading Effective Meetings — 207
    Chapter 17: Effective Listening Skills — 225
    Chapter 18: Giving and Receiving Feedback — 237
    Chapter 19: Dialogue: Thinking Together — 245
    Chapter 20: Improving Team Dynamics — 259

Glossary — 274
Index — 281
About the Author — 283

# FORWARD

VON Canada is a 115 year old home health care service organization with a rich history of serving communities across Canada. Lady Aberdeen founded the Victorian Order of Nurses by recognizing the needs of women to have care in their homes for childbirth, care for ill children and general health care. Our legacy is caring for people in their homes and in the community.

Over the past years VON has faced a number of challenges due to the changing landscape of health care in Canada, the need to eliminate wasteful bureaucracy, and the need to attract and retain the best nursing and health care staff. VON is rising to this challenge by creating a new culture of continuous improvement. HealthCare Lean is giving all staff a common lens and way to manage our organization.

I have had the honor and privilege of leading the Health Care Service Delivery project at VON Canada, introducing the organization to Lean thinking, and the concept of Whole-System Architecture. Using Lean principles and tools, focusing on client and customer needs, and listening carefully to our staff, we co-created with staff and our customers a service delivery change that has resulted in a culture change, reduced errors and waste, better outcomes and much greater satisfaction from our funders, clients and staff. The elimination of waste has freed our managers to devote their energies to truly value-adding work – delivering safe and high quality health care.

The results have been dramatic. For example, we have seen the time required to schedule a nurse's visit drop from an average of five hours to approximately five minutes. Key performance indicators such as referral acceptance, missed visits, continuity of service and others have all shown significant improvement. And, equally important, managers and staff are enjoying their work more than before.

I want to thank Larry Miller for his sage counsel and friendship throughout this process. Both the more dramatic whole-system architecture process and the more gradual continuous improvement process have worked at VON. With the transformation of the health care service delivery process and the introduction of lean culture and management at VON I believe the sky is the limit for VON's future.

Sharon Goodwin RN(EC) MN DHA (c)
Vice President, Quality & Risk
Chief Practice Executive
VON Canada

# INTRODUCTION

There are many models of excellent health care service and they have a few elements in common.

The Mayo Clinic has long been a model of superior health care service. Their core competence has been described as "teamwork."[1] A recent book on the Mayo Clinic described their culture this way:

> "Mayo Clinic is a collaborative organization, a pliable institution that assembles the expert care teams for individual patients. Imagine a huge store that sells everything, with experts in every department who work together to help customers. This is how Mayo Clinic is designed for medical customers. Patients don't get just a doctor; they get, in effect, the 'whole company.' Some patients see more than one Clinic physician. Typically, the first doctor to treat a patient is responsible for coordinating the care plan with other Mayo clinicians and the patient's hometown physician."[2]

Teamwork at the Mayo Clinic is not optional. It is the system you join when you agree to work there. One of the Clinic's doctors described it this way. "The Mayo culture attracts individuals who see and practice medicine best delivered when there is an integration of medical specialties functioning as a team. It is what we do best and most of us love to do it."[3]

But the Mayo Clinic is not alone in this regard. As *lean management* becomes more prominent in healthcare the emphasis on teamwork and continuous improvement will become the new normal. ThedaCare, a four hospital healthcare system in Wisconsin has become a model for lean management implementation in healthcare. Here is how they describe their new normal process:

> "Instead of responding to hierarchy and heroically firefighting in an environment of shame and blame, Collaborative Care teams now meet in daily huddles to review any issue with patients or work flows. When problems arise such as a medication error or a patient fall, team members use PDSA (plan, do, study, act) cycles to determine what happened, find a corrective plan,

---

[1] Berry, Leanard L., Seltman, Kent D. *Management Lessons from May Clinic.* McGraw Hill, New York, 2008, p.49.
[2] Ibid. p. 50.
[3] Ibid. p. 52.

implement it, and study the results on the process. Teams then create new standard work or if the change did not achieve the desired results, the PDSA cycle begins again."[4]

It is not hard to see why the future success of your health care organization will require a culture of teamwork, processes designed and improved by teams, and primary care teams whose focus is on how to provide the best possible care to their clients. To the degree that we can all work together, seamlessly, without interruptions, walls or silos between groups, we will meet the needs of those who matter most – our clients. That is the purpose of the workbook.

The team in an organization is like the family in a society. It is the fundamental building block of trust and competence. Lean organizations are a social system, a culture, as well as a technical system. At the heart of that social system is the team.

The term "lean" is one you will hear often. It originated in a study of the world's best manufacturing organizations, particularly the auto assembly plants of Toyota and Honda. A group at MIT studied the differences between those auto plants producing the highest quality cars and achieving the greatest efficiency, versus those who were not. They called these "lean plants" because the term "lean" implied the elimination of unnecessary activities. And, here is what they found at the heart of those plants.

> "What are the truly important organizational features of a lean plant - the specific aspects of plant operations that account for up to half of the overall performance differences among plants across the world? The truly lean plant has two key organizational features: It transfers the maximum number of tasks and responsibilities to those workers actually adding value to the car on the line, and it has in place a system for detecting defects that quickly traces every problem, once discovered, to its ultimate cause....So in the end, *it is the dynamic work team that emerges as the heart of the lean factory.*"[5]

It is important to know that after more than forty years of practice at lean manufacturing, Toyota managers and front-line employees are everyday seeking to find ways to improve how they do their work. They are still on the journey to find the ideal way to build cars.

---

[4] Toussaint, John, Gerard, Roger A., and Adams, Emily. *On the Mend: Revolutionizing Healthcare to Save Lives and Transform the Industry.* Lean Enterprise Institute, Cambridge, MA. 2010. P.28.
[5] Womack, J.P., Jones, D. T., and Roos D. *The Machine That Changed the World.* New York: Rawson Associates, 1990, P. 99.

The process described in this manual has two goals in addition to improving client service. This process will build a foundation to become a *Magnet* health care organization. Creating a culture and the skills of teamwork are essential to both of these goals.

The Magnet healthcare concept began with the recognition that there was an inadequate availability of nurses and nurses tended to change jobs frequently. However, researchers found that certain hospitals did not have this problem. For some reason they were able to act as a "magnet" attracting and retaining quality nurses. In addition, these hospitals were known to be excellent at care delivery and acted as "magnets" to patients seeking to receive care. This research then identified the characteristics of these magnet organizations.

The first magnet hospitals were found to be places where nurses had autonomy and control over their practice settings; good relationships with their colleagues; adequate support services; enough staff to provide high quality care; time to discuss patient problems with their colleagues; the opportunity to participate in policy decisions; a powerful nursing leader; and an environment that recognized the value of their work. Hospitals with these characteristics had significantly lower staff turnover and attracted well-qualified and committed staff.[6] Not surprisingly, the care delivered in these magnet hospitals was superior as well.

It has long been understood that there is a relationship between job satisfaction and retention of staff. A study of nursing work environments highlighted the relationship between the work environment of nurses and their trust in the management of their organization.

> "The results of this study support the proposition that features of nursing work environments such as autonomy, control over the practice environment, and collaboration with physicians have an impact on staff nurses trust in management and ultimately influence nurses' job satisfaction and their assessment of patient care quality. The results suggest that both trust in management and emotional exhaustion are important mediators of job satisfaction and perceptions of quality. These findings highlight the importance of creating environments which empower nurses to accomplish their work and generate positive feelings about their work and its effects on patient outcomes."[7]

---

[6] "Magnet Hospitals: What's the Attraction?" Fiona Armstrong in the Australian Nursing Journal; March 2005.

[7] *"Impact of Magnet Hospital Characteristics on Nurses' Perceptions of Trust, Burnout, Quality of Care, and Work Satisfaction."* Heather K. Spence Laschinger, Judith Shamian, Donna Thomson. Nursing Economics, Vol.19/No. 5. October, 2001.

In other words, the ability of health care workers to exert control on their environment is directly related to trust, satisfaction and the quality of care. This is exactly consistent with the idea that workers in a manufacturing setting, when respected for their work, given the control and ability to improve their work, will produce better cars or any other product. This is an essential philosophy of the Toyota Production System, or lean manufacturing.

Another pursuit that is related to the development of effective teamwork is the movement toward population based holistic care. This population based care model will require health care professionals to practice teamwork.

> "A predominant focus of population-based health care is health promotion and disease prevention. Many vulnerable populations have chronic health problems. They may seek medical care only when they absolutely have to, however, and by that time, the chronic condition has not only exacerbated, it may be confounded by new acute conditions. Population based nursing care is holistic in nature, with nurses attempting to understand the client from a variety of perspectives, including socio-economic, cultural, racial, religious, gender, abilities, and sexual affiliation. The application of the nursing process greatly assists the nurse in providing holistic care on the community, health system, and population levels."[8]

> "Population based care is the 'development, provision and evaluation of the multidisciplinary health care services to population groups experiencing increased health risks or disparities.' Population based care works closely and collaboratively with community and health care team members who make up a community."[9]

It must be obvious that providing this type of health care intervention is not something done by individual practitioners alone. Rather, it requires close collaboration, teamwork, among a group of professionals who may work for a number of different organizations, as well as collaboration with members of the community to be served. It is not a process of the expert dictating the remedy. That will not work. It will require the skills of dialogue and teamwork. The skills learned in this manual are essential skills for us to move into a new era of more collaborative service delivery based on the needs, not only of individuals, but of focused populations in our communities.

---

[8] Polifko-Harris, Karin. *Applications in Nursing Leadership & Management.* Thomson-Delmar Learning, 2004. P. 39.
[9] Ibid. p. 40.

# Introduction

The parent of lean management is the total quality management movement. The work of Dr. Deming, Juran and Shewart all influenced the development of the Toyota Production System. The importance of quality management, the reduction of errors, cannot be overemphasized in the healthcare environment. Errors, delays, and poor processes not only can kill patients, but they do kill patients.

"The Institute of Medicine's 1999 report *To Err Is Human* estimated that 44,000 to 98,000 Americans die in hospitals each year from preventable medical errors. Despite the widespread attention this report received, little progress has been made. The Fourth Annual Patient Safety in American Hospitals Study, released by HealthGrades in April 2007, found that 1.16 million preventable patient safety incidents for Medicare-covered hospitalizations occurred between 2003 and 2005, at a cost of $8.6 billion. The total patient safety incident rate in 2005 had two more incidents per 1,000 hospitalizations than in 2003, according to the study. The 2006 Institute of Medicine report Preventing Medication Errors stated that the way in which medications are prescribed, administered, and taken harms 1.5 million people each year at a cost of $3.5 billion."[10]

These conditions extract a huge cost to the entire healthcare industry as well as endangering patients. Lean practices absolutely will reduce errors and save lives if properly applied. Just as the quality of every car sold in the world has dramatically improved over the past twenty years, the quality and safety of health care will equally improve.

Why? If you follow the method in this workbook every employee, from top to bottom of your organization will be on a natural work team that will take responsibility for continually improve the process for which they are responsible. Every team will maintain a scorecard that will include safety, customer satisfaction, and other key measures. Every team will meet regularly to discuss how to improve their work, on-the-spot, and in real time. They will experience the joy of feeling like a genuine team, winning their game of continuous improvement. This is not a theory. It has been proven over and over again, in healthcare as well as manufacturing and other industries.

This manual is an attempt to present the most essential practices and skills of effective teams. It is intended for teams at every level of the organization. It is based on both best practices in lean organizations, Magnet health care organization and the history of self-directed or high performance teams.

---

[10] Land, Trudy and Stefl, Mary E. Healthcare Financial Management, July, 2007

# Chapter 1

# Revolution or Evolution?

I was speaking at a Toyota supplier's conference a few years back and observed a presentation by the president of one of Toyota's U.S. suppliers. He was a young man and a bit nervous in his presentation. He had been offered help by Toyota and was visibly shaken from the experience. Toyota has an internal consulting group that works with their suppliers. This group is made up of highly experienced lean experts, experts in the Toyota Production System.

This young president described how the Toyota change agents had required that he would give them free reign in his plant and would stand to the side while they redesigned the work flow and job assignments. They shut the plant down for about one week. He stood by in horror as the Toyota engineers literally ripped his equipment out of the floor, re-arranged every piece of gear, changed the flow of the work and redefined the jobs of everyone in the plant, including himself! It was not what he regarded as a warm and fuzzy experience.

At lunch I sat with these Toyota consultants and discussed how they go about their work. For many years I had been implementing change in the processes and culture of organizations, but this conversation made me question my own methods. I explained to them that when I go into a client organization I ask the senior managers to form a steering committee and write a charter for change that defines the goals, principles, boundaries, etc. I then form design teams of frontline employees and managers and I then facilitate the process by which they redesign both their technical system (work flow) and their social system that includes how decisions are made, the organization structure, teams, sources of motivation, etc.

They looked puzzled. They asked me why I would ask them to redesign their own work. I explained that in our culture it was important to gain "buy-in" and commitment. Then, one of these Japanese engineers looked at me and said rather forcefully and unapologetically, "But, they don't know! We do know! Asking them would be useless."

It took me a while to put this in perspective. Clearly, these Toyota manufacturing engineers did know. They knew how to layout the equipment and assign work in a plant that bends metal, repetitively, every day. But, at the same time the owner of the company was still traumatized by the event.

This was NOT continuous improvement. This was radical, revolutionary, and whole-system change, imposed from outside the organization. I am still looking for the client who will allow me to walk in and say "I know and you don't, so just do what I tell you." In our culture, and particularly in health care in which most of the "workers" are well educated and highly motivated, you must engage them in the co-creation of change, even when it is revolutionary change. Health care is not bending metal in a highly repetitive process. It requires careful evaluation of every client that passes through the health care process, customized therapies, and it demands the full understanding and engagement of every care provider.

Many health care organizations today are in need of revolutionary change, but it must be a revolution that is created from within.

## WHOLE-SYSTEM ARCHITECTURE

There are two types of change that can lead to lean processes and lean culture. One is "Whole-System Architecture" in which you step back and consider the entire system of the organization and ask fundamental questions. Why do we do this process at all? What is our core work? How does this add value? You consider the current state and design the future state of both the technical system, the work flow, and the social system that surrounds and enables that work flow. Too many lean implementations are focused solely on the technical system and fail to redesign the social system. The problems in organizations are more likely to be the result of a social system that fails to encourage innovation, teamwork and open dialogue then any particular failure of a work process.

Whole-System Architecture presents a useful metaphor. When you walk into a great cathedral your head goes back and you look up into the heavens of stained glass and flying buttresses. You marvel at the construction. And your first impulse is to focus on the physical thing of the structure. But, the architect had an end in mind. The architect understood that the nature of physical space, the interior structure of the cathedral, has an effect on the human spirit, emotions, and possibly behavior. And, so too does the structure of your organization. But in most cases the effect is unintentional and often stifling, rather than uplifting of the human spirit. We must become architects of our organizations to promote the spirit of service to customers and the habits of innovation.

Changing the culture means changing "real stuff" that drives behavior. One way of addressing these is to address the 5S's of any organization – **Structure, Systems, Skills, Style** and **Symbols**. These five S's should not be confused with the 5S's that are most often promoted to create an orderly workplace. While those are important, they do not address the most important things that drive the culture.

You cannot fix the work processes unless you fix the culture. All current deficiencies in your work process are derived from cultural assumptions and behavior. The root cause is the culture, and particularly the culture of management.

The basic structure of organizations often creates silos that prevent teamwork. The purpose of organization structure is to enhance the flow of work, not to inhibit that flow. How are medical teams organized? Are they organized by specialty, by geography, by patient population? Is there only one team structure or are their multiple structures that promote different types of knowledge sharing and decision-making? Structure matters. Most continuous improvement efforts attempt to work within existing structures and fail to ask

## Types of Change

| Whole-System Architecture | Continuous Improvement |
|---|---|
| - Revolutionary/re-engineering | - Evolutionary |
| - Rethinking the whole system to create stability. | - Change within a stable system. |
| - Big and rapid change to create major improvements. | - Gradual, small improvements. |
| - Changes in both work system and social system. | - Generally changes in work process. |
| - Must begin and end with the customer/client view. | - May be internally focused or customer focused. |
| - Involve all stakeholders including the customer. | - Generally involves those who directly do the work. |
| **This is required now to respond with urgency.** | **This will be required after major change.** |

fundamental questions about the nature of our organizations.

The systems of information flow are similar to the nervous system in the body, constantly sending messages that trigger behavior and emotions. The systems of hiring, reward and recognition, promotion, training and development, budgeting and sharing financial information all drive performance. Who designed these systems? When they did, what was their intention or philosophy? Were they designed to maximize decision-making ability of front line care providers? Were they designed to promote teamwork? Do they reinforce experimentation and continuous improvement? It is likely that they do not. And, it is even more likely that they were each designed by experts in IT, HR or Finance who were focused on their expert knowledge, and not focused on achieving the outcome of superior patient care. They were not integrated as a whole-system with common purpose and principles. They are most likely "dis-integrated" and misaligned and that is the cause of a huge amount of waste in our organizations.

The purpose of whole system change is to align the systems, structure and other factors to promote teamwork and continuous improvement, to knock down the walls that interrupt flow and create delays and waste. All systems should be aligned to serve the needs of patients or clients.

You can think of Whole-System Architecture as "Macro Lean." And it should generally come before the process of continuous improvement. But, we aren't always that smart and we discover the need for changes in systems and structure along the path of continuous improvement.

# Implementing Lean Health Care

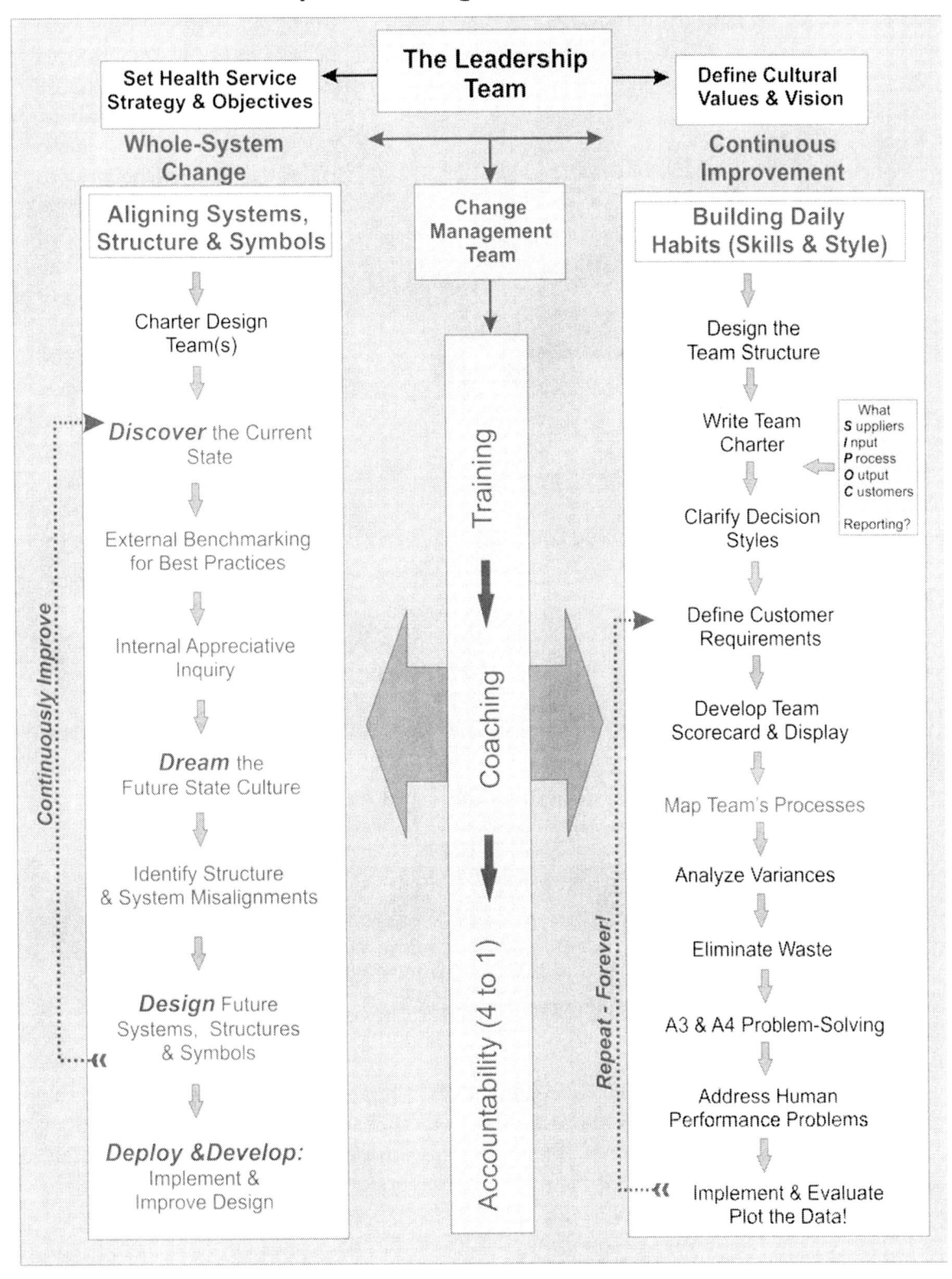

**The Leadership Team**

Set Health Service Strategy & Objectives ← → Define Cultural Values & Vision

**Whole-System Change** | **Continuous Improvement**

Change Management Team

## Aligning Systems, Structure & Symbols

- Charter Design Team(s)
- *Discover* the Current State
- External Benchmarking for Best Practices
- Internal Appreciative Inquiry
- *Dream* the Future State Culture
- Identify Structure & System Misalignments
- *Design* Future Systems, Structures & Symbols
- *Deploy & Develop:* Implement & Improve Design

*Continuously Improve*

## Building Daily Habits (Skills & Style)

- Design the Team Structure
- Write Team Charter
- Clarify Decision Styles
- Define Customer Requirements
- Develop Team Scorecard & Display
- Map Team's Processes
- Analyze Variances
- Eliminate Waste
- A3 & A4 Problem-Solving
- Address Human Performance Problems
- Implement & Evaluate Plot the Data!

What
**S**uppliers
**I**nput
**P**rocess
**O**utput
**C**ustomers

Reporting?

Training · Coaching · Accountability (4 to 1)

*Repeat - Forever!*

At VON Canada it was critical that a whole-system change was undertaken prior to instituting the practices of continuous improvement described in the following chapters. There had been prior improvement efforts, but those efforts were conducted inside the walls of functional silos and no team was empowered to knock down the walls and focus the flow of work on the needs of clients and customers. Managers were often frustrated and felt helpless to create change. In the new organization, teams are organized to manage the process from the moment a funder calls with a request for service through to the completion of that service. Responsibility is unified and the time wasted in resolving conflicts and errors has been dramatically reduced. Now the managers can focus on what they were trained to do – provide great care to clients.

**The Old Way:**
**The VON The Core Work Process Creating Interruptions and Delays**

**The New Way**
**The VON Core Work Process**
**Promoting Teamwork and Continuous Improvement**

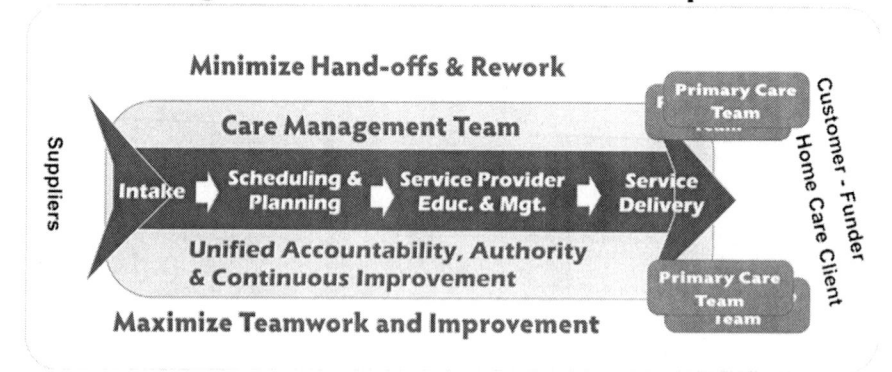

A critical component of Whole-System Architecture is the psychology of co-creation. In numerous organizations I have had design teams go visit with their customers or ask their customers to come meet with the design team. The customers are simply asked, "How can we better meet your needs? What changes would you like to see in how we serve you?" No customer has ever objected to this question. The second question is, "Will you give us feedback on the process we redesign to be sure that it meets your needs?" They always answer "Yes." The act of engaging the customer in the design of the process that will serve them is the best "sales call" your organization will ever make. It never fails. When they feel that you are listening to them and changing to meet their needs, they will support your efforts and feel a greater bond with your organization.

The exact same psychology of co-creation is true with employees and managers in all functions. When the managers of any group in any organization seek to listen and design their work to meet the needs of their customers, they will immediately gain greater support from those customers. It never fails.

I worked with a major Southern university to redesign all of their business services that served both their hospital complex and their academic departments and student body. At the outset, these two major groups of customers both were extremely dissatisfied with the services they received from human resources, information technology, property management, and financial services. I encouraged them to listen deeply to their customer's expression of their needs, rather than their own assumptions and belief in their own expertise. They went out and interviewed the Chairs of each academic department and the leaders of each department or function in the hospital complex. They then not only redesigned each of their core processes to better meet their customer's

## University Campus and Hospital Center Business Services

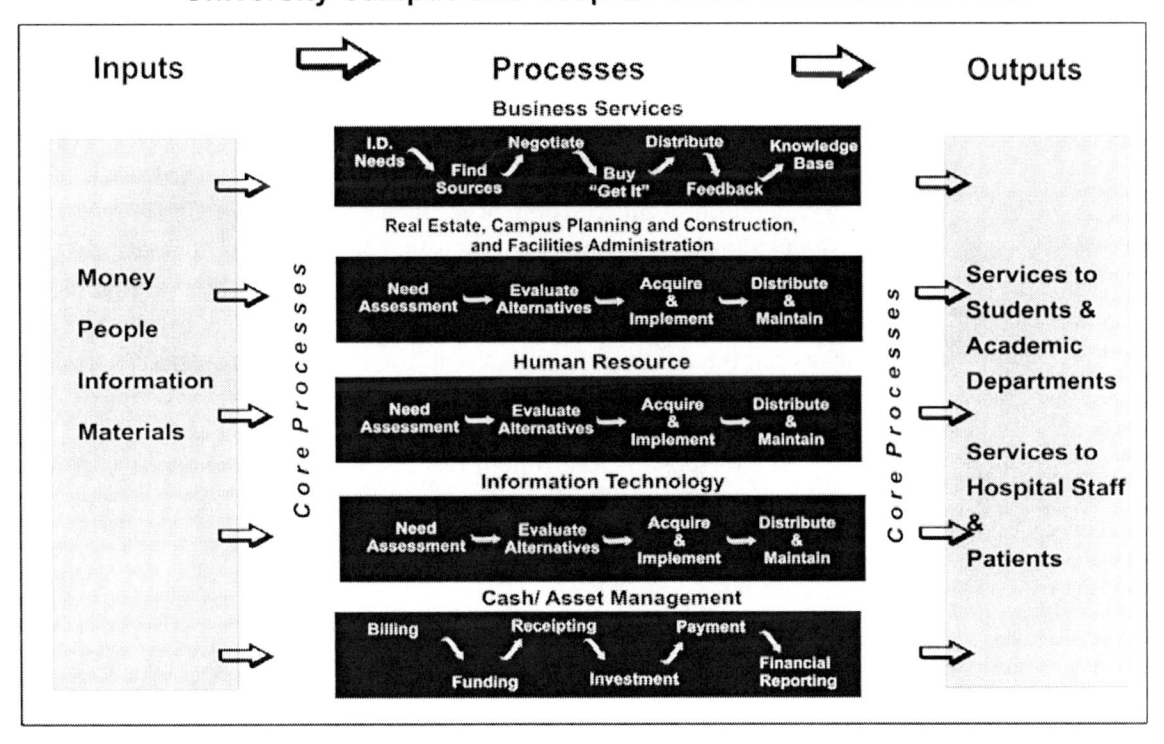

**Inputs** ⇒ **Processes** ⇒ **Outputs**

Business Services: I.D. Needs → Find Sources → Negotiate → Buy "Get It" → Distribute → Feedback → Knowledge Base

Real Estate, Campus Planning and Construction, and Facilities Administration: Need Assessment → Evaluate Alternatives → Acquire & Implement → Distribute & Maintain

Human Resource: Need Assessment → Evaluate Alternatives → Acquire & Implement → Distribute & Maintain

Information Technology: Need Assessment → Evaluate Alternatives → Acquire & Implement → Distribute & Maintain

Cash/Asset Management: Billing → Receipting → Payment, Funding → Investment → Financial Reporting

Inputs: Money, People, Information, Materials (Core Processes)

Outputs: Services to Students & Academic Departments; Services to Hospital Staff & Patients (Core Processes)

needs, they also restructured their own management team so that the leaders of each major process served as a member of the management team. They became process owners and process focused.

It is hard to say which had a greater effect on the satisfaction of the hospital and academic staff – the actual improvements in the work process, or the simple fact of being fully engaged in co-creating those services.

## FROM WHOLE-SYSTEM TO CONTINUOUS IMPROVEMENT

When the revolution is over the hard work begins. Most revolutions in nations fail to produce the future desired by the revolutionaries. Why? Because the habits of daily life were conditioned by the old system. My son was in Iraq working on building the first election process after the fall of Saddam Hussein. One night on Skype I asked him the question everyone wanted to know. "Do you think this will really work?" His answer was equally simple: "Yes, if they can just learn to listen to each other." He explained that during the days of Saddam anyone in a position of responsibility had learned not to say what they really thought, but to say what they thought was safe. If those habits continued and if they could not truly listen and talk to each other, democracy cannot work.

Democracy requires a whole-system. It requires the laws and structure of an election process. But, it also requires a way of life – a way of thinking and acting in which the citizens take responsibility for their own government. It is not so easy.

Lean management, whether in manufacturing or health care, first requires a system in which decisions can be made by those who do the work. It requires the systems of information sharing and the structures of teams that knock down walls within the core work process. But, then it requires the effort and the habits of every member of every team, from top to bottom, to practice shared decision-making, a focus on data, a focus on the needs of customers, and the continual experimentation that is at the heart of lean management.

The purpose of the remainder of this book is to assist you in the development of those habits.[11]

---

[11] More information on Whole-System Architecture can be found in *Lean Culture – The Leader's Guide.*

# Chapter 2

# Action-Learning: The Process of Changing Habits

Many of the methods of training and development are designed for the convenience of the trainer, not the learner. Come and sit in front of me for three days or a week, pay me, and good luck trying to make it work! Unfortunately that is the predominant model of training and development in our organizations. It doesn't work and represents a huge amount of waste!

Adults learn in much the same way as does the child learning to play the piano. A very small amount of knowledge, followed by practice, followed by praise will yield more results than long lectures or thick books.

How we develop continuous improvement for teams and individuals should follow a cycle of action-learning. Health care professionals, more than most, are under great pressure of time and are focused on the real world problems they find in front of them each day. The process of learning and change must be shaped by this reality.

The best methods and the best of intentions can easily fail unless we take into account how adults learn in our organizations. During World War II a process that has become known as Training Within Industry (TWI) and its component Job Instruction (JI) was developed and was then adopted by Toyota as it developed its system of production. For management development Toyota and other Japanese companies added the role of the *sensei* or coach. These methods are effective because they are consistent with action-learning that recognizes the reality of how adults learn.

Malcom Knowles who pioneered the field of adult learning identified the following principles as critical to adult learning:

- Adults are autonomous and self-directed. They need to be free to direct themselves. Their teachers must actively involve adult participants in the learning process and serve as facilitators for them. They must show participants how the learning experience will help them reach their goals.
- Adults have accumulated a foundation of life experiences and knowledge that may include work-related activities, family responsibilities, and previous education. They need to connect learning to this knowledge/experience base.
- Adults are goal-oriented. Instructors must show participants how this class will help them attain their goals.
- Adults are relevancy-oriented. They must see a reason for learning something. Learning has to be applicable to their work or other responsibilities to be of value to them.
- Adults are practical, focusing on the aspects of a lesson most useful to them in their work. They may not be interested in knowledge for its own sake. Instructors must tell participants explicitly how the lesson will be useful to them on the job.
- As do all learners, adults need to be shown respect. Instructors must acknowledge the wealth of experiences that adult participants bring to the classroom. These adults should be treated as equals in experience and knowledge and allowed to voice their opinions freely.

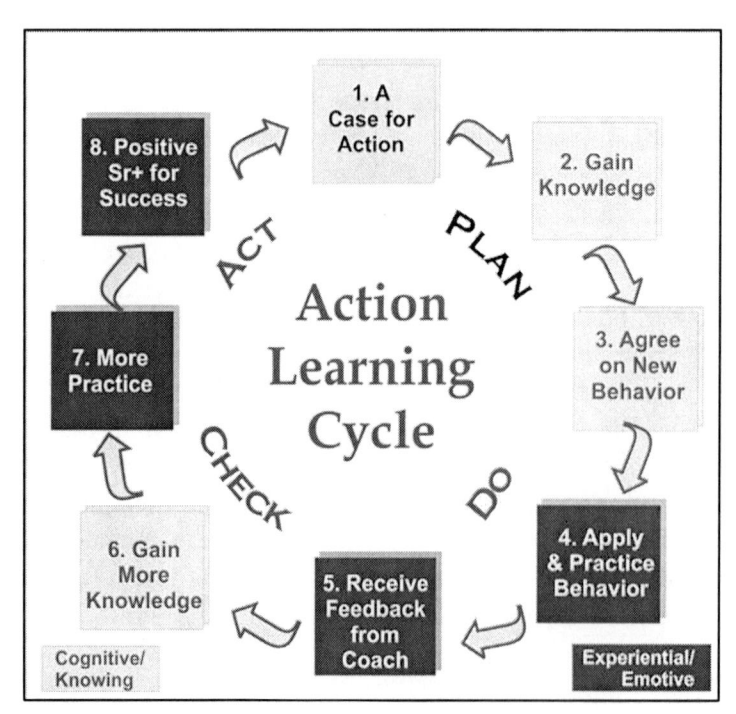

What has proven most effective is to apply this action learning model to team development. The eight steps illustrated here constitute a cycle of learning and continuous improvement. In many ways they correspond to the PDCA cycle of improvement. However, they are a bit more specific to the actions required for effective learning and incorporate the role of sensei or coach.

The steps illustrated in grey are primarily knowing/gaining knowledge steps. The steps in black are more experiential and have more impact on how the learner feels. Knowledge and emotions are equally important in gaining sustained change in individual behavior or in the culture of the organization. Too often our training methods focus more on knowing, and too little on the emotive aspect of learning which is more likely to occur from experience. Often we assume that "if they know, they will do" and this is a false assumption.

### 1. BUILD A CASE FOR ACTION:

The administrators of the hospital, clinic or home care system must develop a clear case for action. Why do we need to change? How will working as a team may my life better? How will it improve patient care?

As management embarks on a process of continuous improvement they need to point to competitors, best practices, financial benchmarks and the voice of the customers who are telling us that we need to improve. And, it helps to make clear that learning and practicing the new skills will be a component of everyone's appraisal process. In other words, it is the job of managers and coaches to make change matter!

### 2. GAIN KNOWLEDGE:

Transferring knowledge is what most corporate trainers do best. It is what classrooms are best designed to accomplish. It is why we have books and websites. However, knowledge very often does not result in behavioral change. It is the difference between taking a history course in which knowledge acquisition is the goal in itself; as opposed to learning to play the guitar. The former is primarily about cognition/knowledge, the latter is about habits or changes in behavior gained through experience and feelings of comfort with that new behavior.

If we are training teams to solve problems effectively, knowing the steps in a problem-solving model is important, but it is only the beginning of employing that knowledge for continuous improvement. Knowledge without action will not change habits or culture.

### 3. AGREE ON NEW BEHAVIOR:

Intention is the beginning of change. The guitar instructor may teach a chord position or scale on the fret board. By itself, that is useless knowledge. It only becomes useful when practiced. The student must agree to practice the chords or scales.

What can a team in the hospital do to immediately start solving problems together? How can they quickly initiate action steps to improve hospital cleanliness or reduce wait times for patients? Doing something and measuring the outcome is when learning is most likely to occur.

The way I have designed this training manual is so that each chapter, beginning with Part One, is a training module and each training module corresponds to a deliverable – a desired performance or behavior. For example, the fourth chapter is on writing the team's charter. The deliverable or action step is to write their charter and gain approval of the sponsoring manager. Another chapter is on defining customer requirements. Of course, the team then brainstorms customer requirements, interviews customers, and agrees on customer requirements. So, each bit of knowledge and training then asks for a new behavior to be performed the team agrees on the behavior and then takes action.

### 4. APPLY & PRACTICE NEW BEHAVIOR:

Imagine learning to play a musical instrument. How much knowledge of the keyboard or fret board is useful without then putting your hands on the instrument and practicing? The answer is very little. The important learning comes from playing the instrument, hearing the sounds, trying out different positions and chords and experiencing their difference. At one point I had the idea that I would learn to play the banjo and I bought a lesson book by Pete Seeger. When asked how often you should practice his answer was "Never. Just play!" What he understood was that the learning will come from the joy of playing, not from doing exercises or turning the experience into a painful task.

Practicing, evaluating, improving becomes a way of life. A Fast Company article (6/2/2009) on Toyota's Georgetown, KY plant described the reflection of one worker in the plant: "Artrip has been at Georgetown for 19 years. The way he does his work is so compelling it has become part of his personal life. 'When I'm mowing the grass, I'm thinking about the best way to do it. I'm trying different turns to see if I can do it faster,' he says." This is a clear sign that continuous improvement has become ingrained in the culture.

### 5. RECEIVE FEEDBACK FROM COACH:

The role of the sensei has become understood as an element of Toyota culture. A sensei is, essentially, a personal coach and mentor. Someone who can guide, observes, and gives feedback and encouragement. It is worth noting that in every sport, whether the emphasis is on team performance or individual performance, there is always a coach. And coaches are not reserved for children or new learners. The best professional quarterbacks, tennis stars, professional golfers and opera singers all have personal coaches even though they are at the top of their game.

In a May, 2004 Harvard Business Review article (Learning to Lead at Toyota) Steven J. Spear does an excellent job of describing how a new manager is hired and trained at Toyota. His coach introduces him to the organization with structured observation and debriefing on what he sees. He is asked to find improvements, many each day, just from observing. Then he is asked to work on the line with an assembly team. He is asked to find improvements and work with the team implementing them. He is then taken to Japan to again work with a frontline team and implement improvements, even in the very plant where the Toyota Production System began its development. At each step the sensei is encouraging him, guiding, and debriefing with him on the lessons he is learning. It is intensely personal and direct training and coaching. But, the sensei does little instructing in the traditional sense. Rather, he is creating experiences, asking questions, encouraging reflection.

Now consider how you develop teams in your own organization. Do they have a coach? Do they follow a structured learning process? Do they receive guidance, encouragement and feedback from a coach? Let me suggest that this is a necessity for the development of teams at every level of the organization.

### 6. Gain More Knowledge:

And now, the cycle becomes obvious. After each lesson learned, action or deliverable completed, the team receives feedback from the coach and then goes on to learn the next element of development: how to develop a balanced scorecard; how to map their work process; how to recognize variances of common versus special cause; how to reduce waste and cycle time, etc. And again this leads to practicing those skills.

### 7. More Practice:

The team and their coach should map out a series of ten to twenty steps that the team or individual will learn then do, then gain feedback and reflection. These steps should be those that lead to the complete set of behaviors you want a team to perform.

### 8. Positive Reinforcement from Coach and the Natural Environment:

As teams practice the skills of continuous improvement they begin to have an impact on actual performance. They should be able to see this impact on measured performance, on graphs. This is in itself, positive reinforcement and strengthens the learned behavior. It is the job of both the coach and the manager to assure that new skills and desired behavior lead to good outcomes for both individuals and teams. These outcomes can be as simple a certification that you are a High Performing Team, or the opportunity to present the results of your efforts to senior managers. There are a hundred ways to "make it matter" to strengthen the behavior of continuous improvement and this reinforcement should be part of the designed learning process.

While there is nothing entirely new about the eight steps of this action-learning cycle, it is a key to establishing lean management and culture that is too often overlooked.

## WHO TRAINS AND COACHES WHO?

Every hospital or health care system should develop internal expertise in continuous improvement. Develop your own cadre of coaches, rather than becoming consultant dependent. A consultant should help you develop your internal resources.

I have found it best to serve as the coach to a team of internal coaches who then use this workbook and other training resources to train every team of nurses, administrators, and support teams in the organization.

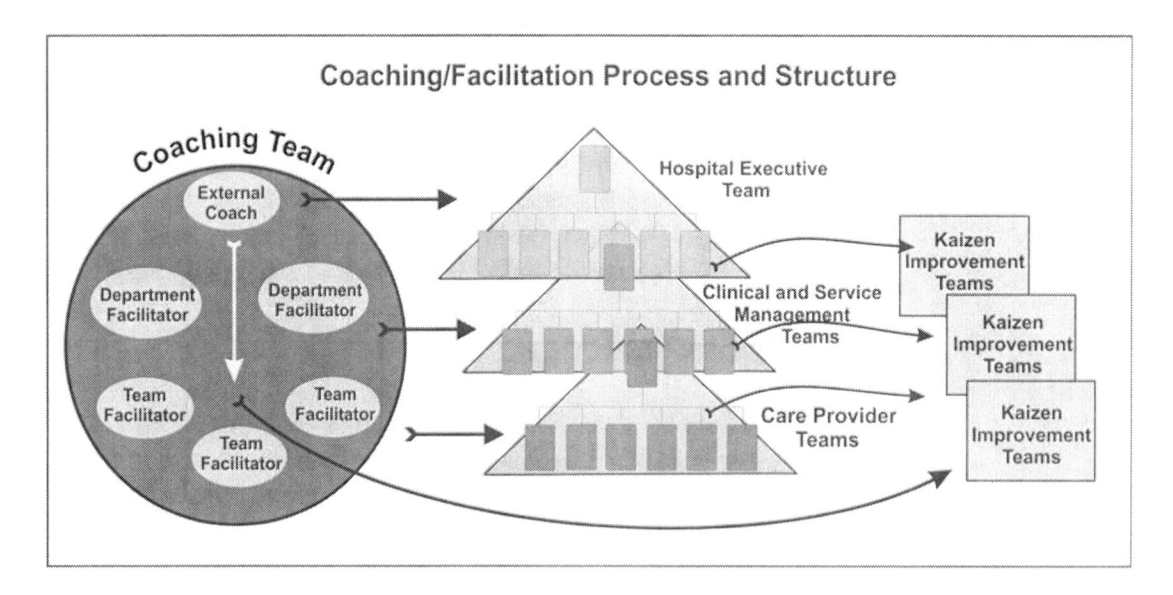

**Coaching/Facilitation Process and Structure**

### THE ROLE OF TEAM COACH:

- The coach will provide training in a sequence of modules that guide the teams through their development to becoming a high performance team.
- The coach will meet with the team leader to plan meetings and to provide feedback to the leader on her own leadership of the team.

- The coach will assist in customizing training modules and materials to best suit her teams.
- The coach will participate on a team of coaches who will evaluate the process of developing teams and work to improve that process.

## THE QUALITIES AND COMPETENCIES OF A COACH:

- The coach should possess excellent communication skills, both the ability to present to small groups and the ability to effectively listen and provide feedback.
- The coach will be an effective team member herself.
- She will be well organized and able to plan meetings effectively.
- She will be respected by her peers for her ability to work well with others.
- She will be humble in her presentation, yet forthright and honest in her willingness to give her opinion on the progress of the group and its members.

# Part One
# Getting Organized

# Chapter 3

# What is Lean? Principles and Purpose

The purpose of this chapter is to present the basic principles, purpose and practices of lean management in health care and for your team to begin the consider ways of applying the basic principles of lean to your area of responsibility.

## Objectives:

1. Understand the over-arching purpose of Lean Teams and how it may be applied to your organization.
2. Understand the synthesis of prior methods, theories and practices and how we are seeking to incorporate all of this learning as we implement a lean culture.

# What is Lean Management and Culture?

Lean is a moving target. Because, at its heart, lean is a process of learning and improvement it cannot be defined as something that is standing still or fixed. It is not simply mimicking what happened at Toyota or anywhere else.

The short answer to "what is lean?" is simply that lean is the generic application of the Toyota Production System (or The Honda Way). It is not one thing but a set of things that are best captured as a philosophy rather than as particular method or technique. If you don't have the philosophy, you don't get it.

Here are some ways of describing lean:

- Lean is a culture of continuous improvement practiced at every level of the organization and by every team.

- Lean is the application of the scientific method of experimentation and study of work processes and systems to find improvements.

- Lean is respect for people. It is respect for the voice of the customer and it is respect for those who do the work, who are "on-the-spot" and are, therefore, the "world's greatest experts" in their work.

- Lean is the elimination of waste in all its forms. Lean is the ability to distinguish between work that actually adds value to your customers and work that does not. By eliminating waste, you free resources to devote to value-adding activity that serves your customers.

- Lean is a work environment that assures the quality and safety of all work for both clients and staff.

- Lean is a focus on improving the work process and not on blaming people or creating fear.

- Lean is a culture of teamwork, shared responsibility and ownership that cuts through organization walls or silos.

- Lean is a culture that returns the joy to work. Honda speaks of the three joys of buying, selling and making the product. We do our best work when we have joy in our work.

- Lean is flow. Lean is an interruption free process that flows from beginning to end without interruption.

## LEAN MANAGEMENT AND CULTURE IN HEALTH CARE

If you examine each of these characteristics of a lean organization you will find that it is not hard to apply them to a hospital or other health care organization.

- *Continuous Improvement:* Health care, more than any other field of work or knowledge, has practiced and developed through a process of continuous improvement. Imagine if doctor or nurses were doing their job today the same way it was done ten, twenty or fifty years ago. Every day there is improvement in health care services. It is the job of everyone, every team member and every manager, to participate in continuous improvement.

- *Experimentation:* Health care, in all its forms, has emerged from the scientific method of controlled experimentation. Applying the principles of experimentation to daily work practices in a hospital, long term care facility, or home care, should be a natural process for those who are trained in any health or healing profession.

- *Respect for People:* Most of those who enter the health and healing professions do so, not for selfish reasons, but to do something noble, to be of service to others. You have probably learned that there is no more reliable source of information about the health of an individual than their own voice, the voice of the customer. The best health care organizations demonstrate respect for the expertise and the spirit of those who chose to work in this profession.

- *The Elimination of Waste:* Everyone knows that health care organizations are experiencing tremendous pressure to reduce costs, from the university where we are educated to end-of-life services. What lean implementation has proven is that costs can be reduced while at the same time providing improved service to clients. If one form can be completed on a computer and be maintained by the client, rather than filling out multiple forms that provide the same information and consume the time of patient and staff, fill filing cabinets, and represent a source of error, costs can be reduced while at the same time reducing the frustration of patients. There are many forms of waste that can be eliminated in most health care organizations.

- *Assure Quality and Safety, First!* In healthcare we know that our first responsibility is to do no harm. Unfortunately, too often harm is done. That harm may be in the spread of infection in the hospital. It may be in a failure of diagnosis. It may be a delay in diagnosis or treatment. Quality and safety must be the first priority of any lean initiative. As in manufacturing, quality and safety cannot be achieved through a special committee or individual. It must be the responsibility of every single associate. This is accomplished by every team being clear of their area of responsibility and their measures of quality and safety.

- *Blame the Process, not the People:* A culture of blame and shame destroys motivation and creates fear. This destroys the capacity for experimentation and learning. Dr. Deming said that 95% of the problems are in the process, but more often we blame the people and fail to fix the process. Too often in health care organizations there is a tendency to search for the "guilty party" when the real blame lies in a process that is too confusing, too difficult, or that leads to errors. Every manager and every team of clinicians and service providers must become experts in their processes and focus on process improvement.

- *A Culture of Teamwork:* The Mayo Clinic, ThedaCare, VON Canada and other organizations that are demonstrating superior results are doing so through a culture of teamwork. Clinicians are organized into teams to provide the best possible care, as are service providers from those in the cafeteria to those who assure clean facilities.

- *Joy at Work:* You only go around once in life. Why not get all the joy you can? What is "joy?" Joy is the happiness that is derived by putting your strengths to work for a worthy purpose. You joined the health care field because you intuitively felt that you would derive joy from your work. Every time you see a patient get well it brings you joy. Every time you see a client that needed home nursing or support become independent it brings you joy. Unfortunately, that joy is often countered by bureaucratic procedures, sources of frustration to your clients, and fear created by management practices and behavior that are based on faulty assumptions about human nature.

- *Lean is Interruption Free Flow:* Several times in factories I have had teams take incoming material off the delivery truck and then stand there as the box stands there. When it is opened and stored, they move to the warehouse or storage area and wait. Then they move from production station to production station and stand there and wait as long as the actual part stands there and waits. This can be an incredibly frustrating experience. I ask them to imagine that the material never stopped moving, but continually flowed from beginning to end. Now follow the patient who feels a pain in her stomach. Where does she go? Stand there with her. Follow her to the next office, the next form, the next professional, the next phone call, the next waiting room, etc. How long does it take? Every second during which she is not receiving direct care for her illness, is an interruption and is non-value adding waste. It is more than waste. It is a source of risk.

Now do an exercise with your team. Take each of these principles and identify how they are currently being practiced in your area of work and how they could be applied in the future.

When you do this, you will understand the purpose of everything else that will follow in this workbook and in the work of your team.

| Lean Characteristics | How Do We Practice this Today? | How Could We Practice this Tomorrow? |
|---|---|---|
| Continuous Improvement | | |
| Experimentation | | |
| Respect for People | | |
| Elimination of Waste | | |
| Assure Quality and Safety, First! | | |
| Blame the Process, Not People | | |
| A Culture of Teamwork | | |
| Joy at Work | | |
| Interruption Free Flow | | |

# You Don't Know Where You Are Unless You Know Where You've Been: A Brief History of Work Organizations

You may think health care organizations are unique. And, in some respects they are. But, you may be surprised at the degree to which the organization structure, systems, culture and processes has followed the same path followed by factories, education, and other work systems.

Healthcare delivery has followed many of the same trends as other types of organizations. Healthcare began with small organizations, individual doctors and small clinics, much like the family farm and small craft shops. It evolved to big organizations with bureaucracies and the loss of intimacy that was felt in earlier days. It is worth understanding this history because it puts in context everything hospitals and other health care organizations are doing to become lean.

At the heart of lean culture is the small team seeking serve their customers in better ways. There is nothing new about small groups of people taking responsibility for performance. In fact, it is the most ancient form of organization, the origin of business. For thousands of years the work place was the home, and the work revolved around the home. The original corporation was not some impersonal legal entity with distant owners. It was the family, the family farm or small craft shop.

When you needed health care, your health care provider looked a lot like that small craft shop.

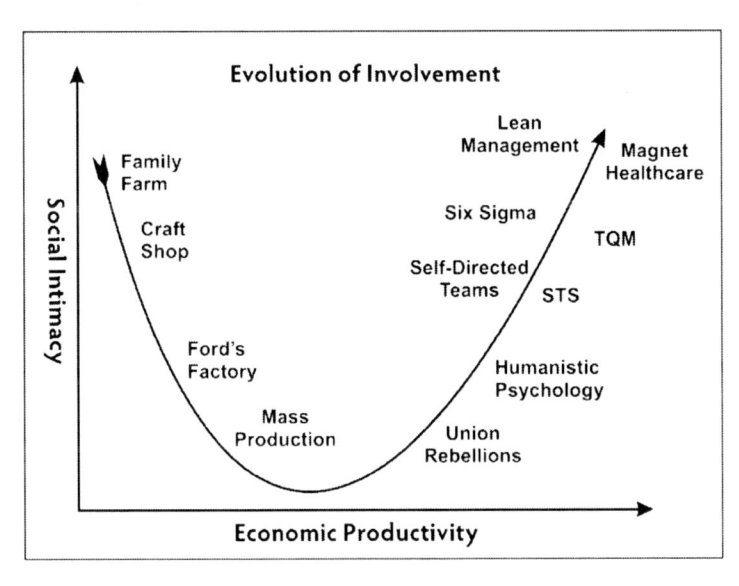

In the beginning, the people who did the work owned the work. It was their responsibility to think about their methods and the quality of their product, and they directly spoke with their customers. This direct contact and direct responsibility, along with the natural consequences of wealth or poverty, assured the motivation of those who did the work and their concern for customer satisfaction.

Family farms and craft shops used what we would now regard as highly inefficient methods. They had little technology, few economies of scale, and little opportunity for training and development or sharing best practices. The productivity, output per unit of input, was low. Bushels of corn per working hour, compared to any modern farm were horribly low. Therefore, the cost of food or goods was high and relative wealth low.

With the development of the combine and tractor, productivity increased, and the need for labor decreased. Workers moved from the rural family structure to the organized, specialized, structure of the cities and factories. In the last quarter of the nineteenth century and the first quarter of the twentieth century, every business learned the value of two things: economies of scale, or "mass production" and the application of the scientific method, or industrial engineering. These two methods, both of which increased productivity, also destroyed intimacy, the social relationships between employees and with their customer.

The same was true in healthcare. The doctor in the small town had little access to resources, information, and technology and could see relatively few patients each day. The efficiency of healthcare organizations has increased dramatically. But, in that gain of efficiency, something may have been lost. It may be that feeling of intimacy between doctor and patient and the intimacy between colleagues.

In the craft shop, the worker making a piece of furniture would sign his name to his work, like a personalized piece of art. Workers on the family farm and craft shop did "whole" work. They made a whole piece of furniture, a whole chair, not just a leg, a seat or a back to be assembled elsewhere. The social aspect of the craft and family farm system was unnoticed and not understood, but it was just as important as any economic understanding. It kept the family together. It united workers, management and customers. Once this was broken it would take a hundred years to repair.

The key element of the mass production system was the simplification of the work into standardized tasks, long production runs of standardized parts, and the close supervision of each worker so he would conform to the exact motions and speed defined by the new class of managers and supervisors. With this tight supervision and simplified work, there was no need for multi-skilled workers. This created the great divide between management and labor, thinker and worker, salaried and hourly.

This creation of division, a class system in the organization, was the beginning of a cancer that would eat at the culture for a hundred years. Hospitals would not be exempt from this same disease.

The first industrialist to make full use of this system was Henry Ford. Initially it took 14 hours to assemble a Model T car. By improving his mass production methods, Ford reduced this to 1 hour 33 minutes. This lowered the overall cost of each car and enabled Ford to undercut the price of other cars on the market. Between 1908 and 1916 the selling price of the Model T fell from $1,000 to $360. Following the success of Ford's low-priced cars, other companies began introducing mass production methods to produce cheaper goods. This changed the fundamental theory by which every organization was managed.

Frederick Taylor, the father of industrial engineering, developed the system of work standards and measurements to continuously improve the efficiency of mass production. Taylor's methods that emphasized the definition of one "right way" to perform a job led to a top-down rigidity that prohibited worker input to decision-making. It was the lack of moderation in the application of these methods that contributed to dehumanizing the workplace and a counter reaction. During the early part of this century, the workplace gained efficiency at the cost of intimacy and individual initiative.

One counter reaction to the industrial system of Taylor and Ford was the rise of the union movement, a rebellion not just for wages, but for dignity, a voice, a recognition that the human beings employed in the factory were not just subjects of engineering.

Managers would claim that there was a "union problem," but the real problem wasn't the unions; it was the system that produced them, a system that was, after thousands of years in which people worked in the family structure, a completely unnatural system, one that denied the basic human need for self-worth and self-control. When workers went down to the union hall, they called each other "brother" and "sister" and called for solidarity, brotherhood, and unity. They were calling for those things that had been taken away, the feelings of the family farm.

The development of humanistic psychology and its applications in organization development were a response to the alienation that had developed between management and workers. The field of organization development (OD) emerged primarily from the work of social psychologists. Social psychology focused on human needs, feelings, and the dynamics between people in groups. Researchers and writers such as Kurt Lewin and Carl Rogers developed models to describe the interaction within groups and the patterns of communication between individuals. During World War II the need to increase the rate of creativity led to research on group behavior and how best to increase the flow of ideas. What we now call "brainstorming" and other group techniques resulted from this effort.

In the 1940's Abraham Maslow defined seven stages of human motivation or needs.[12] This structure was useful in helping managers understand the significance of motivational influences beyond the simple need for survival and money. Maslow's work and the work of Herzberg[13] and McGregor[14] further developed the understanding of the relationship between organizational systems, management styles (Theory X and Theory Y), and employee motivation. This work became the foundation upon which numerous management and organization development practices were built. Job enrichment[15], Blake and Mouton's Managerial Grid, and various forms of group training and team building all have their foundation in the principles and values promoted by social and humanistic psychology.

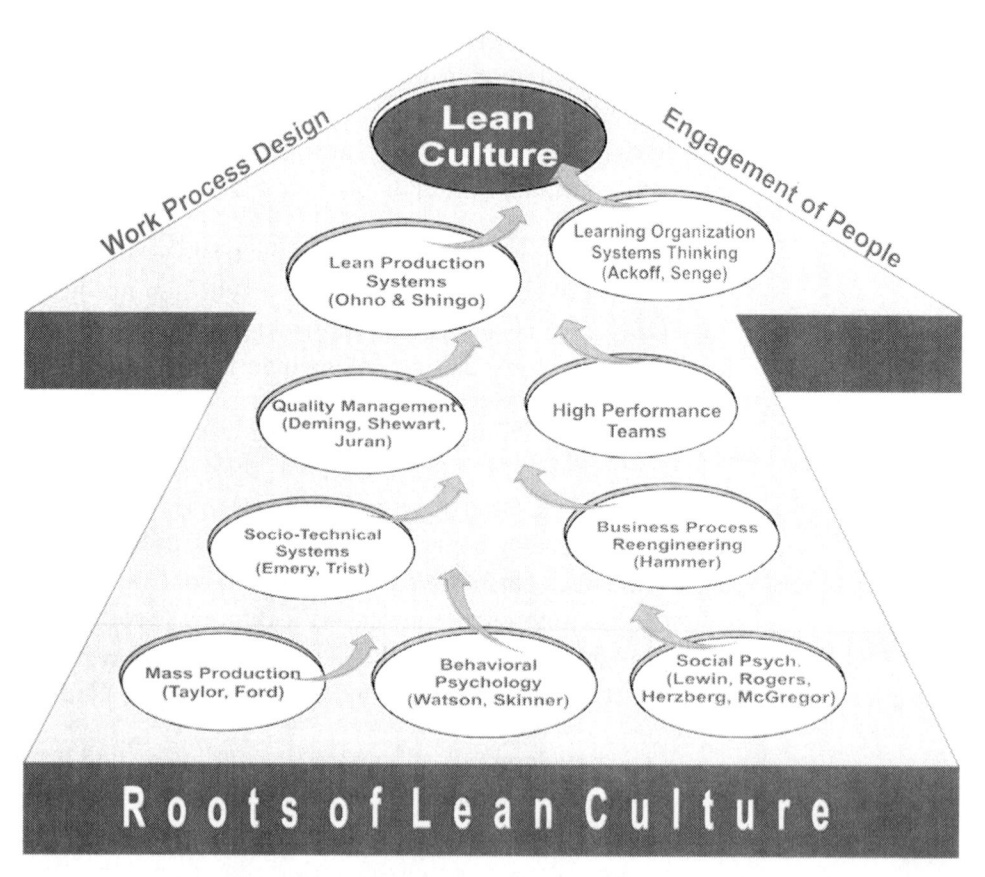

*Roots of Lean Culture*

- Work Process Design
- Engagement of People
- Lean Culture
- Lean Production Systems (Ohno & Shingo)
- Learning Organization Systems Thinking (Ackoff, Senge)
- Quality Management (Deming, Shewart, Juran)
- High Performance Teams
- Socio-Technical Systems (Emery, Trist)
- Business Process Reengineering (Hammer)
- Mass Production (Taylor, Ford)
- Behavioral Psychology (Watson, Skinner)
- Social Psych. (Lewin, Rogers, Herzberg, McGregor)

The development of Quality Circles in Japan can be traced back to the research in group dynamics and decision-making conducted in the 1950s in the United States. The quality movement was founded on the convergence of two disciplines, the discipline of group problem-solving and that of statistical process control.

---

[12] Maslow, Abraham. "A Theory of Motivation." Psychological Review, 50, 1943, pp. 370-396.
[13] Herzberg, Frederick. *Work and the Nature of Man.* World Publishing Company, 1966.
[14] McGregor, Douglas M. *The Human Side of Enterprise.* New York: McGraw-Hill Book Company, Inc. 1960.
[15] Meyer, M. Scott. *Every Employee A Manager.* New York: McGraw-Hill Book Company. 1970.

After World War II several Americans were invited to Japan to assist in the rebuilding of Japanese industry. Their teachings, filtered through the prism of Japanese culture, led to much of modern **total quality management**. Among these teachers were W. Edwards Deming, Walter A. Shewhart and Joseph Juran. Shewhart's *Economic Control of Quality of Manufactured Products*[16] may be the most important book on quality or manufacturing ever written, and the seminars of these three fathers of modern quality management created much of the foundation of what is now regarded as lean management.

From Dr. Deming and Dr. Juran we learned to place the emphasis on performance to customer requirements, to define performance in terms of customer satisfaction, and to provide feedback to suppliers.[17] Dr. Deming and his disciples emphasized the importance of variability in process and of gaining statistical knowledge and control of the process. These views complemented the emphasis on teamwork and employee satisfaction that was emerging from the humanistic school of management.

Dr. Deming repeatedly emphasized the power of the system and the importance of managing the system. Unfortunately, Dr. Deming and the quality advocates provided no method for analyzing and changing the system of the organization. But, at the same time that Dr. Deming was becoming recognized in Japan, Eric Trist at the Tavistock Institute[18] in London began studying the environment of organizations and the interaction of the technical system of work and the social systems. The foundation study of **socio-technical systems (STS) design** was conducted by Trist in British coal mines. He found that the traditional culture of the mines was one of small, self-selected, and highly interdependent groups of workers, often members of the same family. When new technology was introduced into the mines, workers were assigned to single tasks controlled by external supervisors. The reactions of workers to this mass production culture were negative and led to high absenteeism, safety problems and low productivity. When workers were allowed to design their own organization, they duplicated their more traditional small self-managing work group. Productivity went up, safety problems and absenteeism went down.

What Trist did in coal mines was very simply to re-establish some of the patterns found in the family farm, combined with modern technology. This was a breakthrough. STS became the methodology for

---

[16] Shewhart, W.A. *Economic Control of Quality of Manufactured Product*. New York, D. Van Nostrand Company, Inc. 1931.

[17] Deming, W. Edwards. *Out of the Crisis*, Cambridge, MA, MIT Center for Advanced Engineering Studies, 1986.

[18] Trist, E., Higgins, C., Murray, H., & Pollock, A. *Organizational Choice*. London, Tavistock Institute, 1963.

creation of a new organization in manufacturing plants, the self-managing, self-directed, or high performing team. This proved so successful that it was adopted in all Proctor and Gamble plants. STS and TQM were operating in completely separate but parallel worlds, competing for management attention. Yet, there was an obvious synergy. TQM and Lean required the redesign of the work and organizational system. However, they had no systematic process to achieve that redesign. My colleagues and I combined these into what we termed "Whole System Architecture." This provided a methodology to redesign the system as Dr. Deming encouraged.

As the wave of Japanese automobiles became increasingly popular in the United States, closer examination of the system of production developed by Toyota led to increasing adoption of what we now call "lean manufacturing."

The evolution of production systems occurred in three stages (which have been well described in *The Machine That Changed the World*, the result of a five-year MIT comparative study of the global auto industry).[19] These stages are 1) craft production, 2) mass production, and 3) lean production.

The fathers of the Toyota Production System were Taiichi Ohno and Shigeo Shingo. Ohno was the production manager, later the Vice President, of Production at Toyota, while Shingo was the manufacturing engineer who is responsible for the development of many of the tools of what we now call "lean."

Shingo began his revolutionary work focusing on the die change process at Toyota, the key process in stamping metal parts. Large production lots were required because die change at Ford required 24 hours, by a separate group of workers, organized in a separate department, with separate managers and supervisors. For many years Shingo worked at speeding die change. But, the truth is that Shingo did not know how to speed the die change process. What he did was to ask questions and challenge the workers who were on-the-spot. It was these front-line workers, given encouragement, challenge, feedback and support to experiment, who made the breakthroughs. This process is important. Eventually die change was accomplished in minutes rather than days.

In accomplishing this quick die change, which became known as SMED (Single Minute Exchange of Dies), Ohno and Shingo had established a pattern that would be replicated throughout the factory.

---

[19] Womack, James P., Jones, Daniel T., & Roos, Daniel. *The Machine That Changed The World,* New York, Rawson Associates, 1990

Small groups of workers would be treated as full partners in the process, responsible for their own work, able to improve and modify their process, and having knowledge of the previous and next stages of production (their internal customers and suppliers) so that they would understand the requirements and effect of their work. Ohno found that these work groups, given the necessary information, worked to continuously improve their work process. This became the cultural assumption at Toyota, and it was entirely different than the cultural assumptions prevalent in traditional factories. This difference in culture is the primary explanation for the rise of Japanese automobile companies and the decline of the U.S. auto industry.

If you understand what Shingo did, you will understand that this exact same process can be applied within a hospital or any other health care organization. It is more about human nature that it is about the nature of a stamping press.

On the assembly line, Ohno formed workers into teams with a working team leader rather than a foreman. Teams were given a set of assembly steps and told to work together to devise the best possible ways to accomplish the assembly. The team leader would participate in the work, stepping in to help where needed. These teams soon accepted responsibility for housekeeping, small machine repair, maintenance, and checking their own quality. The teams would meet periodically to find ways to continuously improve (Kaizen) their process.

The total system in the Japanese plants became distinctly different than those in American auto plants. Lots were small, and quick change-to-order was a priority. They achieved the combination of efficiency and small production runs which American producers assumed to be contradictory. This was accomplished only by completely redefining the system of work and worker responsibility.

The task now for all managers, including those in healthcare, is to combine the best of all the improvement efforts, to renew the human bonds and sense of responsibility that was present on the family farm without eliminating any of the efficiencies of lean production. *This is the purpose the Healthcare Lean.*

Healthcare Lean begins with an assumption about human nature. That assumption is that when given responsibility, when given the facts, when given a way of keeping score and making decisions, the overwhelming majority of individuals will rise to the occasion and accept responsibility to improve performance. This is a truth about human nature whether it is in a factory, a hospital or with community based health care practitioners.

The philosophy underlying lean management and Magnet healthcare organizations is that we must respect the expertise and good intentions of all of our staff. And, when working together in teams they will create collective wisdom and collective responsibility around providing exceptional client care.

The distinction between those who manage and those who do "work" is not useful anymore and will gradually be eliminated; it divides and de-motivates. But our structures and systems, our practices of management, have preserve the dead carcass of that system and hold back the gains that come when people are working as one body.

# CHAPTER 4

# WRITING YOUR TEAM'S CHARTER

The purpose of this chapter is to help team members reach agreement on their purpose as a team and the principles that will guide their behavior. Your Charter will define your responsibilities and relationships.

### OBJECTIVES

- To engage the team in a discussion about why they are a team and their responsibilities as a team.
- To have the team develop a charter that will define their work and responsibility as they serve their clients.
- To have the team establish a code of conduct, or principles to live by.

## WRITING A TEAM CHARTER

Whether your team is a health care service delivery team or whether it is a care management or supporting team, your team should have a clearly defined charter that clarifies boundaries and responsibilities. Every team has boundaries. No team (including the CEO's team) can do anything it wants. Every team has a field of action and boundaries that define that field. This charter creates a rational linkage between your team and the rest of the organization.

Developing the team charter should be done when a team is first formed. It should be jointly developed by the team itself and the team or manager to whom the team is responsible. One of the advantages of developing a charter comes from the conversation itself. Team members need to have this conversation so they developed a shared understanding.

The following are the seven components that should be in a team charter:

1. Statement of Purpose: Why do we exist as a team?

2. Process Responsibility: What is the definition of the process that this team "owns" and is responsible for measuring and improving?

3. Process Boundaries: Where does this process begin, and where does it end? Who hands off stuff to us, and to whom do we hand off our finished stuff?

4. Communication Responsibility -- Managers, Clients, Customers, Suppliers and Other Teams: Whom should we keep informed and about what? From whom do we get feedback, and to whom do we give feedback? What information do we need to provide to a manager, and when?

5. Performance Responsibilities: What are the primary measures of performance for which we are responsible? This should not define specific measures, but the general categories of performance.

6. Membership and Sponsorship: What positions or functions serve as members of this team? Who gives us the authority to take action, make decisions, and to whom do we report?

## DEFINING YOUR TEAM'S PURPOSE

Individuals have a personal need to find their purpose and to create their own energy source; they may find it in their faith, family or career. Teams are structured around a common purpose and manage their work to be of service to their clients and customers, those who care about their work. Purpose may be found in genuine caring for those you serve in your healthcare service delivery and fellow team members. The purpose of a larger organization should be found in its statement of mission and strategy. Why does the company exist? What will it contribute to the world at large, its customers, shareholders, and employees?

## THE HIERARCHY OF PURPOSE

There is a hierarchy of purpose from the eternal to the instant, from the spiritual to the material. We can visualize this as a pyramid. At the top of the pyramid is our largest understanding of our existence. Most of us gain understanding of our purpose from our religion or our parents. The concept of purpose is a spiritual concept. It is not merely intellectual, and it is certainly not material.

**Hierarchy of Purpose**

- Purpose of Life — Long Term
- Career Ambitions — Spiritual
- Job Aspirations
- Job Goals
- Work Task — Material — Short Term Situational

The concept of purpose creates a link between spiritual capital and financial, social and other forms of capital. Spiritual capital can be viewed as including both one's connection to a higher source of purpose, for most God, and to a strong commitment to moral values. A team or larger organization can possess spiritual capital to the degree that the members share both an ennobling purpose and moral or ethical values. In healthcare organizations we do share a noble or worthy purpose and this should be reflected in how we do our work each day.

Many people have great difficulty relating spiritual purpose to their daily work-life. Yet, merely struggling with the question of how my work fulfills my spiritual purpose is, in itself, a step forward. Spiritual progress always comes from the internal struggle to resolve questions. If one has no questions, one has no spiritual progress. By asking this question we are seeking connection; we are seeking meaning; we are seeking unity between our spiritual and material lives; we are seeking an integrated life. Job satisfaction, particularly in a healthcare organization, is in part a function of how we understand our personal and organization's purpose.

This is the first subject your team should decide together. Why do you exist, as a team? Who cares about the work you do? How can you have a positive influence on others?

1. How might this team contribute to my meeting my own purpose as an individual?

   _____
   _____
   _____

2. Who are this team's primary clients or customers, those who make use of and care about the work we do? Where does our work go, and why is it important?

   _____
   _____
   _____

3. How do we contribute to the larger goals and purpose of our organization?

   _____
   _____
   _____

4. What influence do we have on our community? Do we fulfill any purpose that is related to the needs and requirements of the community?

   _____
   _____
   _____

5. Imagine your ideal world. If you could make anything happen, if you had a magic wand that you could wave, what would you like your team to accomplish?

_____

_____

_____

6. Now, consult together with the members of your team. Use a flip chart and make a page for each of the six questions above. Have each member of your team go to the wall, and write down the most important answer they developed individually for each of these questions. Now discuss each of them. From the list that was put up by all of the team members, which items stand out as the most important and motivating answers. Feel free to combine and consolidate the answers.

7. From the consolidated list that is on the wall, discuss which answers represent the most important purpose of your team. Select three to five sentences that best define the purpose of your team. These answers should be motivating to you, and they should create a unity of effort on the part of all team members.

   Our most significant purpose is…

_____

_____

_____

_____

## DEFINING OUR CORE WORK PROCESSES

The work of teams is to manage and improve their work process. The charter should define what processes you "own."

It is important that the team take time at this point to define the basic landscape within which it works. For every team there are inputs and outputs. Someone or some group supplies the team with what it needs to do its work and someone receives its work.

Every team adds value by transforming input to output. It is the team's processes that achieve this transformation. In other words, if your team is a restaurant team, you receive raw food as input. You slice and dice, mix and stir, cook and prepare the food for serving. That is a process that adds value. You serve the food to customers who receive your output and are willing to pay for the value that you have added to the raw input. Almost every team does something similar, although perhaps more complicated than this restaurant team.

This flow, from input to output, is typically described as the team's SIPOC: Suppliers, Input, Process, Output, and Clients and Customers. In later chapters we will analyze these elements of the system, particularly the work process, in much greater detail. But, for the purpose of defining

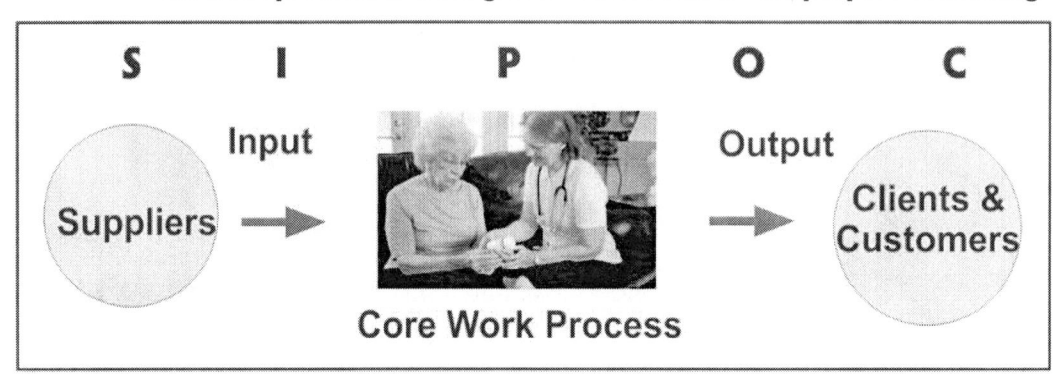

your charter, it will be helpful at this stage to define the basic elements of your SIPOC and particularly the processes for which you are responsible.

# My Team's SIPOC

| Suppliers | Inputs | Core Work Processes | Outputs | Clients & Customers |
|---|---|---|---|---|
| | → | → | → | → |

## Communication Responsibilities

No team is an island and it has a responsibility to communicate its progress and problems to others. It is important to define to whom the team needs to communicate and how frequently.

You may find it helpful to fill in the following chart as you define your communication responsibilities:

| To Whom Will We Communicate? | How Frequently? | What Information? |
|---|---|---|
|  |  |  |

## Performance Responsibilities

What are the primary measures of performance for which we are responsible? This should not define specific measures, but the general categories of performance and potential risks of failure.

To discuss this it will be worth reading the work of the Health care Service Delivery Design Team. They have proposed measures and performance responsibilities for teams. Take a look at these and see if they fit for your team, or if you feel you need to modify them, make them more specific, you should do that.

## Membership and Sponsorship

In many cases it is obvious who the team members will be. However, in many organizations there will be teams that include members who are permanently assigned to a different department, but who come together to provide a service or accomplish some other performance. For example in a manufacturing plant there may be a "technical operations" team made up of engineers, chemists and quality experts who work together with line manufacturing employees to manage technical aspects of the work.

Define the members of your team by position or function rather than by name. Over time, the names will change, while the team will continue to fulfill its purpose.

Also define the "sponsor," the position that will approve this charter and authorize the work of the team.

## Gaining Charter Approval

It is important that the sponsor, whether an individual or a team, review the charter and provide the team with any needed feedback. This "sign-off" will indicate ownership and commitment to the team by the leaders above.

## CREATING A STATEMENT OF TEAM PRINCIPLES

Most teams have found it helpful to agree on a set of guiding principles that is an agreement on how they will behave as a team. On an athletic team there will be agreements to attend practice every day and to be there on time. Agreements like these are agreements to respect each other times, each other's right to have a voice and to be heard respectfully.

It is a little bit like rules of the road, such as slower cars drive in the right lane. Most people would agree that these traffic laws and "rules of the road," which may appear to limit our freedoms, actually allow us a greater degree of freedom. If there were no traffic laws, we would be driving very slowly to make sure no one was flying through the next street corner. We can travel in relative safety and ease because we all agree to adhere to some common rules of the road.

If you did the exercise in the previous chapter in which you looked at a best and worst case team, you can now use that to say "how do we want to behave as a team?" and develop a statement of principles from this.

If not, follow the questions below to arrive at a set of team principles by which you agree to live:

1. Describe the best team experience you ever had. How did people behave on this team that led to this good experience?

   _____
   _____
   _____

2. Describe the worst team experience you have ever had. How did people behave on this team that led to this experience?

   _____
   _____
   _____

3. What role did the team leader, or facilitator, play that contributed to the good performance of the team?

   _____
   _____
   _____

4. Place two flip charts on the wall. Label one of them "Best Team"; and the other one "Worst Team." Now have each team member share the behavior that was characteristics of best and worst team experiences.

5. Now, discuss the two lists and from them, make a third list. This list could be labeled "How We Agree to Behave;" or, "Our Team Principles." Ask the group to reach consensus on the five to ten key behaviors that lead to successful teamwork.

_____

_____

_____

_____

So, now what do you do with this list of team principles, and the statement of purpose?

It is easy to put these aside and forget about them. This is almost a natural tendency as we dive into our daily work. Here are a couple suggestions that have proven to help teams live by their purpose and principles:

- Make a permanent flip chart, or some other kind of chart, that you can put on the wall each time your team meets. Just making these visible will serve as a reminder (like a traffic sign) and help the members of the team behave according to those principles.

- Sometimes the most subtle reminder is helpful. You may find that the team is in a heated discussion about some matter, and two or three members are interrupting each other, or two other members are carrying on their own conversation as if the group wasn't even there. The facilitator, or any member of the team, could stand up; go over to the list of principles, and just point at the principle that says, "We will listen respectfully, while others speak," or the one that says "We agree not to interrupt each other." The other members of the team will stop and take notice, and hopefully, bring their behavior into conformance with the principles.

- It is a very good idea for the team to periodically "process" how it is functioning as a team. Every fourth or fifth meeting, for example, your team leader might ask the group, "How do you think we are doing as a team?" The members can then look at the team's purpose and list of principles and ask themselves whether they are living up to their own agreements. If your team is like most teams, you will find that you are sometimes not living up to an agreement such as "Give every member an opportunity to be heard;" or, "Be sure to clarify our decisions and action agreements." This reminder will be both to the facilitator and the entire team. These gentle conversations are much better than anyone admonishing or punishing the team or its members. Remember that we are all learning how to function well in a team. This is just part of that process.

# Chapter 5

# Organizing Your Team

The purpose of this chapter is to develop the basic structure, roles and responsibilities on your team.

## Objectives

1. To understand the role of different types of teams at that you may employ in your organization.

2. To understand what type of a team I belong to and what that means for me.

3. To discuss and agree on the different roles on our team.

Let us assume that your team has just been formed. You have been given responsibility for a process, or set of processes. You know who the other team members are. Now, what do you do to turn this group of people into a genuine high performing team?

> There are several things you need to do:
>
> - First, define the different roles and responsibilities on the team.
>
> - Second, clarify the roles or relationships with those who are connected to your team.
>
> - Third, agree on your schedule of meetings, when, where and who.
>
> - Fourth, create a standard agenda that you will modify for each meeting.
>
> - And, fifth, plan for the team's learning and development. This is just the beginning.

## DIFFERENT TYPES OF TEAMS, FULFILLING DIFFERENT ROLES

A hospital, like most organizations, is a living organism. It changes shape and structure and sometimes it even changes direction. It is part of a larger ecology of healthcare systems in your country and like any organism it must adapt to that changing ecology. It is also a learning organization, which means that as lessons are learned from trial and error, it will change its structure and systems to incorporate new learning. Therefore, teams will come and go, and some will be more permanent than others. For example, there will always be a senior management team, although members change. And, there will always be frontline or primary care teams to address the needs of your clients. And these will also change membership and shape as needs change.

What is important to understand is that changes in team structure, or the creation of new teams, will be easy and efficient when the members have learned the skills of functioning well in teams. If they know how to create and follow an agenda, if they know how to engage in effective dialogue and solve problems, if they have good facilitation skills, changes in team structure are quick and easy. Therefore, everyone learning these skills is an asset to the entire organization. In fact, wherever your career takes you, you will carry these skills with you.

Teams can be organized in more than one way, for more than one purpose. It is important to be clear which kind of team you are organizing. A team may be an on-going core client service team, an enabling or support team, a project improvement team, a coordinating team to work on some problem that cuts across the work of many teams; or a management or executive team.

## CORE CLIENT SERVICE TEAMS

These may also be called primary care teams, nursing or home support teams. In a real sense they are the most important teams in the organization. They are teams that do the core work of caring for our clients. Most organizations are a chain of process management teams that follow the flow of the process from input to output. Lean organizations have organized all front line employees into teams who take ownership of their work process.

The basic idea of Healthcare Lean is that all levels of the organization are formed into teams that engage in continuous improvement of their work. These teams are linked together, with each team getting feedback from their clients and customers, while management levels provide coordination and leadership to the teams. The goals, scorecards, and work of these teams are all linked together to create a unity of energy and effort.

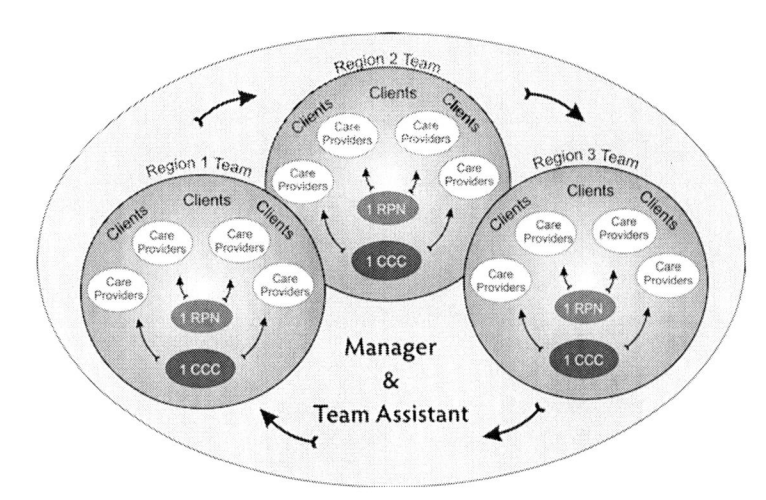

This illustration is of the client service teams designed for home health care delivery. You will see that there are several levels of teams. First there is the overall team led by a manager. Then there are geographic teams that are actually a cluster of sub-teams. The exact numbers of these teams will change as the process develops. But, you can see that everyone who serves clients is a member of a team and they will all participate in supporting one another, sharing information, solving problems and improving continuity and the quality of care delivered to their clients. They are all doing the core work of the organization.

Who facilitates or leads these teams? It may be their formal manager at the next level, or the team may have developed its skills so that they become increasingly "self-managing," relying on a facilitator from within the team. Generally, the more self-managing a team can be the better. This means that they must assume responsibility for their own performance.

You are probably used to seeing organization charts drawn as boxes and solid lines going from top to bottom. Instead, we have drawn the organization charts as sets of interlocking circles that better represent the reality of teamwork and collaborative relationships.

Are teams ever entirely self-managing? No. We may use that term, but it never means that a team is actually without any management. Everyone reports to someone else and is accountable to someone else.

## Enabling or Support Teams

In addition to the teams doing the core work there are critical support activities that enable the core work. Human resource management, technology services, quality management, financial support, and education and practice improvement are all essential activities to providing excellent client service. Just as it is beneficial for those in the core service delivery work to function well in teams, it is equally beneficial for those who work in these support groups to also function well as teams, both within their function as a team members supporting or participating on service delivery or managing teams.

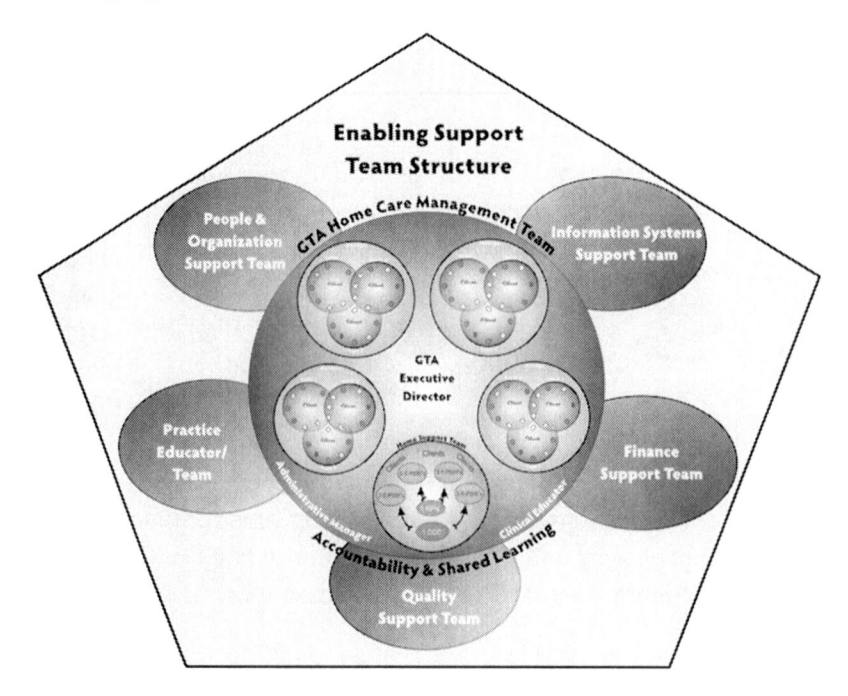

This illustration is intended to describe the relationship between these enabling teams and one health care management team. The specifics of the diagram are not important, simply the idea of how these teams overlap and interact with one another.

## LEADERSHIP TEAMS

Just as every care provider doing front line work should be a member of a team, every manager should also be a member of a team. If you think about it, the Board of Directors of a company is a team. The CEO and the senior business unit leaders are, or should be, a team. Each of these teams has responsibility for managing the on-going operations and that means that they are engaged in continuous improvement of operations. Their ability to collaborate, so solve problems and implement action plans, will all depend on how well they function together as a team.

It is also important that leadership or managing teams serve as a model for the culture, a model for the behavior that they wish to see throughout the organization. This is a key aspect of leadership.

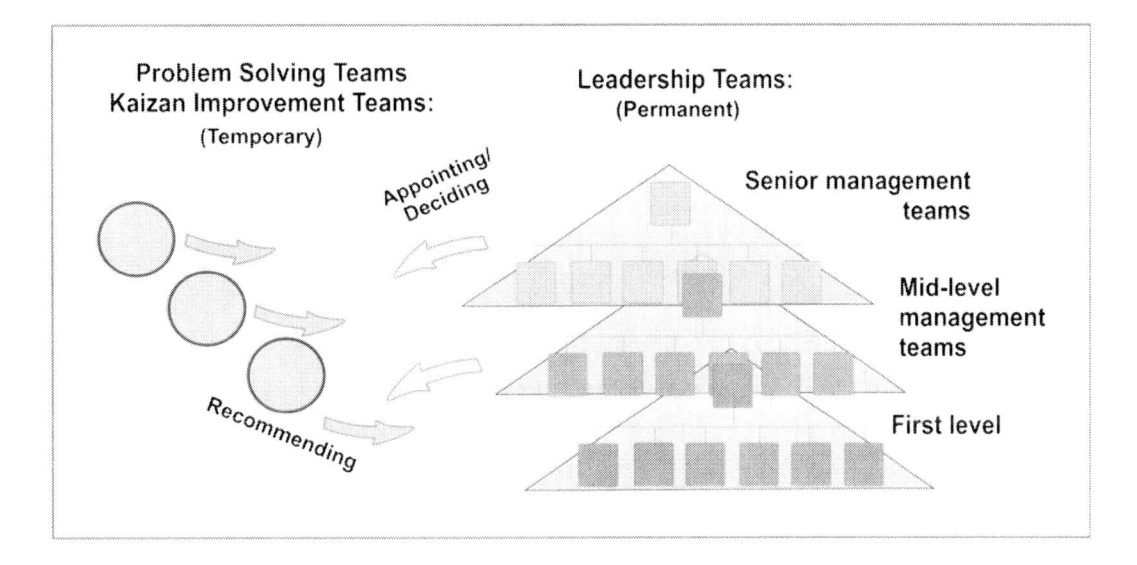

Just as health care delivery teams and enabling teams have responsibilities for process improvement, leadership teams have this same responsibility. For example, there is a process of strategic planning. There is a budgeting and financial management process. There is a process for exploring new opportunities for new healthcare services. Each of these processes is critical to the success of any organization. Studying and improving these processes is the work of leadership teams.

Too often executives and managers see themselves as "Lone Rangers" riding through the organization to find the bad guys and solve problems on their own. Many research studies have demonstrated that successful leaders are those who are successful at building a strong team around them, working well with that team, and giving credit to the team. In other words, they are good team leaders. The Lone Ranger was a mythical character, a figment of imagination. The idea that managers can ride into town and find the bad guys and then ride out of town is equally a myth.

## KAIZEN, PROJECT IMPROVEMENT OR PROBLEM-SOLVING TEAMS

The design team that created the new health care delivery process was a temporary team. It was, in lean management terms, a Kaizen team. You can also call it a project improvement or problem-solving team.

From time to time it is advantageous to put together a team comprised of members from different functions, different levels, or different regions of the organization to solve some problem or make improvement that cuts across many teams. Some problems cannot be solved within one care delivery team or one management team alone.

Project improvement teams are temporary. They are not the primary job of any member, but members who work on different teams will serve on a project team to find a solution to a particular problem.

Project teams may be chosen to work on a problem by the management team, or permanent care delivery teams may identify a problem beyond their control and request that a project team be formed to attack that problem.

Unlike managing teams, these teams are not deciding teams, they are formed to study, analyze and develop recommendations that are then approved by a managing team.

Which of the above types of teams do you belong to?

---

What other teams does your team interact with in the organization? What kind of teams are these?

_____

_____

What are the key differences between your team and other types of teams in the organization?

_____

_____

## MEMBER ROLES AND RESPONSIBILITIES

A baseball team or a health care service team succeeds because the players play their position with skill and enthusiasm. Outfielders, pitchers and infielders know their job, their particular contribution to the success of the team. On a team at work there are also distinct and important roles that need to be played.

When teams become mature and skilled it is common to rotate or share these roles. But first, we should understand the roles, practice them, and develop our skills. As we do, the performance of the entire team will improve.

### THE FACILITATOR

Have you ever been in a meeting and sat there wondering just what the topic was and feeling like no one else knew either?

Have you been in a meeting when you felt that everyone was already in agreement, but people just kept talking and no one seemed able to just close the discussion?

Have you been in a meeting where a couple people did all the talking and others were never able to get a word in?

These are just some of the symptoms of poor facilitation that plague meetings. The ability to facilitate a meeting has nothing to do with rank in the organization. I have seen hourly employees on the shop floor do a fantastic job of facilitating a group and I have seen company presidents with virtually no ability to facilitate a meeting. Facilitation is a particular skill that can be learned by anyone, and someone on every team must be a skilled facilitator. Neither formal rank nor formal education guarantees that someone is a good facilitator.

What is facilitation? *To facilitate is to make something easy for others.* To facilitate a group is to help others in the group make their contribution. Facilitation can be as complicated as planning out an entire series of meetings or it can be the simple act of asking a member of the group if they would like to say something. But most of all, it is the concern for others, the sensitivity to recognize that some are talking so much that others are unable to express their opinions, or the sensitivity to recognize when the group has reached a point of agreement. It is the courage to bring order to what may be the chaos of conversation. It is the most frequent act of leadership that is most needed in organizations today.

And who is the facilitator? There is almost always someone who has the formal role of facilitation in a group. However, and this is extremely important, the actual act of facilitating, of making it easy for others to contribute, is something that every member of the group can and should do. Any member of the group can ask the question "Has everyone had an opportunity to give their opinion?" Or say "It feels like we are in agreement, are we ready to decide?" These are the types of facilitating questions or statements that "move things along" in a group and any member can help make it easy for others or the group to move along.

What is the function of the facilitator? It can be summarized in the following points.

## Organizing Your Team

> **Facilitation is...**
>
> - To create a clear agenda and help the group follow the agreed upon agenda.
>
> - To state the topic and help the members of the group stay on the topic.
>
> - To create an environment that is encouraging and safe for all to contribute.
>
> - To help others contribute by inviting or encouraging them in a manner that is helpful to them.
>
> - To be sure that contributions are heard by the group.
>
> - To bring topics to a close or decision when the need for dialogue or discussion is complete.
>
> - To restate or clarify decisions in a manner that creates unity of understanding.
>
> - To resolve conflicts that may arise in the group.

We are most likely to think of meetings led by the formal leader or manager of a group and assume that this formal leader will facilitate the group. This is the (F-L) Facilitator-Leader role. This is the way that most traditional meetings are facilitated. But, is there a rule that says that the formal manager must facilitate the meeting? Maybe it would be better in some circumstances for the formal manager to sit back, observe, and participate. When the formal manager leads the discussion it is difficult for her to avoid biasing the group in a direction. The conversation is more likely to be open and creative when the facilitator is not the formal manager.

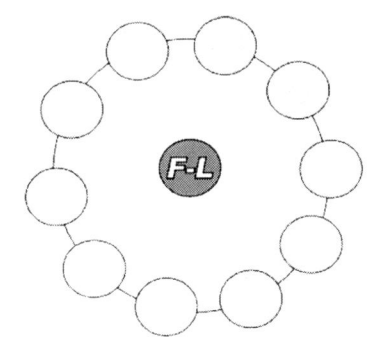

If it is clear that the formal manager of the group wishes to take charge or does not feel that the group is ready to take responsibility, this arrangement may be the best. It may also be the best in a development or training stage when the leader has the intention of modeling, demonstrating, good group leadership skills so others can learn.

It is often the case that the facilitator is not the formal leader or manager. It may be that a number of

Page 65

individuals on the team have been trained in the skills of leading meetings and the function of facilitation can be rotated among them. In some senior management teams where all the senior managers had been trained in the team process and all were leaders of their next level teams the senior management may happy to rotate the role of facilitator, or "chair" of the meeting, to a different person each month. Or, in some cases it is useful to have a facilitator who is not a permanent member of a team, but someone who is completely unbiased and is participating without any intention of contributing to substantive matters. If the group wants to discuss how it works together as a group, its internal process, it may be helpful to have an outside facilitator.

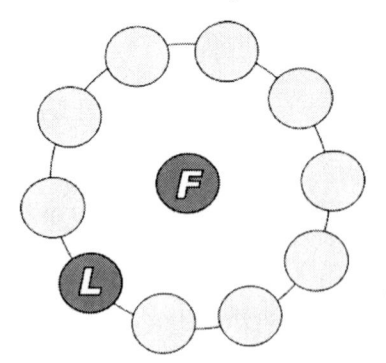

It is worth considering the different roles a facilitator may play in relation to the other members of the team. If a team is relatively inexperienced in the team process, it is likely that the team will be very dependent on the facilitator to make progress. In this case the facilitator plays a central role. However, as the team gains experience and maturity, the role of facilitation becomes increasingly less dominant and shared by other members of the team. In this case both the leader and facilitator may be pictured as part of the circle, but not in the center of the circle.

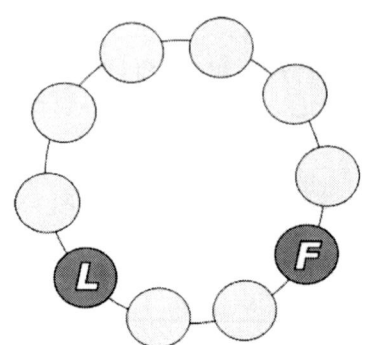

## The Scribe

It is very useful to have someone other than the facilitator designated as the "scribe" or note keeper of the group. This person will take minutes and distribute those minutes to all of the members of the group. It is helpful if the scribe has a laptop computer and composes the minutes during the meeting. At the end of the meeting he may read the decisions and action steps that were agreed to and check with the group to be sure that he has recorded them correctly. In many organizations the meeting room is connected with wireless Internet access and the scribe can email the minutes to the members of the team before leaving the room.

The nature of minutes is important. Some note keepers have a tendency to write down everything that is said, as if they were a court recorder. That is **not** what the scribe should do. In a team meeting the members should feel free to say things that are just ideas, and then change their mind as the dialogue progresses. If each comment is being recorded, this will create a hesitancy to offer ideas in a free manner and then to change one's position as new ideas are shared. The scribe should simply record the topics, the decisions, and the action steps that were agreed to.

The scribe may also maintain a "parking lot." A parking lot may be on a flipchart or in the minutes. This simply is a place to put things that we don't want to discuss now, but we should discuss at some later time. It is very normal for members of the group to think of things that are important, but, if discussed now, might take the group off their current topic.

## THE TIMEKEEPER

It is usually assumed that the facilitator or chair of a meeting, who has her eye on the agenda, will take the responsibility of keeping the group on time. However, it is often the case that the facilitator is not a "pure" facilitator, but is an active member of the group, fully engaged in the conversation. In this case, it may be useful to have someone serve as the timekeeper.

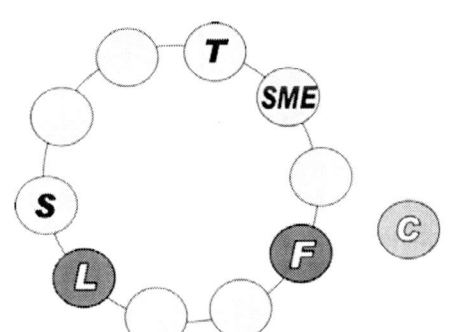

If your meeting is planned for two hours, you may have five topics and each of these is allocated a planned amount of time by the group. It is very helpful if the timekeeper has his own flip chart. At the beginning of a topic, the timekeeper writes on the flip chart "30" if the topic has been allocated 30 minutes. With ten minutes to go, the timekeeper can get up and cross out "30" and write "10" on the flip chart without interrupting the conversation. He can do the same with five minutes and two minutes left. With two minutes left he might just stand by the flip chart, still without saying anything, but you can be sure that the group will be very conscious of the time. When time has run out, he then crosses off that last number of writes "0". At this point the facilitator will ask the group if this topic requires more time, and if so, does that mean they will extend the meeting longer, or take time from another topic. If your group has trouble getting through your agenda, you may find this method helpful.

## SUBJECT MATTER EXPERTS (SME'S)

Many teams have found it helpful to ask a member to specialize in some area of knowledge or some function, that is helpful to the group, but in which it is not necessary for every member to be involved. For example, there may be one person designated as the data management Subject Matter Expert (SME); this could be the member of the team who knows where to get the data for the team's scorecard. He or she will plot that data on graphs and report that data to the team at each team meeting.

Another member of the group may take on the role of helping others with computers and software. In virtually every office there is a computer/software SME, informally recognized as "the person you go to" when you need help with your new computer or software. This person is acting as an SME, even though there may be no formal recognition of this role.

There can be an SME for communicating with customers and suppliers, one for training new members, or one for communicating with management or subordinates. It will be helpful to think about what regularly occurring tasks are important to the team and ask whether it will be helpful to ask a member to take on the role of SME for that task, function or knowledge area. It is a good idea to plan a schedule of rotation for SME roles. This will give team members the opportunity to develop different skills.

## COACH

As teams are developing their skills, it is helpful to have a coach. For the same reasons an athlete benefits from the experience and skill of a coach, a management or work team can also benefit. A coach is not a member of the team. It is very important that the coach not be from within the immediate "power structure" so that he is not hindered by concerns about being "politic" in his feedback to the team. A coach does not go out on the field and play. A coach is on the sidelines and observes the play, and from this perspective can give objective feedback. The coach may meet with the facilitator or leader before a meeting and ask for observations as to the progress and functioning of the team. The coach will then observe and may give the entire team feedback and may also meet with the leader or facilitator to give feedback on how performance of that role can be improved.

It is important that the coach be sensitive to the need to encourage the team, to provide positive feedback on the progress they are making. If the coach only gives feedback on areas in which the team can improve, his advice will soon not be welcomed. It is also important that the coach does not overwhelm the team with thirty things they need to do differently. No one, nor any group, works on thirty things at once. It is great if they work on two or three. Sometime later they can work on the others.

Coaches may be internal or external consultants who are hired to help with the process of developing the team's skills. When teams are senior management teams, it is desirable for the coaches to be external consultants who have both independence and extensive experience. However, with most teams, it is desirable to develop the internal capacity in the organization for an on-going coaching process.

Organizing Your Team

Now it is time for you to define the roles on your team:

1. Who is the formal "leader" or "manager" of your team?

2. Who will facilitate your meetings? Is this a permanent assignment, or will this rotate among members?

3. Who will be the "scribe" or note taker for your team?

4. Who will be the timekeeper?

5. Are their subject matter experts who will attend your meetings? When?

6. Who will coach and provide feedback to your team?

## SIMPLE THINGS THAT MAKE A DIFFERENCE

Sometimes very simple things can make a large difference in the success of a team and the effectiveness of meetings. The following are some issues you should check off to be sure you aren't overlooking these simple things.

It is very helpful if your team meeting becomes a pattern, a recognizable "drum beat" predictable, easy to remember and easy to find. If the time and place of the meeting are constantly changing it is not realistic to expect the members to show up reliably.

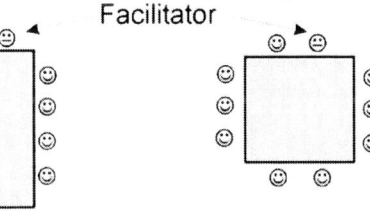

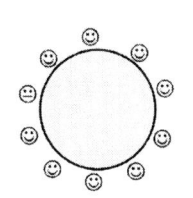

Be sure that the place where you meet is quiet and a place that is least likely to be subject to interruptions. Hopefully, the room you meet in will be well lit, comfortable and have enough room. If the room is too small, it has a negative effect on the emotions of the group. It is important to have extra room for flip charts and for members of the group to stand up and cluster around a chart or other group exercise.

To minimize distractions it is important that everyone turn off cell phones or beepers and it is wise to put a "meeting-in-progress" sign on the door. It is also important that the members of the team tell those who might interrupt them (whoever answers the telephone!) that they are not to be interrupted unless it is a personal emergency (family member in the hospital), or the president of the company calling.

Page 69

The room arrangement does matter. Look at the following possible seating arrangements for a team meeting. Note the position of the facilitator as well as the team members. Ask yourself the following questions about each of these arrangements:

- Which arrangement is likely to give the facilitator a greater sense of authority?

- Which will cause the members to defer to the facilitator?

- Which arrangement is likely to cause some members to feel more powerful?

- Which arrangement is likely to cause most of the member to feel comfortable contributing to the group?

- If you came into a meeting with each of these arrangements, where would you choose to sit?

- Which arrangement do you feel would be most conducive to reaching consensus? Why?

Choose a seating arrangement that reduces perceptions of unequal power if you want to encourage openness, sharing and the ability to reach consensus.

When planning a team meeting, you should think of any things you may need to use in the meeting. It is usually desirable to have two flip charts in the room, with tape to post pages on the walls (unless you have the self-sticking variety or walls with magnets). Be sure to have sufficient markers. And, you may wish to have "Post-it-notes" available for brainstorming activities.

When should team meetings be held? It is important to establish a regular schedule. In most work environments a weekly meeting is desirable. However, many teams these days are comprised of people who travel, live in different cities, or otherwise find it difficult to be in the same place at the same time. This may require a once a month meeting or virtual meetings.

Virtual meetings, either on the phone, or using some Internet meeting software or web site, are increasingly common. Regardless, establish a schedule that is predictable and at close enough intervals to provide for frequent review of your scorecard, solving problems promptly, and creating unity of effort among the team.

Let's make a plan for our meetings:

When and how often will our team meet?

Where will our team meet?

_____

Which types of topics will we plan to discuss in virtual meetings (on the phone) and which will we reserve for face-to-face meetings?

_____

_____

**Checklist of Simple Things**

- ✓ Establish a "rhythm"
- ✓ Predictable place and time
- ✓ Interruption free Environment
- ✓ Arrange the Room for Maximum Participation
- ✓ Make Necessary Tools Available in Advance
- ✓ Plan Frequency for Short Interval Problem-solving

# CHAPTER 6

# STAGES OF TEAM DEVELOPMENT

The purpose of this chapter is to assist the team to recognize normal patterns of development or stages of maturity that most teams pass through.

## OBJECTIVES:

1. To recognize the characteristics of a mature and well-functioning team.
2. To recognize the current level of maturity of your team.
3. To identify specific ways that your team may advance to a higher level of maturity and performance.

As every team begins to practice and develop its skills it will pass through stages of growth. Whether you are on a primary care team or a leadership team you are likely to witness some behavior that you may at times find to be "adolescent" or which you may describe in some other way. It's OK! Just as your own offspring must go through some stages of exploration, testing, and learning to cooperate, teams go through very similar stages.

In 1965, Bruce Tuckman wrote that there are normal, even necessary stages of development that a team passes through as it matures. These stages - forming, storming, norming and performing - are often presented as if you MUST go through them as you must go through childhood and adolescence. It is true that there is a normal progression in the social development of a team, but there is nothing certain about these stages. In our work settings it is normal that teams may have already established some form of relationship, may have worked on other teams, and may go quickly and relatively painlessly toward maturity.

It is still a useful framework to consider your own development. Read through the description of these stages and then ask yourselves, "Where are we in this process?"

## FORMING

In the first stages of team building, the *forming* of the team takes place. The team meets and learns about the opportunity and challenges, agrees on goals, and begins to tackle the tasks. Team members tend to behave quite independently. They may be motivated but are usually relatively uninformed of the issues and objectives of the team. Team members are usually on their best behavior but very focused on themselves. Mature team members begin to model appropriate behavior even at this early phase.

Leaders of the team tend to need to be directive during this phase.

The forming stage of any team is important because in this stage the members of the team get to know one another and make new friends. This is also a good opportunity to see how each member of the team works as an individual and how each responds to pressure. Trust is being established, and this will be the basis of their future work.

## STORMING

Groups are then likely to enter the *storming* stage in which different ideas and individuals compete for consideration. The team addresses issues such as what problems they are really supposed to solve, how they will function independently and together and what leadership model they will accept. Team members open up to each other and confront each other's ideas and perspectives.

In some cases *storming* can be resolved quickly. In others, the team never leaves this stage. The maturity of some team members usually determines whether the team will ever move out of this stage. Some team members will focus on minutiae to evade real issues.

The *storming* stage may be necessary to the growth of the team. It can be contentious, unpleasant and even painful to members of the team who are averse to conflict. Tolerance of each team member and their differences needs to be emphasized. Without tolerance and patience, the team will fail. This phase can become destructive to the team and will lower motivation if allowed to get out of control.

This is the stage during which coaching and facilitation may be most critical. The team and individuals may benefit from feedback by an objective third party.

## Norming

At some point, the team will likely enter the *norming* stage. Team members adjust their behavior to each other as they develop work habits that make teamwork seem more natural and fluid. Team members often work through this stage by agreeing on rules, values, professional behavior, shared methods, working tools and even taboos. During this phase, team members begin to trust each other. Motivation increases as the team gets more acquainted with the project or process for which the team is responsible.

Teams in this phase may lose their creativity if the norming behaviors become too strong and begin to stifle healthy dissent and the team begins to exhibit groupthink.

Leaders of the team during this phase tend to be participative more than in the earlier stages. The team members can be expected to take more responsibility for making decisions and for their professional behavior.

## Performing

Hopefully, your team will reach the *performing* stage. These high-performing teams are able to function as a unit as they find ways to get the job done smoothly and effectively without inappropriate conflict or the need for external supervision. Team members have become interdependent. By this time they are motivated and knowledgeable. The team members are now competent, autonomous and able to handle the decision-making process without supervision. Dissent is expected and allowed as long as it is channeled through means acceptable to the team.

Leaders of the team during this phase are almost always participative. The facilitation of the team may now rotate among members. The team will make most of the necessary decisions. Even the most high-performing teams will revert to earlier stages in certain circumstances. Many long-standing teams will go through these cycles many times as they react to changing circumstances. For example, a change in leadership may cause the team to revert to *storming* as the new people challenge the existing norms and dynamics of the team.

In which stage is your team? What are some of the signs or behavior that indicates its stage of development?

_____

_____

What are some things you can do to help the team move through the current stage and get to the performing stage?

_____

_____

## TEAM MATURITY AND DECISION-MAKING

Another way to understand the maturing of a team is to consider the degree to which the team takes responsibility for its own performance and how managers react to their maturity.

When a team acts as a truly high performing team, initiating action to communicate with clients and customers, measuring its own performance, and acting with self-initiative to make improvements, it may be said to have high "performance initiative." Many teams when they are first formed are waiting to be told what to do. They are looking to do what is acceptable, not to initiate improvements.

If you look at the next diagram, you will see a matrix with Performance Initiative on one axis. On the other axis is the control of decisions – who is making the decisions? An easy way to think of this is to think about a child growing into adolescence, and then into mature adulthood. Every parent has struggled with the issue of how much freedom to allow a teenager. Of course, every teenager wants more freedom to decide when to come home at night, whom to associate with, etc. How does the parent know when to let go and "delegate" these kinds of decisions to the young person? The answer lies in performance. The more maturely teenagers behave, the more reasonable it is to allow them to make their own decisions. The parent moves through a progression from telling, through advising, to delegating.

What happens if the parent gives up control of decision-making too soon? This can lead to poor performance. The teenager may not be ready to make his own decisions and may make unwise ones. Or, what happens if the teenager is ready to make her own decisions, but the parent is over-controlling? This is de-motivating to the young person and is likely to lead to rebellious behavior.

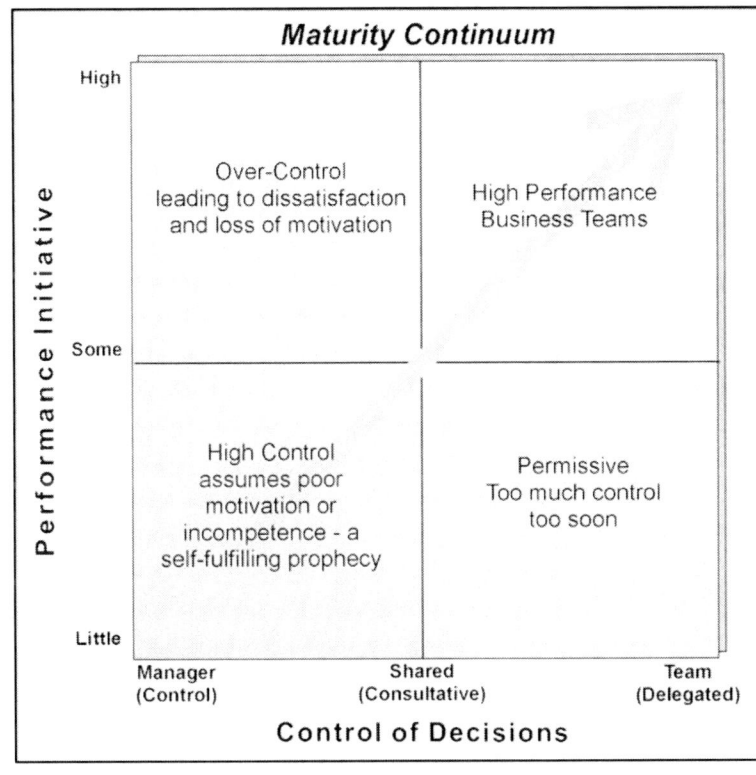

*Maturity Continuum*

| | Manager (Control) | Shared (Consultative) | Team (Delegated) |
|---|---|---|---|
| **High** | Over-Control leading to dissatisfaction and loss of motivation | | High Performance Business Teams |
| **Some** | | | |
| **Little** | High Control assumes poor motivation or incompetence - a self-fulfilling prophecy | | Permissive Too much control too soon |

Performance Initiative (vertical axis)
Control of Decisions (horizontal axis)

Teams are not that different. When teams take responsibility for their own performance, the manager should assert less control and delegate more. On the other hand, if the team fails to take ownership of its performance or fails to initiate improvement efforts, the manager has a responsibility to be more directive.

What sometimes happens when implementing teams is that the manager is told that he "is supposed to let go." So he does, even though he may be very uncomfortable with this. His gut may have told him the truth, that the team was not ready to take responsibility on its own. This is a common cause of failure. Of course, failure also occurs because of over-control and the subsequent de-motivation of the team.

A human life progresses from dependence through independence to interdependence. In other words an infant, when born, is entirely dependent on the parents. Human beings are one of the least independent of infants. Fish are more capable at birth. But, as the infant matures in childhood she gains degrees of independence, walking, feeding, and learning to dress herself. The primary characteristic of teenagers is their declaration of independence – "I can do it myself!" But, that is not yet maturity. When you enter marriage you enter an agreement to be interdependent. In maturity individuals, teams, even companies and countries recognize the need for close collaboration, mutual interests, and development of the behavior required for effective interdependence.

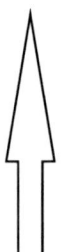

---

**Interdependence** ⟹ *Adulthood*

Teams collaborate with clients, customers and other functional areas to make decisions that are in the best interest of all.

**Independence** ⟹ *Adolescence*

The team exerts autonomy and begins to take control of performance. They act in the best interest of the team, but don't necessarily think about how the team's actions affect overall performance and do not involve "outsiders" to help make the best decisions.

**Dependence** ⟹ *Childhood*

Members depend on managers to worry about the overall performance of the team. They are only concerned that they do *their* job well, and that their personal needs are met.

# Chapter 7

# Clarifying Decision Styles

The purpose of this chapter is to provide the team facilitator and all team members with the skills to assist others in making their contribution to the team and to create an orderly process within the team.

## Objectives:

1. To clarify how decisions are made and should be made in different situations.

2. To understand the relationship between decision-making styles and the culture of the organization.

As you build a lean culture it will be necessary to shift how decisions are made throughout your organization. You will increasingly become a high-trust culture as primary care teams and other teams demonstrate their maturity and their ability to improve service to their clients.

This is a normal transition as everyone learns to focus on the process, rather than blaming people, and everyone develops a unity of effort around providing the best possible care to clients and customers.

The reality of health care and home health care in particular, is that each individual is making decisions each day that affect the life and well-being of clients. We must trust in the responsible nature of each care provider. Similarly, we must learn to develop trust in primary care teams and managing teams at every level to solve problems and make decisions that serve the interests of both customers and clients.

## CLARIFY WHO MAKES WHAT DECISION AND HOW:

A true lean culture is one in which consensus decision-making is valued. The value of creating ownership for a decision and assuring that a decision is of the highest possible quality is more important than making it quickly.

What has happened is that the decisions around the new process and social systems were made by those who must implement those decisions. They now understand why they were made, why they make sense, what they mean to the clients and customers, and they are committed to their implementation. Too often an outside expert is called upon to make decisions or an internal manager who thinks she or he knows best, but the decisions are not "owned" by those who must then implement them. The implementation process then becomes one of constant selling, controlling, demanding and blaming. Taking the time to develop consensus, ownership by those _who know_, _who care_, and _who must act_, is almost always a wise investment.

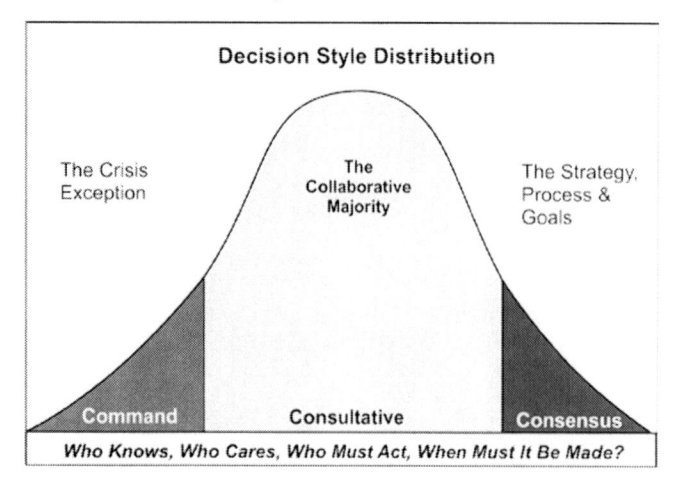

Members of a team want to understand how decisions are made and who makes them. Many of the conflicts that arise around teams involve a failure to create this clarity. If team members think they are going to make a decision, and a manager then makes the decision alone, they will be upset even if they don't disagree with the decision. Disunity results from differing expectations and feeling betrayed that an agreement (real or imagined) isn't being followed.

In my own company we had a once a month team meeting when all of the consultants and administrative staff would meet for the day, share learning, discuss the company's finances, marketing, etc. More than once, I would put an issue before the group and ask for input. Frequently, one of the consultants would ask me, "Larry, are you asking us for input so you can make the decision, or are you asking us to reach a consensus and make the decision?" Good question. Sometimes I wasn't sure and needed to clarify this in my own mind. Several times, I asked them whether they thought I should make the decision or let the group reach a decision. On most of those occasions, they preferred that I make the decision after listening to their input. They didn't want to spend the time to reach a consensus. It is not true that team members want to be involved in making every decision, but they do want input, and they want to know how those decisions are made.

Here is a quick primer on assigning decision responsibility: Consider three types of decisions: Command, consultative and consensus. The criteria for deciding which to use are *who knows, who cares, who acts,* and *when must it be made?*

## COMMAND DECISIONS

Command decisions are those made by an individual. Individual command authority is not dead and not merely a left over dinosaur of the Roman Legions. Of course, command worked well on the battlefield on which quick decisions were required and obedience won battles. Even today, if the building is burning down, if the machine is spitting smoke and oil, if the customer calls and is furious that he got the wrong material delivered – is the right answer to call a meeting? Definitely not! These are decisions in which speed is more important than reaching consensus. These decisions are best left to individuals who are on-the-spot and have expert knowledge.

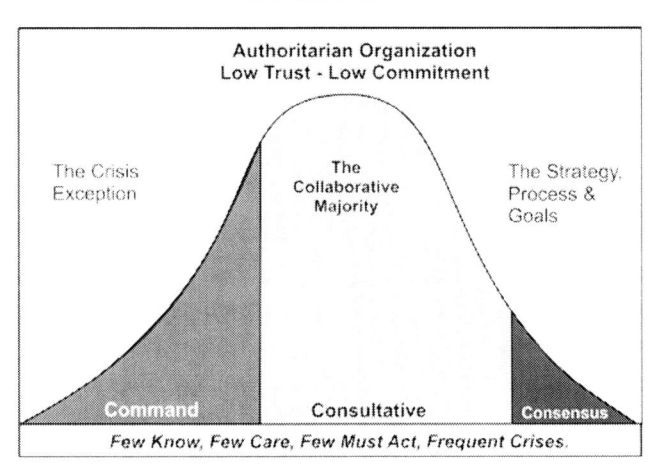

Speed and expert knowledge are two reasons for command to be the preferred decision style. In the operating room, with the patient cut open and the cardiologist holding a heart in his hand that has just stopped beating – do you want him to call a meeting to get help through consensus decision-making?

Not if it's your heart! Of course, you want him to use his expert knowledge and make a decision, fast! The greater the degree of knowledge an individual has compared to others on a team, the more likely a command decision is appropriate. The greater the required speed, the more likely it is that command decision-making is appropriate.

An organization in which command decision-making is predominant is an organization that lives in frequent crisis. This raises serious questions about the ability of the leaders to plan, engage in systematic action, and develop the people below them. Or it is an organization dominated by personalities whose egos prevent them from letting go of decisions and trusting others. Predominance of command decision-making reflects low trust and will soon de-motivate employees.

## CONSULTATIVE OR SHARED DECISIONS

Consultative decisions involve selective involvement by those who know, care, or must act. If a referring health care agency calls and a client is in need of an emergency visit, they do not want to be told that you will put that on the agenda for your next team meeting! They need to know whether you can respond appropriately NOW! But, if you say, "I understand and I will contact me team immediately and get back to with fifteen minutes to let you know if we can meet their needs, this will likely satisfy the requesting agency. They will understand the need to consult others quickly. But, they must know that you are in control of the decision and you are taking responsibility.

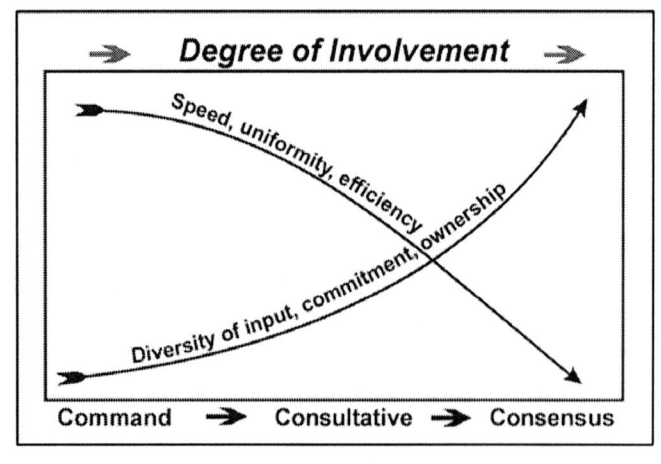

This is consultative decision-making. Consultative decisions are those when an individual maintains responsibility for getting a decision made, but takes time to consult with those who know, who care, and who must act.

## CONSENSUS DECISIONS

Consensus decisions are true team decisions where you turn over the decision to the group. When do you do this? First, when the conditions of speed and individual expertise are not the most important factors. When the quality of the decision, commitment of the players, and unified action are most important, it is time to use consensus decision-making. Consensus decisions involve a cost – the cost of time, energy of the group, and the risk that you may not like the decision.

When do you employ consensus decision-making? For those decisions that involve long-term goals, and how we do things, our ongoing processes. All members of the group have an investment in the goals of the group and the "how" and "why" we do our work. Involvement in these types of decisions gains commitment, gains the wisdom of the group, and provides for shared learning.

Ask your team which decisions should be command, consultative or consensus. You can create a great deal of clarity and have the group focus on those things that add most value for the group. The time and energy of teams is often wasted with trivial and inappropriate decisions. Use common sense.

The Health care Service Delivery Design Team developed a set of proposed decision-making processes, defining which decision they felt that primary care teams and other teams would be making and how they should be made. However, this is only a proposed starting point. It is important that you take the proposal they developed, or others have found to work successfully, and clarify your own decision-making process.

## Exercise: Clarify Decision Styles

Make a list of decisions that get made by your team. You might brainstorm this and make a list on a flip chart in a team meeting. Then look at the decision style criteria on the previous pages and make a list of which decisions should be command, which consultative, and which consensus. Also indicate who is involved in each:

1. Command Decisions:

_____

_____

_____

_____

2. Consultative Decisions:

_____

_____

_____

_____

3. Consensus Decisions:

_____

_____

_____

_____

# Chapter 8

# Standard Work

The purpose of this chapter is to familiarize you with the concept of *Standard Work* and *Leader Standard Work* and give you an opportunity to define the standard work among your team members.

## Objectives:

1. To define that work or behavior on the part of team members that should be standard, regular or periodic behavior that will support the effort of the team.
2. To establish those patterns of behavior that will not only assure the effectiveness of the team in meeting its objectives, but to assure that optimum care is provided to our clients.

One of the aspects of lean management that has been adopted from manufacturing, and has proven effective in many different settings, is the idea of standard work and leader standard work. The idea is very simple. You can imagine on an auto assembly line that a standard way is developed to accomplish the task of painting the body, or installing the engine or other component. Similarly, in a health care setting, you can imagine that in a hospital there may be a standard way to insert an IV, or to prepare a patient for an operation, or to clean a patient's room..

These standard work procedures reduce error and reduce the need for "reinventing the wheel" over and over again. Similarly, to support the work of your primary care team or a management team, there may be standard work, standard activities or behavior that should be done daily, weekly, or monthly.

Developing standard work should not be confused with making things rigid or bureaucratic. There is a balance between continuous improvement and standard work. Lean organizations are constantly seeking to improve the way they do things. Therefore the standard work changes as soon as someone or some team demonstrate a better way. In fact, Taichii Ohno, one of the founders of lean management said "Where there is no standard work, there can be no kaizen (continuous improvement)."

When we all know our standard work it can reduce misunderstandings and reduce errors when one person needs to step in to cover for another person.

To achieve a significant change in organization culture it is necessary to reconsider the work of all employees, at all levels. One of the most common mistakes made when implementing lean management is to assume that the change is one that must occur at the first level, and not at management levels. In fact, the changes at management levels are just as important as the changes at the first level. How managers think, act, set the example, and take personal responsibility for improvement, will determine the success of the organization.

## What is Standard Work?

One way to understand standard work is to think about your personal life or non-work activities. For example, when you are preparing a meal there is a standard way that you set the table. You do not have to spend time thinking about what utensils to put on the table or where they are placed because long ago you developed or accepted a standard way to set a table. When you start to prepare a meal that you have prepared many times before you have probably developed a standard way of preparing that meal. And, when you get up in the morning or go to bed at night, you most likely have standard things you do to prepare yourself for the day or the night. All of these are personal and informal standard work.

At any healthcare organization, much of the work we do has very significant consequences in terms of the health, safety and well-being of our clients. In healthcare there has been a traditional culture of individual expertise and individual decision-making as to how to conduct procedures and how to assist clients. This is understandable when doctors each pride themselves on their expertise and do not want to be restricted or instructed as to how to do their work. But, freedom for everyone to decide has its price. We agree on the standard behavior of stopping at a red light and going on green. Does this restrict our freedom or increase our ability to move swiftly from one point to another?

Here are some types of activities for a healthcare or health care service provider that might be worth considering for standard work:

- The time and nature of pre-visit communications with a client.
- Questions asked of the client in initial interviews.
- Preparation for visits, such as information gathering and acquiring or assuring the proper supplies.
- Initial activities during each visit, such as washing hands, asking the client questions, and checking charts.
- Method and nature of reporting on each visit.
- Questions to ask the client in regard to their comfort and satisfaction.

Standard work is not for care providers alone. It is also for team leaders, managers and even executives of the organization. The culture of management, like the culture of medical professionals, has often been one of feeling superior to the need for any routine or standard work. Yet, in fact, the CEO of an organization has standard meetings that he or she must attend, standard reports to review, and standard activities that support and encourage the work below. This is *leader standard work*.

Leader standard work typically does the following:

- It reviews standard work at the next level.
- It reviews the quality of healthcare performance and the conditions that impact performance.
- It considers the environment, cleanliness, and orderliness of the work environment.
- It includes a check on visual controls.
- It includes listening, learning, and seeking to understand.

- It incorporates the responsibility to motivate and encourage employees.
- It includes a focus on process, not just results.
- It documents the job of "lean management."

Leader standard work creates a disciplined process of management. If you are the coach of a professional football team, for example, it is important that your own behavior creates a model of disciplined action. You expect your players to eat properly, run a certain amount each day, and practice their routines and plays, in a disciplined manner. They are like the front line workers in an organization. By seeing that you adhere to a disciplined process of management yourself, this encourages them to do the same. Military officers understand this same principle. You cannot expect better behavior below than you demonstrate yourself.

## How Much Time is devoted to Standard Work?

There is no one right answer to how much time should be devoted to standard work. However, it is logical to assume that at lower levels a higher percent of time is devoted to standard work and at higher levels a greater percent to unique work.

It is true that at more senior levels a greater majority of time is spent on unique activity, planning new business activity and solving larger problems. It is reasonable to assume that from the first level employee to the CEO there is a progression from more standard work to more unique work.

| Position | % Time Devoted to Standard Work |
|---|---|
| Executive Management | 5-15% |
| Regional Management | 15-25% |
| District Managers | 20-40% |
| First Level Managers | 30-50% |
| Team Leaders | 60-80% |
| Care Providers | 80-100% |

# Deciding on Standard Work

## Standard Work for Health care Providers

Your team coach will be able to provide you with a list, form and categories of standard work that has been developed by other health care delivery teams and other leadership teams. These are a good starting point for you to develop your own standard work.

Here are some categories of standard work that you might consider for your health care delivery team:

1. Health care Visit Practices
    a. Environmental scan for health and safety factors
    b. A script for standard introduction and questions.
    c. Standard practices as per body mechanics.
2. Planning and Communication with Clients and Funders:
    a. Periodic checking for communication from your Client Care Coordinator, clients or managers.
    b. Pre visit questions to ask.
    c. In visit charting and reporting.
    d. Initial progress reports.
    e. Post visit reporting and communication.
3. Team Member Activities
    a. Daily or Weekly team huddles
    b. Information sharing with your team
    c. Follow up on action items.

## Leader Standard

As you develop lean management practices standard work for leaders will become clearer and the usefulness of standard work will be demonstrated at the management levels of the organization.

It is important that your management think through the important tasks for each position. However, at each level the focus should be on helping, facilitating, encouraging, and supporting the work of the next level below. Ultimately it is the first level that does the most to serve the clients and customers.

Some initial work developing leader standard work has been done and the following categories were developed. You can use this as a beginning point for your own development of your leader standard work.

1. Observing Work Practices
    a. Observe KPI data on dashboard and visual display.
    b. Check to see that visual displays of key performance data are up-to-date.
    c. Periodic observation of care providers visits.
    d. Observe the standard work of the next level
    e. Provide feedback and recognition.
    f. See and reinforce improvement made by those doing the work.
2. Planning:
    a. Plan weekly management meetings
    b. Budget review and budget planning
    c. Personnel resource planning
    d. Attend planning meetings
3. Reporting and Communicating Activities
    a. Review occurrence reports
    b. Reporting and liaison with funders
    c. KPI review meetings
    d. Town hall or other employee meetings
    e. Attend weekly management meetings
    f. Business plan and financial reviews.
4. Managing Others and Problem-solving
    a. Personal development plans
    b. Provide recognition.
    c. Assist others in problem-solving

The above categories are just a starting point or suggestions. It will be very useful for your team coach to assist you by sharing work developed by other teams or best practices from practice leaders in the organization.

The following pages present a worksheet that may be used in developing and maintaining leader standard work practices. This form would be developed for each level of work, including team members and senior managers. Your coach has copies of forms both in paper and electronic format.

# Standard Work - Worksheet

Position: _____ Name: _____ Date: _____

| Tasks: Work Practices | Time of Day | Daily Completion | Weekly Completion |
|---|---|---|---|
| 1. | | | |
| 2. | | | |
| 3. | | | |
| 4. | | | |
| 5. | | | |
| 6. | | | |
| 7. | | | |
| 8. | | | |
| 9. | | | |

Notes on possible improvement actions:

| Tasks: Observe Performance and Visual Display | Time of Day | Daily Completion | Weekly Completion |
|---|---|---|---|
| 1. | | | |
| 2. | | | |
| 3. | | | |
| 4. | | | |
| 5. | | | |
| 6. | | | |
| 7. | | | |
| 8. | | | |
| 9. | | | |

Notes on possible improvement actions:

HealthCare Lean

| Tasks: Observe Safety and Environmental Behavior | Time of Day | Daily Completion | Weekly Completion |
|---|---|---|---|
| 1. | | | |
| 2. | | | |
| 3. | | | |
| 4. | | | |
| 5. | | | |
| 6. | | | |
| 7. | | | |
| 8. | | | |

Notes on possible improvement actions:

| Tasks: Meeting & Problem-solving Observations | Time of Day | Daily Completion | Weekly Completion |
|---|---|---|---|
| 1. | | | |
| 2. | | | |
| 3. | | | |
| 4. | | | |
| 5. | | | |
| 6. | | | |
| 7. | | | |
| 8. | | | |

Notes on possible improvement actions:

# Chapter 9

# Defining Client and Customer Requirements

The purpose of this chapter is to help the team identify their clients and customers and suppliers, know the requirements of their clients and customers, and set broad goals to meet their clients and customers' needs.

## Objectives

1. To identify who you work for, who receives your work, your clients and customers.
2. To identify the types of requirements your clients and customers may have.
3. To identify your suppliers and the type of feedback that would help them serve your team better.
4. To reach agreement with your team on your clients and customers and suppliers.

Our success is directly related to the degree to which we understand and appreciate the needs and requirements of both our clients and of our funders. For many years the pursuit of quality in either products or services has focused on defining exactly what will please, even delight, those who are on the receiving end of those products or services. We often think we know, but often do not know, exactly what it is that creates satisfaction among our clients and customers. During this chapter your team should seek to achieve clarity on those requirements.

There is joy in work when it is done in the spirit of service to someone else. There is joy in work when you feel that you have control over the quality of your work. There is even more joy in work when you know that you are expert and that you are daily striving to improve the quality of your work. All work should have joy. The process of Healthcare Lean can bring that joy to your work. In this chapter, you will begin to establish those conditions that create joy, or the simple satisfaction of knowing that you are doing your work well.

The basic functions of a team are to…

- ✓ Define your clients and customers and their requirements for the work you deliver to them.
- ✓ To define your work process that creates the output of products or services that goes to your customer.
- ✓ To receive feedback on your work and to strive to continuously improve your work process and results.
- ✓ To provide feedback to your suppliers, who provide the input that you need to do your work in the best possible way.

All of these functions can be seen in the following simple diagram and in the acronym SIPOC. In an introductory chapter you defined the components of your SIPOC. Now we are going to be more specific.

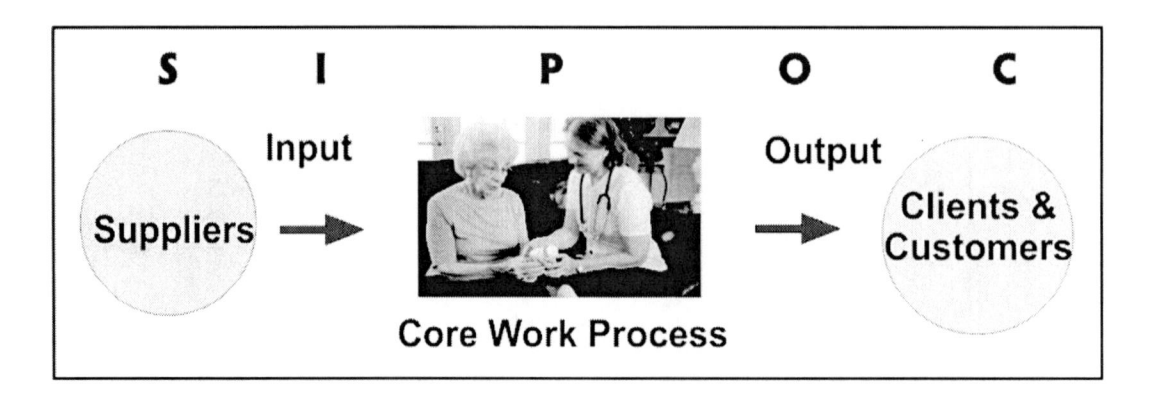

The real work of organizations is horizontal, not vertical. We often think of the work we do as being for our manager, in other words, going up the organization. But the real work is not something that is passed up the organization; it is something that flows through the organization, horizontally. A hospital, like most organizations today, is a chain of customer or client relationships.

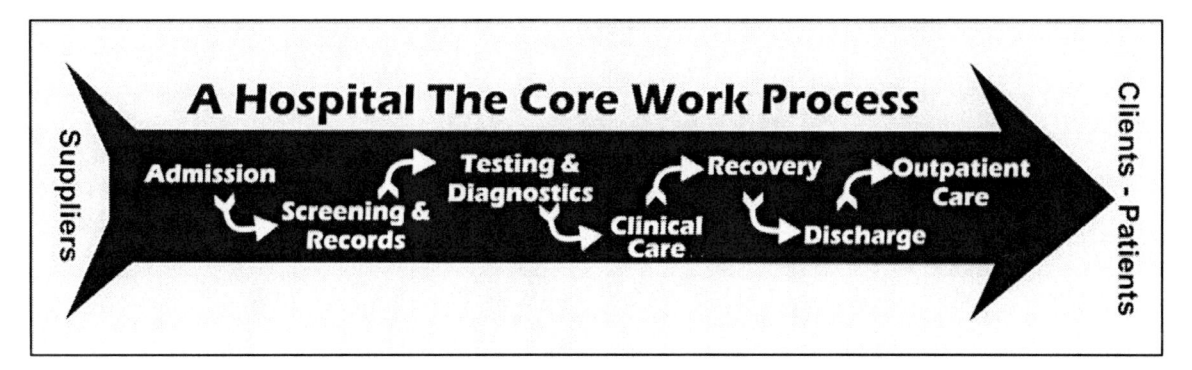

**A Hospital The Core Work Process**

Suppliers → Admission → Screening & Records → Testing & Diagnostics → Clinical Care → Recovery → Discharge → Outpatient Care → Clients - Patients

The above is one way to describe the core work process of a hospital. Each these functions may be a separate department and may be considered one team, or within an area such as clinical care, there are likely numerous teams. But, these teams almost never get their work done alone. They get their work done best by having good customer supplier relationships between each group. Through the eyes of most patients, it is all one big team that is either easy or difficult to navigate.

High performing organizations are passionately focused on managing this flow of work, this core work process that creates the real value of the organization.

## WHO ARE OUR CLIENTS AND CUSTOMERS?

When thinking about your clients and customers, you should consider that some of your customers may be internal in addition to the external clients and customers. Define who some of these internal, as well as customers are.

My team's external clients and customers are…

_____

_____

_____

My team's internal clients and customers are…

| The Work I Do | The Output of My Work (Knowledge, Service, Materials or Information) | Who Receives this Output (These are my customers or clients)? |
|---|---|---|
|  |  |  |
|  |  |  |
|  |  |  |
|  |  |  |
|  |  |  |
|  |  |  |
|  |  |  |

Your clinical care team or management team may have outputs and customers that may be somewhat different than your own. Discuss this with your team members.

| The Work My Team Does | The Output of My Team (Knowledge, Service, Materials or Information) | Who Receives this Output? |
|---|---|---|
|  |  |  |
|  |  |  |
|  |  |  |
|  |  |  |
|  |  |  |
|  |  |  |
|  |  |  |

Now consider which outputs, the result of your work, are most important to your customers and clients.

| My Most Important Care Client (or type of client) | What is the service or output of my work that is most important to them? | What are the criteria for delighting this client? |
|---|---|---|
|  |  |  |
|  |  |  |
|  |  |  |

| My Most Important Customer other than a care client | What is the service or output of my work that is most important to them? | What are the criteria for delighting this client? |
|---|---|---|
|  |  |  |
|  |  |  |
|  |  |  |

# Defining Client and Customer Requirements

Businesses are continually trying to figure out not only what their customers want today, but what they might want tomorrow. Some of the great business success stories, such as Apple Computer, are the result of brilliantly anticipating what will be desired by customers, even before they know anything about it.

A healthcare organization we must not only be thinking carefully about what our clients and customers want and need, but what they will want or need in the future. This is how we must continually improve our services.

The following are common categories of criteria for client or customer satisfaction:

## Specifications

What measurements, define the desired service that our clients and customer considers to be a requirement. In a company that makes things, this may include actual dimensions; tolerances between components; weight of the product; surface characteristics such as smoothness or color; or any other measures they may have. Are there specifications for client care? What outcome measures are most important to your health care organization?

## Reliability

In a service business, such as healthcare, reliability of service providers may be one of the most important criteria. Do you do what you say you will, and do you perform as the client or customer expects? Do you show up when you say you will? Do you call back with an answer when you said you would? In other words, not answering the phone is a reliability problem. It says, "I can't rely on this person or team."

## Timeliness

We have become a "just-in-time" society. We order movies and expect them delivered to our mailbox the next day or instantly over the Internet. We have incredible expectations for things being delivered on time, every time. What are your client's and customer's requirements for timeliness of service delivery?

## COURTESY

Even though patients come to you for clinical needs, they most often judge you by how they feel when they leave. Whether or not they feel that they were treated with courtesy and respect has a halo effect on all of their judgments about your service. Included in courtesy is not just "being nice" but listening well, responding to what the customer is saying, and genuinely having empathy, understanding for the customer's needs. Most customers are willing to forgive errors, but have much more trouble forgiving a service provider who refuses to understand the problem they may be causing. We all want to work with other people, either on our team, or with customers and suppliers, who demonstrate compassion and genuine understanding of our needs.

## INNOVATION

Another requirement that many customers have, particularly in service companies, is for ways of doing things that are innovative. We like to work with suppliers who are not standing still, but are continually developing better ways to do things, or better products.

Now let's consider how these criteria apply to your clients and customers and the services you provide:

| Client or Customer | Service Provided | Requirement |
|---|---|---|
| **SPECIFICATIONS** | | |
| **RELIABILITY** | | |
| **TIMELINESS** | | |
| **COURTESY** | | |
| **INNOVATION** | | |

## WHAT INPUT DO WE NEED TO ADD VALUE

Just as you are the service provider or supplier to others, there are those who provide you with services, information, materials or knowledge. These "suppliers" may be either internal or they may be external suppliers. Let's identify who are the key suppliers that enable you to do your work in the best possible manner.

| My Most Important Input I Need to do my Work | Who Supplies this Input? | What are your key requirements for this Input? |
|---|---|---|
|  |  |  |
|  |  |  |
|  |  |  |
|  |  |  |
|  |  |  |

## THE POWER OF FEEDBACK

All teams, all people, require feedback for their performance to improve. Feedback is the information we receive that tells us that our performance is increasing, decreasing, or the same. It is a primary source of motivation to change. It is why we step on a scale to weigh ourselves. It is why we attend sports events and continually look up at the scoreboard. It is why we have to keep our eyes on the road when we are driving, so we will know if we are drifting to one side or the other and correct. Feedback keeps us on track. All people need feedback in regard to all performance that matters.

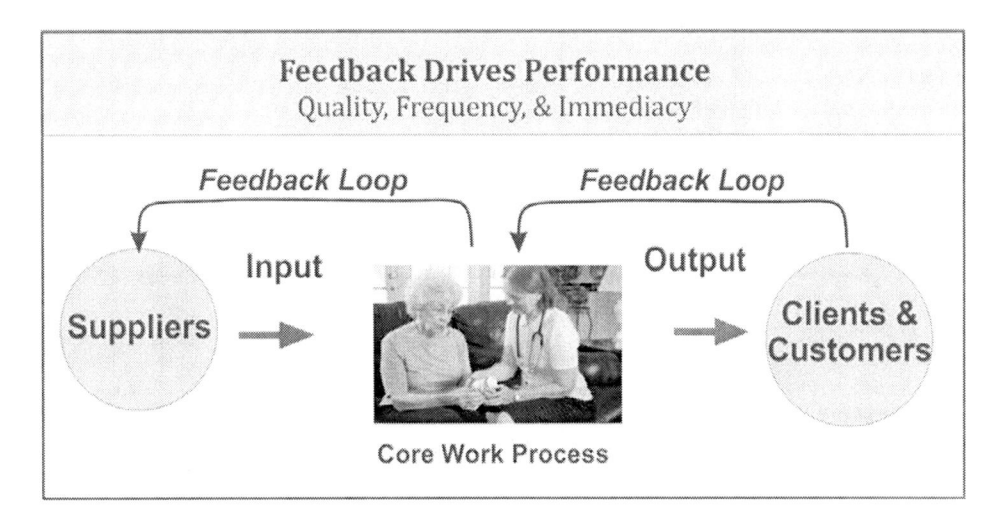

**Feedback Drives Performance**
*Quality, Frequency, & Immediacy*

Suppliers → Input → Core Work Process → Output → Clients & Customers

*Feedback Loop* (from Core Work Process to Suppliers)
*Feedback Loop* (from Clients & Customers to Core Work Process)

Care and service or management teams need feedback for all the same reasons that sports teams need feedback. Where does it come from? Basically, there are only three ways we get feedback: first, we generate measures of performance within the team; second we receive feedback from above; and third, we receive feedback from those who receive our work, our clients and customers.

The purpose of this SIPOC model is to establish sources of feedback that will guide our behavior and increase our ability to be self-managing. And, this is the same reason we need to help our suppliers by giving them feedback.

What are the most important types of feedback that you now receive from your clients and customers? Are these subjective ("Nice job") or are they objective measures of performance that can be used as a scorecard?

| **Feedback Analysis and Improvement** ||||
| Who is the Client or Customer? | What Feedback Do We Receive | Is it *F*requent, *P*eriodic, and is it Visually *D*isplayed? | How could this Feedback be Improved? |
|---|---|---|---|
|  |  |  |  |
|  |  |  |  |
|  |  |  |  |
|  |  |  |  |
|  |  |  |  |
|  |  |  |  |

You feel that is the responsibility of others to provide you with feedback. And, while it is true that your care and service manager should provide feedback, as well as your clients and customers, we are each responsible for our own performance. If you are responsible for your own performance then you will take responsibility for soliciting feedback from whoever may provide feedback that is helpful. This is why most hotels, restaurants and car dealerships don't wait for you to give them feedback – they ask!

# Chapter 10

# Developing Your Team Scorecard and Visual Display

Every high performance team has a clearly defined set of measures and an effective score keeping system. The purpose of this chapter is to provide a guide to establishing that system.

### Objectives

1. To identify the key types of measures that should be on your scorecard.
2. To have the team reach consensus on their 4 to 8 key measures of performance.
3. To understand the importance of a balanced scorecard.
4. To establish a pattern of data collection and review.

Keeping score, taking a count, must be the oldest of all practices of management. Everything that works is not new, and some of the best things are old. Keeping score is as old as the most ancient sport and the most ancient business. Motivation hasn't changed that much in thousands of years. As a hospital implements lean management we must become very good at "playing the game" that makes work like a sport. Keeping score is fun, it makes work interesting, and it leads to improvement.

Healthcare Lean creates a team structure with accountability for performance and makes the adult-to-adult assumption that employees and manager are mature, do want to take responsibility for improving performance, and, if given the information and structure, will rise to that responsibility. This assumption has rarely proven false.

Some years ago my consultants and I were implementing a team process at Eastman Chemicals in Kingsport, Tennessee. I vividly remember a discussion with a department manager when we suggested that financial information on the performance of first level work teams be shared with those teams so they could take responsibility for their business performance. The department manager thought that was ridiculous. He said with great authority "You don't understand these people. These people don't care about that information. They work here just to get their pay check and go home. In fact, you ought to know that most of them consider this their second job."

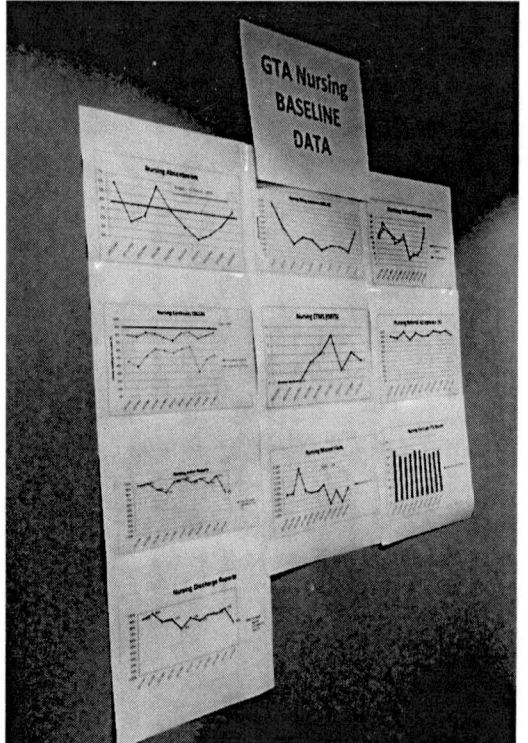

This was puzzling since this "second job" was eight hours a day at least five days a week. I asked, "So what do they consider their first job, if this is their second job?"

He replied "Well, most of them have their own farms, or some other business that they run. That's what they really care about."

This raised a disturbing question. "What causes these employees to feel more motivation about their own farms or small company then working at Eastman Chemicals?"

That led me to ask this department manager, "Do you think they look at the revenue and cost numbers for their first job?"

"Of course, most of them do their own accounting. They know exactly how well they are doing," he replied.

"Do you think they talk to their clients and customers and are concerned about their satisfaction?" I asked. "Of course, they make darn sure they can sell their produce or product, it's their business."

So these same employees who consider this their "second job" and don't care about the numbers, in their other job they run the business, do the accounting, take responsibility for sales, marketing, quality management, process improvement, and everything else that goes into running a business. This only proves that most often motivation is not simply in the person, but is in the system that surrounds the person.

Hundreds, if not thousands, of times I have seen the person change from someone who "just wants a paycheck" to someone who feels and acts like a business owner and manager because of relatively simple changes in the nature of the system that surrounds them. The essence of that change has always been giving them genuine responsibility for managing a piece of the business, with the information, the authority to make decisions, and the accountability for performance inherent in the assumption of being a "business manager."

## SCOREKEEPING IS A SYSTEM OF MOTIVATION

Dr. Deming, the legendary quality leader, used to say that when he visited a manufacturing plant, he wanted to see graphs posted, and he wanted to see dirty fingerprints on the graph. No fingerprints – no good! Why? He wanted to know that those doing the work were literally in touch with the results of their work, their score. Many thought this was a simplistic and foolish idea, but perhaps Dr. Deming understood the same common sense that every team and every coach understands.

In a health care setting, you may not want dirty finger prints on the graphs, but you at least what to know that the care providers are intimately in touch with their measures of performance.

The next time you watch a football, baseball, or basketball game have a notepad in your lap and write down every measurement, every kind of score, that is mentioned. When you reach fifty in one game, you can quit. In all cases there is a constant reference to numbers. Most of the references are about positive, not negative, numbers – the most balls hit over the fence in right field, the most three pointers shot by a left-handed shooter in the fourth quarter of a game! They seem to have scores on everything.

Scorekeeping is also a system that creates unity in groups. Imagine the scoreboard at a basketball or football game – everyone watches it, everyone cheers when it changes, and without it there would be no fans in the stands. What is the magic of the scoreboard? If you understand this, then you understand how to create great scorekeeping systems at work. Something about the way we are internally wired causes us to derive great pleasure in seeing the numbers change; watching the ball go through the hoop, everyone cheers; then their eyes turn to the scoreboard, and they are pleased with the change in score. The entire process helps to bond the team and fans together.

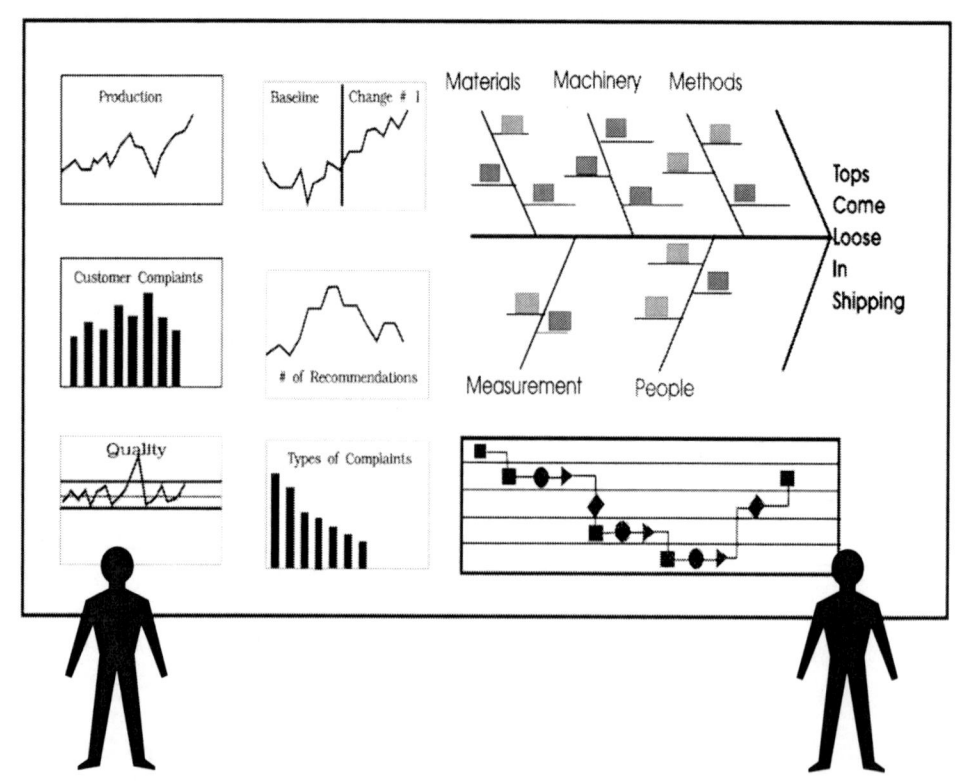

Even those who have no reason to motivate others, but only to motivate themselves, create scorekeeping systems. For example, the lonely runners – those who are able to maintain this behavior for years -- almost all have established a scorekeeping system that keeps them going; minutes per mile; miles per day, week and month; pulse rate after one or five miles. There are dozens of ways to keep score, and those who maintain their motivation maintain a scorekeeping system. It is the single most obvious essence of self-management.

## WHAT GAMES DO YOU PLAY AND WHY?

Think about your own motivation. What do you enjoy doing in your spare time? What sports or games do you enjoy playing?

_____

_____

_____

What are the characteristics of the scorekeeping system in this sport? Think about frequency (how often, visibility, immediacy)?

_____

_____

_____

How do these same characteristics now apply to the system of scorekeeping for your team?

_____

_____

_____

## KEYS TO EFFECTIVE SCOREKEEPING

Here are the keys to scorekeeping that will create the game of Healthcare Lean:

### IMMEDIACY AND FREQUENCY

In basketball, the fans look up at the scoreboard and expect to see a change in one to three seconds after the ball goes through the hoop. In baseball, perhaps because they don't score that often, they have from two to ten seconds. After that amount of time, in either sport, the fans get itchy and may start to show their frustration. If it took an hour to get the score up on the board, how would the fans and players feel? Quickly they would lose motivation and would not show up for the game. How long do your employees or team members wait? The speed and frequency of feedback both increase motivation and increase the effect of a shared experience, and bonding.

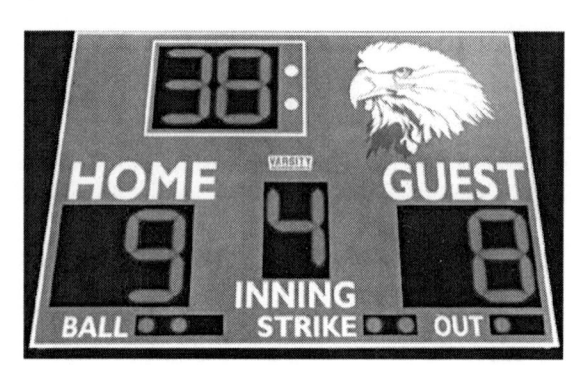

Almost every organization can improve motivation simply by increasing the rate and frequency of feedback. In most organizations, the only reason feedback is delayed is that no one has worked at creating a frequent and immediate feedback system. Investors watch the "real time" ticker and graphs of their investments as they change by the minute or second. With computer technology, creating this kind of feedback is not difficult; we simply need to determine to do it.

## VARIETY

Of course, not all scores can be delivered in seconds. Some scores (monthly sales, quarterly financials) can only be computed in much longer cycles. This is also true in sports. Some scores are annual or career numbers (earned run average over years or career, annual batting average, current batting average, etc.) and many other scores are for that day's game. This is characteristic of all effective motivational systems. Design your scorekeeping system to include individual and team, short-term and long-range scores. But be sure that the information is delivered as quickly as possible to those who perform. Remember, it is not just the fans in the stand (stockholders, analysts, management) that need the information; it is those on the playing field.

## VISIBILITY

The United Way gets it. They place a big thermometer graph right at the entrance to the building where you cannot possibly miss it. And every day as you pass it, you don't know why, but you get some little satisfaction in seeing it move up toward its goal. United Way understands the power of good scorekeeping – or good feedback systems.

Providing graphic feedback has advanced in recent years with the addition of computer-based graphics and reporting.

| **Assess Your Team's Scorekeeping** |||
|---|---|---|
| Scores for Your Team | Characteristic of Effective Scorekeeping | How Can You Improve Effectiveness? |
|  | Immediacy |  |
|  | Frequency |  |
|  | Variety |  |
|  | Visibility |  |
|  | Team Ownership |  |
|  | Balanced |  |

### OWNERSHIP

We are excited by a change in numbers when we feel those numbers are for "my team," when we have ownership of that performance, even if it isn't a direct reflection of our own performance. We don't have to be the athlete, but we do have to feel that it is *our team*. And, if we are the athlete, the one performing, you can bet we want measures of our performance, and not someone else's.

It is common for teams to give themselves a name, create their own logo or mascot, and have some piece of clothing made with their team's logo. It is a normal thing to want to identify with a team, root for a team, and follow the scores of a team. There is no reason why all of this cannot be part of your company's work environment. Imagine any environment in which individuals or teams put forth maximum effort, achieve maximum results, and have fun while they are at it. Inevitably, there will be extremely clear scorekeeping, immediate feedback, and visual display of the score.

## BALANCED

There was a time when some managers felt that the only thing that mattered was financial results. Those who wanted to elevate the importance of quality measures, customer satisfaction, or the performance of processes had to do battle (and usually lost!) with the financial managers.

Two things have worked to alter the view of most managers today. The first is the surge by Japanese car companies and the adoption of the quest for quality by most major U.S. corporations. These have elevated the understanding of quality and process measures. Almost all managers understand that the way you get to financial measures is through effective processes and quality. The second is the book by Kaplan & Norton[20] that promoted the idea of a balanced scorecard; was popular and succeeded in arguing for a system of balanced measures in the organization.

There is nothing complicated about creating a balanced scorecard. (The trick is more in the process than in the "thing.") Here is a diagram that illustrates the possible components of a balanced scorecard. Kaplan and Norton emphasize that their model and definition of a balanced scorecard is not something fixed in stone, but a proposal that they expect others to modify, adapt, and evolve with their own needs and experience.

Any scorekeeping process should enhance learning and process improvement and people development. When developing a scorekeeping

---

[20] Kaplan, Robert S., Norton, David P. *The Balanced Scorecard: Translating Strategy into Action.* Harvard Business School Press, Boston, 1997.

process, the team should identify those questions that will lead to learning and development. For an athletic team, for example, they might ask, "How many seconds does the quarterback take to release the ball? How many seconds does it take the receivers to run the twenty yard dash down field?" The answers to these questions will provide the specific feedback that will promote learning. Learning will not result from looking at the team score at the end of the game. The learning will come from the components of team performance.

At one home healthcare serve a measure of performance may be the number of visits made by a care provider in a day. But, you can imagine a misuse of this measure in which care providers are in such a rush to maximize the number of visits that they fail to fill out charts or properly attend to the client. Obviously, both quality and quantity are important in health care and we should never sacrifice the quality of visits to increase their number.

Both people and processes should be developed as a result of the scorekeeping process. We should measure things that directly impact our financial performance and quality; but we should also measure our development of people, the process of learning.

## BUILDING YOUR SCORECARD

Remember that everything that follows is a suggestion as to how to construct your balanced scorecard. Think! You may think of a better way, of variables that are more important, or a better process. But, the following are steps that have proven to work in other organizations and are a pretty good starting point for your own thoughts.

### THE PROCESS

The process is as important as the decisions. The results are in the process. The following five steps to develop each measure should work for you. Later in this chapter you will see four charts, one for each of the major components of the balanced scorecard. These charts have the process on one axis and the variables specific to each category of the scorecard. These variables are merely suggestions. You may find that different financial measures or process measures will be more relevant or important to your team. But, the idea is fill in or check off the process steps for each variable.

1. **Define the Score**

For each variable, for specifications for example, there may be dozens of specifications for your product. It can be measured a hundred ways. But from your interviews with clients and customers, you learned something about which specifications are most important. Define the few specifications that are most important to customer satisfaction.

When developing your team scorecard, you do not want to have twenty different scores. You want to have four to eight (approximately) scores that are a balanced representation of your team's performance. It is almost always true that, if a team selects twenty different scores, in a short time they will lose track of them and not plot their data on a consistent basis. Constancy of purpose is important when developing your scorecard. Be realistic.

2. **Baseline Data**

How do you know when you have improved? Before you change anything to seek improvement, it is very helpful to have baseline data that will give you a basis to determine whether or not you are making changes that are paying off.

Below you will see a graph with baseline data recorded and then the data after the team has made a change in their work process. You can see that the baseline performance is stable. This is important because if there is already an upward trend in performance, how will you know that a new change is making a difference? It is better to let that trend play out; let it get to the point of achieving stability. Then you can implement a change to your process and you will be able to see the difference.

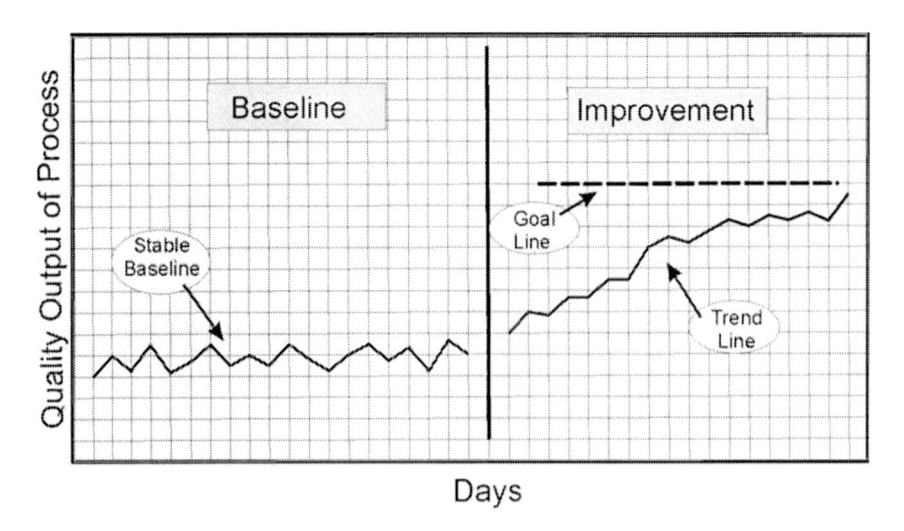

Most importantly, notice how easy it is to see the point of improvement on the graph. Clearly whatever the team did made a positive difference. By seeing the change occur on the graph after they have made a change, the team is learning. They are learning by using the scientific method, which is simply to know the facts of performance by collecting data, then making a change that might affect performance, and then observing the "post-intervention" data.

You can also see that there is a goal line on the graph. When a team sets a goal that they put on the graph, it gives them something to shoot for, something to celebrate when they succeed. Again, seeing it on the graph is extremely helpful to motivate the team.

3. **Set Objectives and Visualize**

We are not talking about "management-by-objectives here. We are talking about YOUR team setting objectives for YOUR own performance. It is the difference between being "managed" and "self-managing." Look at the graph of your performance. Then look at what improvements you think you need to make based on the feedback you received from your clients and customers. In later chapters, we will discuss problem-solving methods that will help you make these improvements.

4. **Change**

In later chapters you will look more thoroughly at specific problems you will find in your process and institute changes. Your period of implementing changes may be days or months. The important thing is that you are going to plot your data and keep track of the effect of your changes as a team.

5. **Evaluate**

The focus of your team meetings should be on this scorecard, what you are doing to improve it, and watching your data. You should be discussing whether or not your changes are having the desired affect and whether or not the data is stable or trending in one direction or another.

## BRAINSTORM AND DECIDE ON SCORECARD MEASURES

You scorecard should be a living thing. In other words, as you learn and develop the skills of team management you will modify and improve your scorecard.

Now it is time for your team to consult together, brainstorm together, and reach consensus together on the scores that would be most indicative of your team's performance.

Remember that you do not want more than six to eight scores that you monitor as a team. Also, please remember to make the score visible. Graph it!!! Post it on the wall where your team meets or works. Remember the scoreboard at the basketball game. Don't cover it up!

# Build Your Balanced Scorecard

| Category | Measures | Where will Data Come From? | Where, How will it be Displayed? |
|---|---|---|---|
| Customer Satisfaction Measures | | | |
| Process Measures | | | |
| Learning and Development Measures | | | |
| Financial or Productivity Measures | | | |

# Part Two
# Improving Performance

# CHAPTER 11

# SOLVING PROBLEMS

The purpose of this chapter is to provide your team with a simple and effective model of problem-solving. Solving problems is one of the most important functions of a team.

## OBJECTIVES

1. To understand a healthy philosophy of problem-solving.
2. To introduce and practice a general method of problem-solving.

At the heart of the work of every team is solving problems and making improvements in their process and performance. Before exploring methods of problem-solving, it is important to think about the philosophy of problem-solving. Just as thinking about and working toward good health is not something that should be avoided, rather it should be routine and a normal part of life, so to solving problems should simply a routine part of what we do.

Many organizations are crippled by the wrong philosophy, and no methods will overcome the wrong philosophy.

# A Philosophy of Problem-solving

## Problems are Normal!

You should solve problems every day. Your managers should solve problems every day. Solving problems is our job. It is why we come to work. If we had no problems, we would be terrifically bored. Celebrate problems! Every problem is an opportunity for learning.

Unfortunately, in the "old culture" before teams and lean, it was common for managers to punish those who presented problems. They thought you were doing your job if you had no problems and brought no problems to them. I suppose they wanted to sit back at their desk, with their feet up in the air and proclaim that everything was running just fine.

Dr. Deming said that to improve we should "drive out fear." He was addressing this philosophy of problem-solving. Fear hides problems, but it does not solve them. We must have a healthy philosophy of problem-solving. The following are some points to consider when thinking about your own personal approach to problems.

## The Problem is in the Process, Not in the Person

Most problems can be solved by examining how we do things, the work process. Just as health problems are often caused by the routine ways we live, most problems at work are the result of the routine, habitual, ways we get things done. Of course, sometimes they are the result of individuals not being adequately trained or informed. But, this lack of training or lack of information is, itself, a process problem. If you blame individuals for problems, you will again create fear and cause them to hide those problems. It is far better to say "I am sure you wanted to get a better result; let's see what caused the problem." By analyzing the problem, rather than blaming the person, you will find it much easier to make progress.

## Fast is Good and Quicker is Better

Every problem has a cost that occurs in time. Health problems are exactly the same. The longer you ignore or delay solving a health problem, the more likely it is to get worse and be more difficult to solve. If a problem is causing anxiety for a client or customer, with every passing day the probability increases that the client or customer will find another supplier. These costs are usually invisible because client or customers rarely tell you why they chose to buy a competitor's product or service. They generally do not consider that their responsibility. So it is your responsibility to find problems and solve them quickly.

## There Are No Perfect Solutions

Every day of our life is an experiment. We experiment with new items on the menu of a restaurant. We experiment with a new variety of soup when we go to the supermarket. We experiment with a new traffic route, a new television program, or a new website. We are constantly experimenting. This is how we learn.

In our daily life we recognize that we will never find the one right and final website, or the final menu item or food in the grocery store. Why do we think we will find the perfect and final solution to any problem at work?

When we are solving problems, we are only finding the best solution we can find NOW with the facts and information we currently have. A week or month from now we will have new facts or information that may make a different solution seem better. Accepting this reality makes it that much easier to get on with the experimentation of implementing solutions. Every solution is a learning opportunity.

## Address Problems that Your Team Can Control

It is always more fun to find problems that someone else should fix. It is why we enjoy sports or politics. We think politicians should fix everything, and we enjoy pointing out what a terrible job they are doing. This is fun because we are spectators. We don't have to change our self.

Your team should address problems that are within your control.

## Trust in the Power of Collective Intelligence

Let us assume that you are the smartest person on your team. It may even be true. But the reality is that our knowledge and intelligence is only a fraction of the combined knowledge and intelligence of the combined team.

Just imagine if you could somehow lift out of each brain their experience, wisdom, and intelligence and put it in a pile in the middle of a table. Now put your brainpower on the table next to it. Your brainpower will be small in comparison.

The magic of effective group problem-solving is that the collective brain power of the group expands to the degree that it combines. In other words, if you and I have an open conversation about a problem, it is likely that there will emerge from our "thinking together," rather than alone, a solution which will be something that neither of us would have arrived at on our own. We are now both smarter than when we began the conversation. So when we add our knowledge and experience together, that group brain pile is not merely the sum of our brainpower when we began. It doubles.

There is no way that your individual brainpower can match the collective intelligence of the group... if the group is able to create collective intelligence.

Think about how problems are solved in your team. How is the above philosophy of problem-solving practiced, or not? What would you do differently if you adopted this philosophy?

## I Want the Facts, Nothing But the Facts!

Many years ago, before most readers of this workbook were born, there was a television detective show, probably the first "cops and robbers," show called *Dragnet*. Sergeant Friday was the central character. In each show he would interview some witness to a crime, and he would always say "I just want the facts, nothing but the facts."

It is easy to form opinions. The moment someone walks into the room, we form an opinion of them. But we don't know them. We don't know the facts. We don't know what happened at home this morning; we don't know what pain they are suffering; we don't know what they can contribute. Opinions without facts are easy. But effective problem-solving is always based on a period of gathering the facts. Too often we think we know the facts when we only know some small portion of the facts.

## Adopt a Disciplined Model of Problem-solving

For many years, even before the quality movement or

lean management, there were many models of problem-solving. Many writers have defined the five, six, or seven steps to problem-solving. Most of these models include the same or very similar elements. There is no one right model or one best way. All problem-solving processes should include fact finding, brainstorming and investigating the causes of a problem, brainstorming and deciding on solutions, and action planning and follow-up. These are the most critical common elements in all problem-solving models.

When the Total Quality Management process was the primary model improvement model the PDCA (Plan, Do, Check and Act) cycle of problem-solving was very popular. It is also known as the Schewhart Cycle after Walter Schewhart a pioneer in the quality field. However, it was made popular by another quality guru, Dr. Edwards Deming. It was adopted as a common problem-solving model at many companies.

The PDCA cycle is best used for relatively simple problems, although you can place many different methods or steps within these four major steps.

On the next two pages you will see a blank PDCA form you can use, and a form with more detailed steps within each of the four major steps.

- **Plan** to improve your operations first by finding out what things are going wrong (that is identify the problems), and come up with ideas for solving these problems.

- **Do** changes designed to solve the problems on a small or experimental scale first. This minimises disruption to routine activity while testing whether the changes will work or not.

- **Check** whether the small scale or experimental changes are achieving the desired result or not. Also, continuously Check key activities (regardless of any experimentation going on) to ensure that you know what the quality of the output is at all times to identify any new problems when they crop up.

- **Act** to standardize procedures or process and implement changes on a larger scale if the experiment is successful. This means making the changes a routine part of your activity. Also Act to involve other persons (other departments, suppliers, or customers) affected by the changes and whose cooperation you need to implement them on a larger scale, or those who may simply benefit from what you have learned (you may, of course, already have involved these people in the "Do" or trial stage)

# HealthCare Lean

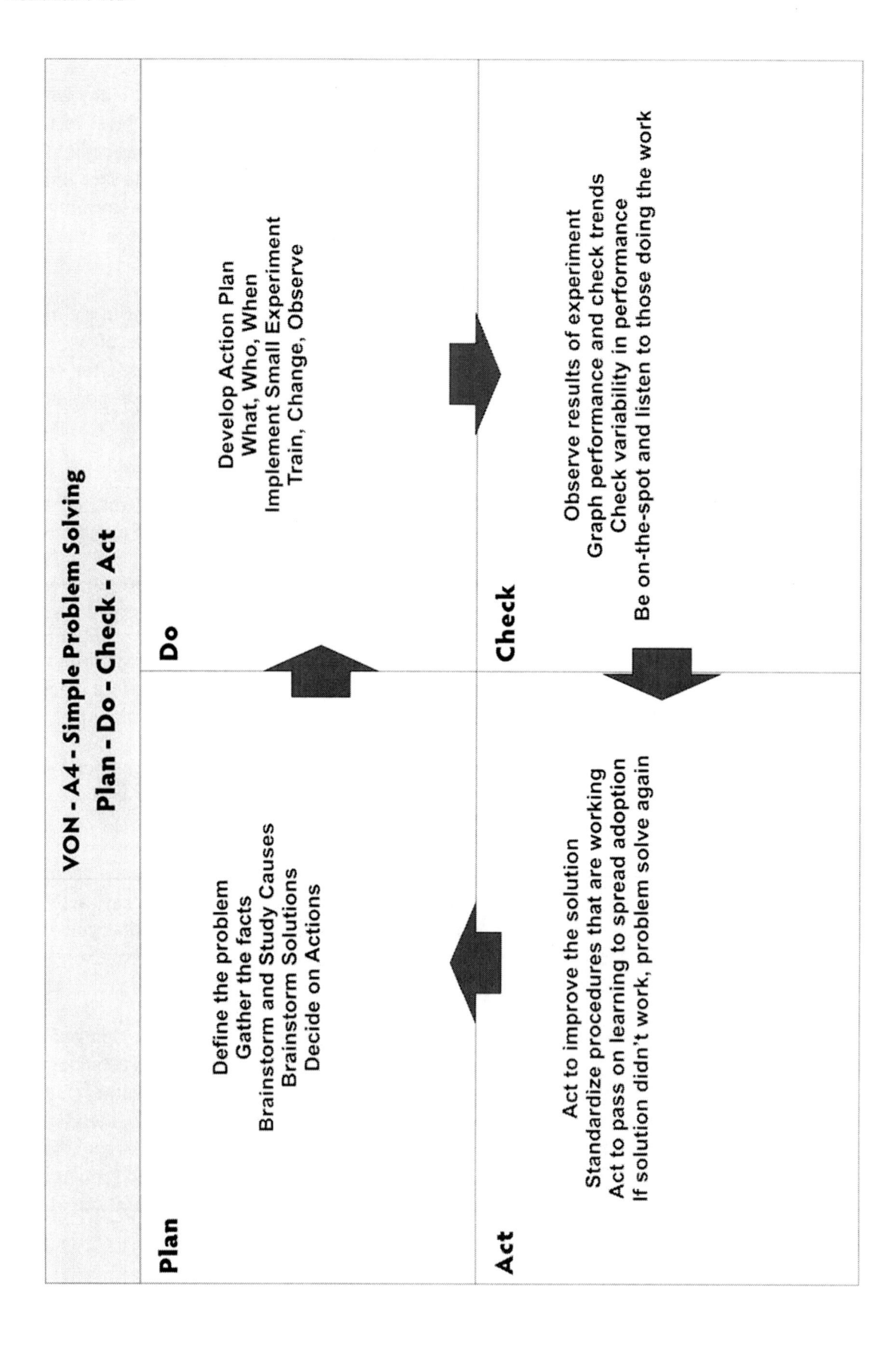

## VON - A4 - Simple Problem Solving
## Plan - Do - Check - Act

**Plan**

Define the problem
Gather the facts
Brainstorm and Study Causes
Brainstorm Solutions
Decide on Actions

**Do**

Develop Action Plan
What, Who, When
Implement Small Experiment
Train, Change, Observe

**Check**

Observe results of experiment
Graph performance and check trends
Check variability in performance
Be on-the-spot and listen to those doing the work

**Act**

Act to improve the solution
Standardize procedures that are working
Act to pass on learning to spread adoption
If solution didn't work, problem solve again

**VON - A4 - Simple Problem Solving
Plan - Do - Check - Act**

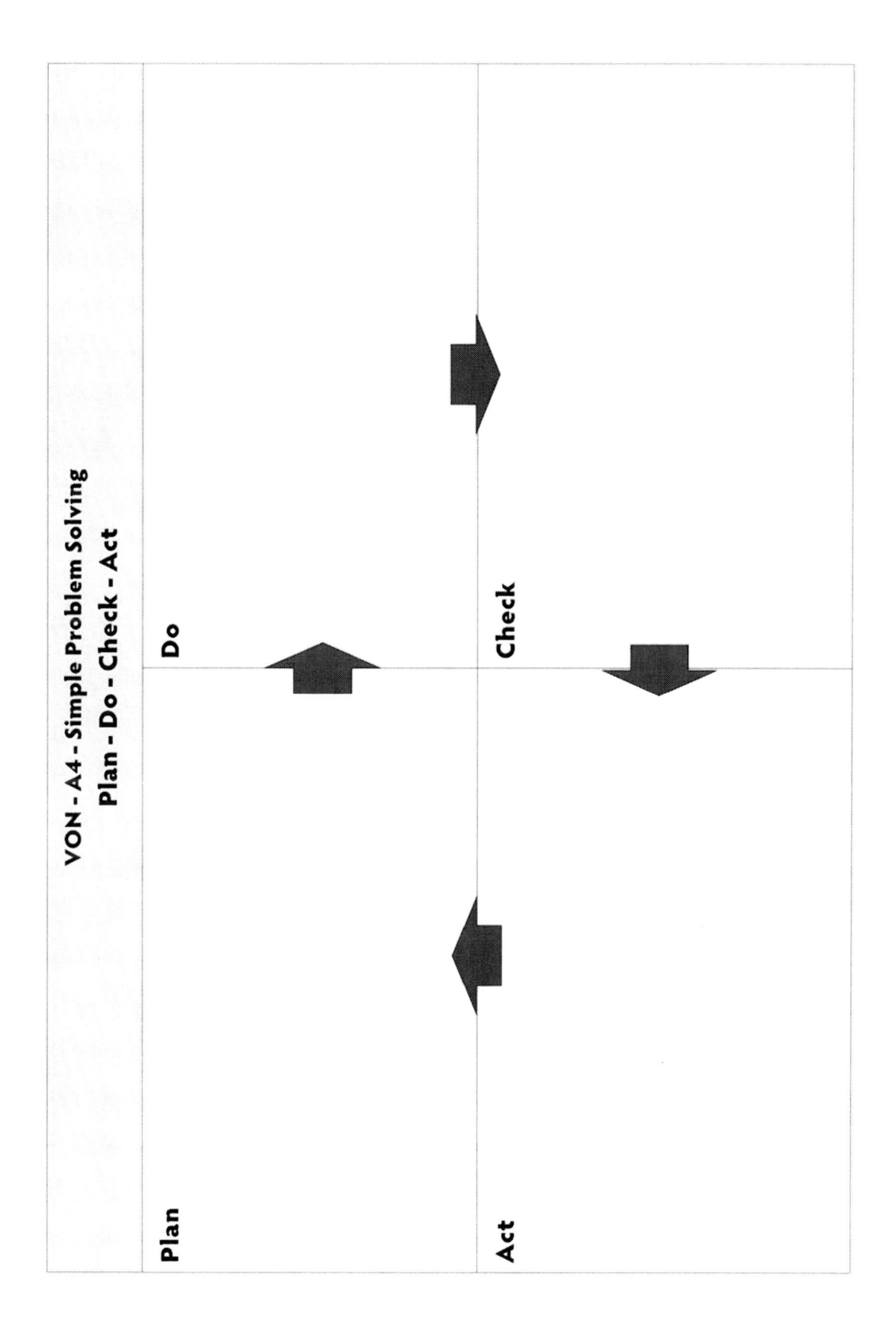

| Plan | Do |
|---|---|
| Act | Check |

The following is a more comprehensive and explicit problem-solving model. It contains all the same elements as the PDCA and a few more. This is recommended for problems that require more in-depth problem-solving.

The PDCA model is simple enough to use on one sheet of paper, and A3 sheet that is about the size of these pages. The following model can also be used on one page, but it fits much better on a larger sheet, an A3. These A3 and A4 forms will be available from your coaches.

This model can be summarized by the acronym DIMPABAC: **Define** the problem to be solved; **Inquire** with all those who have facts regarding the problem to gain different understanding and insight; **Measure** actual performance on the problem; **Principles** should be defined that are important to understanding this problem and its solution; **Analyze** the data and causes of the problem; **Brainstorm** solutions to the problem; Agree to **Act** on a solution; **Control** and standardize the process and evaluate results.

## 1. DEFINE THE PROBLEM

What makes for a good problem definition? Imagine that you are not feeling well and you go to your doctor's office. Now let's imagine that there are three doctors there. Immediately after you walk into the office the three doctors stare at you at the same time. One doctor looks at you and says "Darn, she really looks sick." The second doctor looks at you and says "I don't see it. She looks fine to me." And, the third doctor says, "Well exactly where does it hurt and how long has it felt that way? Let's take some tests and measure a few of your vital signs and then let's make a judgment."

In which of these doctors do you have the most confidence? I think it would be the third one. Why? Because, the first two doctors are telling you how they feel, rather than how you feel, based on little information. Their judgments have as much to do with them as they do with you. The judgment that you look "really sick" is pretty useless. It is a very inadequate problem definition. Every doctor knows that you cannot begin to prescribe a remedy until you have a good definition of the problem – where it hurts, how long it has hurt, exactly where the pain is, etc. Similarly, your problem definition should be specific and it should be based on hard data.

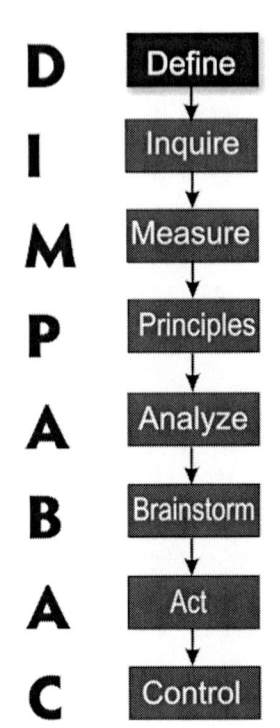

A good problem definition has what is called "inter-observer reliability." This is a fancy way of saying that if three or four people see the same thing, they will be able to reach the same conclusion. The description will allow all of them to know it when they see it. For example, if you are describing a problem of a hitter in baseball, you might say that he is a "weak hitter." This may be true, but there is not likely to be inter-observer reliability. Two observers could easily get into an argument as to whether this player is a "weak" hitter. On the other hand, if you say that this hitter has an on-base percentage of .165, assuming your facts are correct, this is hard to argue with. Two people looking at the facts would agree on this definition of the problem. The problem to be solved is "how to increase his on-base percentage." That definition is a measure of performance.

You could also describe the problem in terms of *pinpointed behavior*. You could describe how this player is slow to get the bat off his shoulder and is late to swing 50% of the time. Two observers, if they were trained and observed carefully, would likely come up with the same definition of the problem or be able to recognize the problem you have described.

These more specific definitions are far more helpful in leading us to a solution than simply to say that this ball player is a "weak" hitter.

Pick a problem that is important to your team. This problem should be one that will improve some measure on your scorecard. You have already interviewed client or customers, you have developed a scorecard, and you have mapped your process. You should be prepared to solve some important problem facing your team. Answer the following questions:

What is the problem definition?

_____

_____

How long has this been a problem?

_____

How does this problem affect performance or business results?

_____

_____

How can you measure this problem in terms of performance or behavior?

_____

_____

### 2. Inquire: Gather the Facts

Sometimes when you begin to solve a problem, you will have all the experts and information in the room. However, it is very common that this is not the case. For most problems, you will have to do a bit more homework to gain input from others. It is almost always true that the team that is in control of the problem (in other words they may be the cause) do not have the same understanding as client or customer, suppliers, or other experts.

Go and see where the problem is. There is no substitute for being on-the-spot and directly observing the problem. In lean management there is a popular term – *Gemba*, or the *Gemba Walk*. It simply means going to where the work is being done. Too often managers make judgments without being on-the-spot.

Who has expertise in this problem - client or customer, supplier, other teams, internal experts?

_____

_____

_____

What information would you like to know about this problem from others?

_____

_____

_____

_____

Who will interview these persons and when?

_____

_____

Have we learned anything that may redefine the problem?

_____

_____

What have we learned that may suggest a solution?

_____

_____

## 3. MEASURE THE PROBLEM

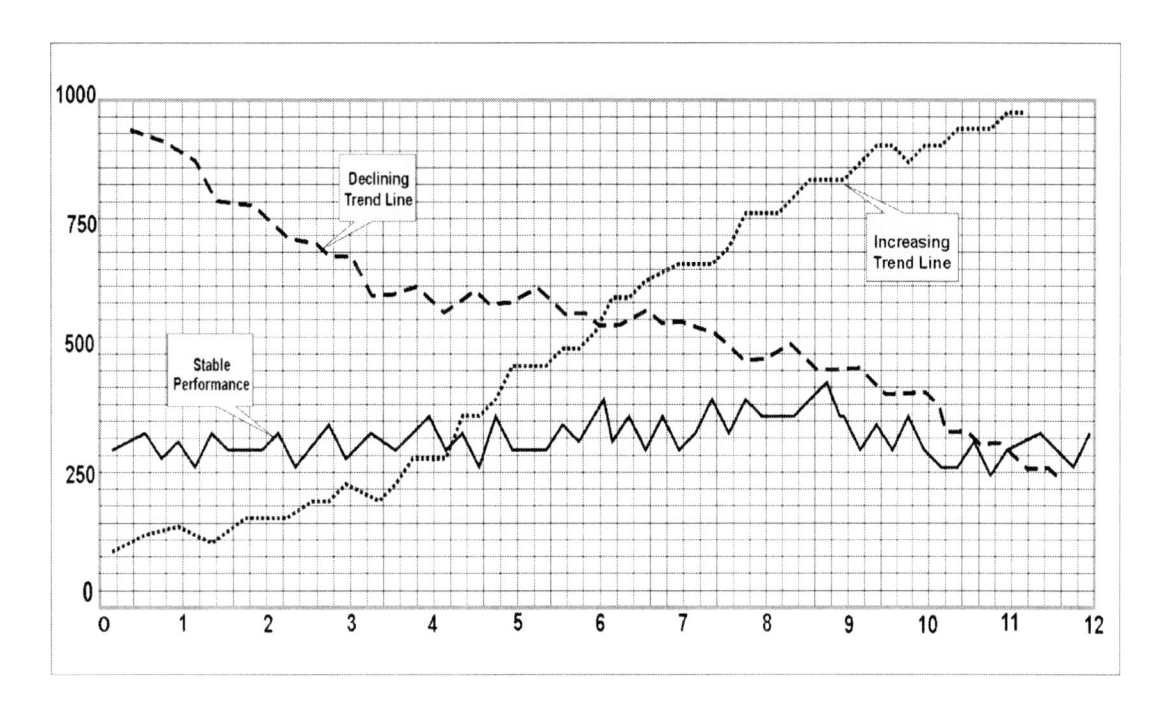

You don't know how serious a problem is until you measure and build a baseline set of data. You will remember in a previous chapter on scorekeeping we discussed the importance of establishing a baseline so that you would then know whether or not you are improving. This will also tell you the severity of the problem.

By looking at a graph of your data you can tell many things that can guide your decisions to make improvement. For example, you may see the variations in performance, and this may point to causes of the problem. You may also see trends. In the following graph you will see three different lines. One of them demonstrates relatively stable performance. Performance is not the same every day; it varies, but it varies in a way that tells you that it is not getting better or getting worse. The other two trend lines show increasing performance or declining performance. It is extremely important that you observe the slope of the trend line before trying to make changes.

If your performance is in an improving trend, should you make a change at all? Perhaps it would be better to let the data continue to improve under the current conditions. Eventually it will come to a level at which it will stabilize or start to decline. If you implement an improvement, while the trend line is already improving, you will have no way to know whether or not your change has had any affect. On the other hand you may wish to make some change quickly to stop a declining trend. However, you should analyze the causes of this decline to understand what conditions are driving down performance.

### 4. Principles: What is Important?

In healthcare, principles are important. Your work is not simply getting things done quickly or making more money. Healthcare professionals must do their work based on core values and principles of ethical treatment of clients. Probably at a hospital, more than in most organizations, it is important to ask "What principles should we take into account while solving this problem."

For example, you may recognize that a solution will require cooperation from other teams, funding agencies or other healthcare professionals or organizations. It may be a principle of solving a problem that you should base your solution on collaboration with these other professionals or agencies.

When looking for problem-solving principles, you should go back to the team's principles and purpose you established in one of the first steps in the team process. How do those values affect the problem you are trying to solve or the solution you are looking for? What other principles should guide your search for a solution?

## Brainstorming – Getting Creative

Brainstorming has been used for many years since WWII when it was developed to stimulate innovation and creativity in research laboratories. The idea is simple. It is our normal habit, when working in groups, to jump to a solution and to immediately start criticizing or judging a solution or ideas offered by someone else. The big breakthrough in brainstorming is the research-proven idea that we will generate more ideas, and more creative ideas, if we suspend judgment or criticism and focus on generating a lot of ideas. One idea stimulates a second idea, which in turn stimulates a third. There is what feels like a chemical reaction between the minds of the team members when they allow themselves the freedom of brainstorming.

Brainstorming requires disciplined leadership. In other words, the facilitator of the brainstorming must be prepared to stop someone who starts to judge the ideas of someone else. This will put the brake on idea generation. Here are some steps to effective brainstorming:

- ☑ Clearly define the problem that is the subject of brainstorming. Ask the group whether they understand the boundaries of the problem.
- ☑ Make it visual. Seeing ideas is essential to stimulating ideas in other team members. Write them on a flip chart, a cause-and-effect diagram, or an affinity diagram (see the next few pages for a description of affinity diagrams).
- ☑ Don't rush. Give it time. It takes time to think.
- ☑ Give everyone an opportunity to contribute. You can go "round-robin" around the room in sequence, use slips of paper, or just "free-wheel" letting anyone speak when they want to. It is often effective to switch between these methods in the same session.
- ☑ Ask clarifying questions when you don't understand someone's idea. "In other words are you saying that ... may be the cause?" And allow the team member to respond with a clarifying statement.
- ☑ The group should feel free to combine ideas or build one idea on top of another.
- ☑ Encourage wild and crazy ideas. Someone might say "I think we should just tear the place down and start over." Rather than saying "Well, you know we can't do that," allow it. Then someone might think, "Well if we did have the freedom to start over, what would we do differently?" And that thought may lead to another, etc. Crazy ideas often generate the most useful ideas.
- ☑ Humor is often the sign of creative thinking. Laughter is good.

## 5. Analyze (Brainstorm) the Root Cause

At this stage you will want to have your team brainstorm all of the possible causes of the problem. Probably the most effective tool for brainstorming causes and solutions is the "fishbone" or "cause-and-effect" diagram. On the following diagram you can see five major categories of potential causes. The original categories were Man, Machine, Materials and Methods. These are not necessarily the most appropriate ones for your team and for this problem. Your team should discuss and reach consensus on the four to six most likely big potential categories of causes. Then, under each of these brainstorm the possible causes.

## Generating Ideas

There are several ways to do this. One way is for the facilitator to simply write down the causes as members of the team think of them. Another way is for everyone to write down possible causes individually on Post-it-Notes, then come up to the wall and place those notes on the fishbone diagram where they belong. It is a good idea to do this silently so members of the team take time to think. As a member of the team sees another member place a note by "Incorrect Information", for example, that may stimulate an idea in his or her head. That may lead to thinking of a different possible cause.

It is usually assumed that this brainstorming will occur in one meeting. However, this may not be the best way to discover causes or solutions to problems. CEDAC is "cause-and-effect-diagrams with the addition of cards". The idea is to put a large fishbone diagram on the wall where everyone can see it. Sometimes it may be in the hall where associates arrive or leave work. On this diagram place the definition of a major problem. In an envelope by the diagram, place a set of large 3"X5" notes. Have notes of two different colors. Indicate a code that blue, for example, are the "cause" cards; while yellow may be "solution" cards. Team members can then think about the problem and place cards there whenever they like.

# Problem Definition

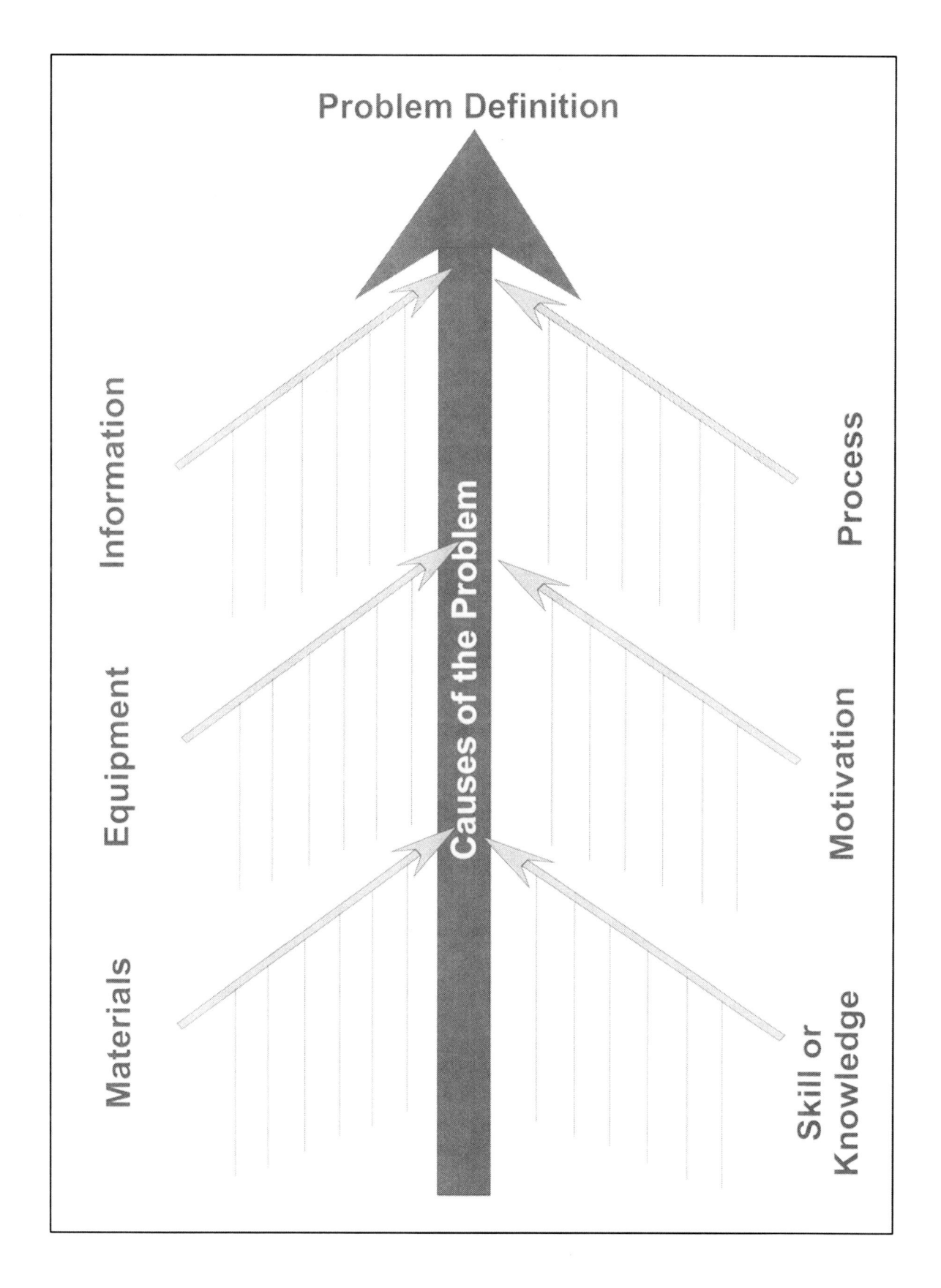

**Causes of the Problem**

- Materials
- Equipment
- Information
- Process
- Motivation
- Skill or Knowledge

Another way to brainstorm is to use an "affinity diagram." This is also a very simple idea. Again, use Post-it-Notes. Members of the team write down what they think are the likely causes of the problem. Each cause is written on a separate note. The team members then just go up to a bare wall and post the notes on the wall in a random manner.

After members have been given some time, perhaps fifteen minutes, to do this, the facilitator then asks them to silently sort them into "like" causes. These like causes may be categories like those on the fishbone diagram. They are organizing the causes into "affinity" groups.

It is contrary to the group's habits to work in silence. But there is a magic to silence. People have to think! Very often we talk first and think later. Now we are being asked to think first, and we will talk later.

The members of the team will move the notes into clusters that they think go together. If one member thinks a note belongs in a different cluster, it can be moved there. If someone else moves it back, then the team may recognize that it can logically belong in more than one cluster, and a duplicate can be made.

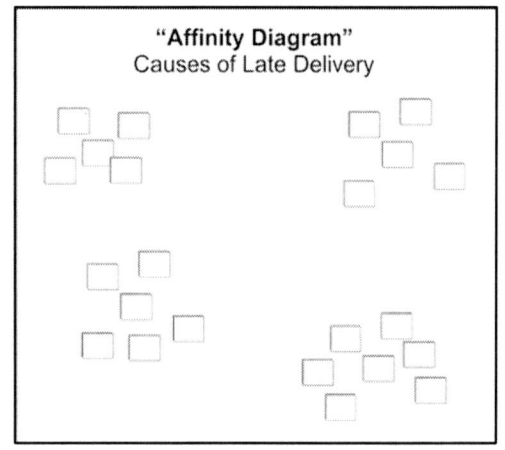

"Affinity Diagram"
Causes of Late Delivery

Once the group is finished, it is time for a discussion of the different clusters.

Why are they clustered together?

What is the common idea or principle that holds a cluster together?

Are the notes truly separate causes or do some of them overlap or duplicate each other?

What are we learning from this?

Are some clusters more important than others? Or are some of them related to each other.

## REACHING CONSENSUS ON PRIORITIES

Now that you have generated many possible causes of a problem, it is time to narrow them down to a critical few. You may also wish to study them further. But, first narrow them so you can focus your energy on solving the most important causes of a problem.

Here is a simple way to reach consensus on priorities.

- Narrow the List

Let us assume that you have a flip chart with a list of twenty-five possible causes of the problem you are trying to solve. Ask the team members to look at this list and pick the five that they think are the most significant causes of the problem. The facilitator can ask the members of the group to come to the flip chart, take a magic marker, and make a small dot by each of the five they have selected. When they have all voted, it will be easy to see which five received the most votes.

At this point it is a good idea to ask the group "Do you all agree that these five are the five most significant priorities for us to work on? Does anyone want to make a case for something else?" Generally, the group will agree, but sometimes someone will feel strongly about another one, and it may be that others do not understand the issue in the same way that he or she does. You can ask the group if they agree to add this as a sixth item.

Now you can decide whether five are too many to pursue further. You may want to get the list down to the two causes to really focus your energies. If this is the case, you can now ask the group to vote again. But, before voting a second time, it is a good idea to ask someone to argue the case for each of the causes remaining on the list. This is often a healthy discussion in which one or two members may be able to provide information that only they have.

- Reach Consensus

Either by voting again, or by a simple show of hands, you may now reach consensus. When reaching consensus, it is important for the leader or facilitator to state the decision being made and ask everyone if they agree. The facilitator should simply look at the group and see if all are nodding their heads. If not, the facilitator should seek clarification.

## Pareto Analysis

The other, and more scientific, way to prioritize is to do a Pareto Analysis. The above process of prioritizing may be based entirely on how the members of the team "feel" about different causes of the problem. Sometimes those feelings are well grounded, and sometimes they are not.

To do a Pareto Analysis you must have data on the different causes of the problem. Once you have narrowed the potential causes down to five or ten, you may decide to go collect data to determine exactly how often the problem is caused by each.

Let's use the example of a team of employees who work in a movie theater. They have a form at the exit from the theater on which client or customers are encouraged to give feedback. You have taken the cards for a one month period and sorted all of the complaints. Here is the list of complaints and the number of each. You will also see the percent this represents of the total.

1. Dirty floors in theater – 97 (45.3%)
2. Dirty rest rooms – 65 (30.3%)
3. Movie started late – 27 (21.6?)
4. Bad popcorn – 13 (06%)
5. Discourteous employees – 7 (.03%)
6. Temperature in theater – 5 (.02%)

Total = 214 complaints

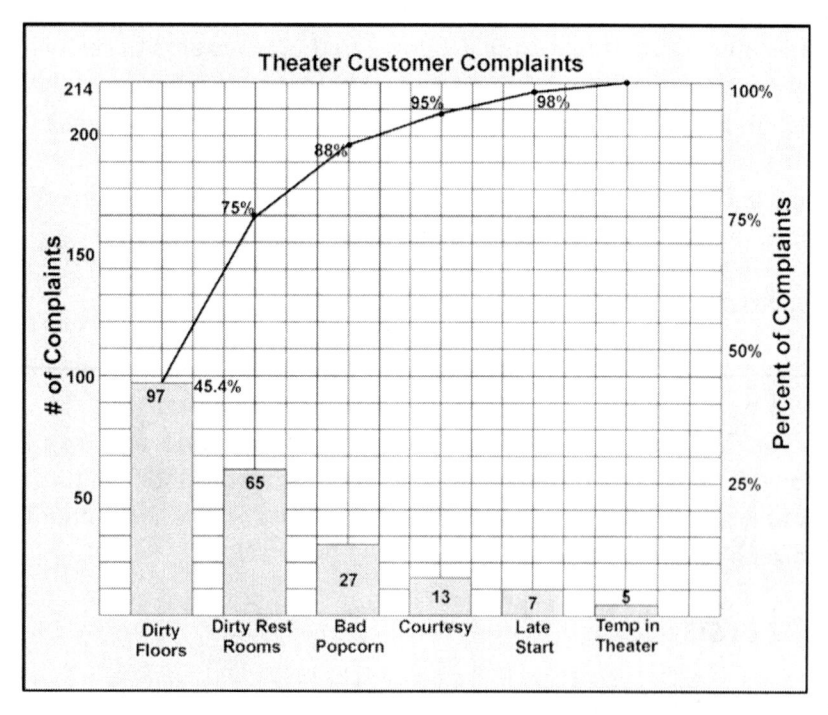

214 complaints equal 100% of the total complaints. Below you can see a bar graph representing the number of complaints by category and a line representing the total percent represented by each column, cumulatively, so it ends at 100%.

Looking at this chart, you can see that the first two "critical few" causes represent 75% of the total complaints. If you could eliminate those two problems you would have eliminated 75% of the causes of dissatisfaction on the part of client or customers. It may be possible to focus on all of the problems. However, on many teams it is not possible to focus on everything at once; rather it is most effective to pick one or two on which to focus your energies. Pareto analysis has proven an effective way of prioritizing problem-solving efforts.

## 6. BRAINSTORM SOLUTIONS

You have now gathered a great deal of information on your problem. You have thought about it a great deal. Now it is time to think about and define those solutions.

Start by brainstorming solutions. Use the same brainstorming techniques, including the fishbone diagram, affinity diagram and other techniques but this time in a search for solutions to the specific causes you have defined.

It is wise to NOT feel that you have to decide on a solution in one meeting. Often you need to study solutions. You may need to consult with an engineer if the solution involves changes in equipment. You may need to consult with human resource professionals regarding the need for additional training if that is part of your solution.

When you consider possible solutions, consider experimenting. Do not assume that you have to "bet" that you have made the one right decision. It is dangerous to tie your ego to a solution. Even with the best problem-solving methods, we are often wrong. It is okay to be wrong if you are willing to take action, evaluate, learn, and modify your solution. Thomas Edison tried thousands of "solutions" before inventing the light bulb. There is no reason to think that you will discover the one "right" solution on your first try. If you become too invested in one solution, it may make you blind to other opportunities or other solutions.

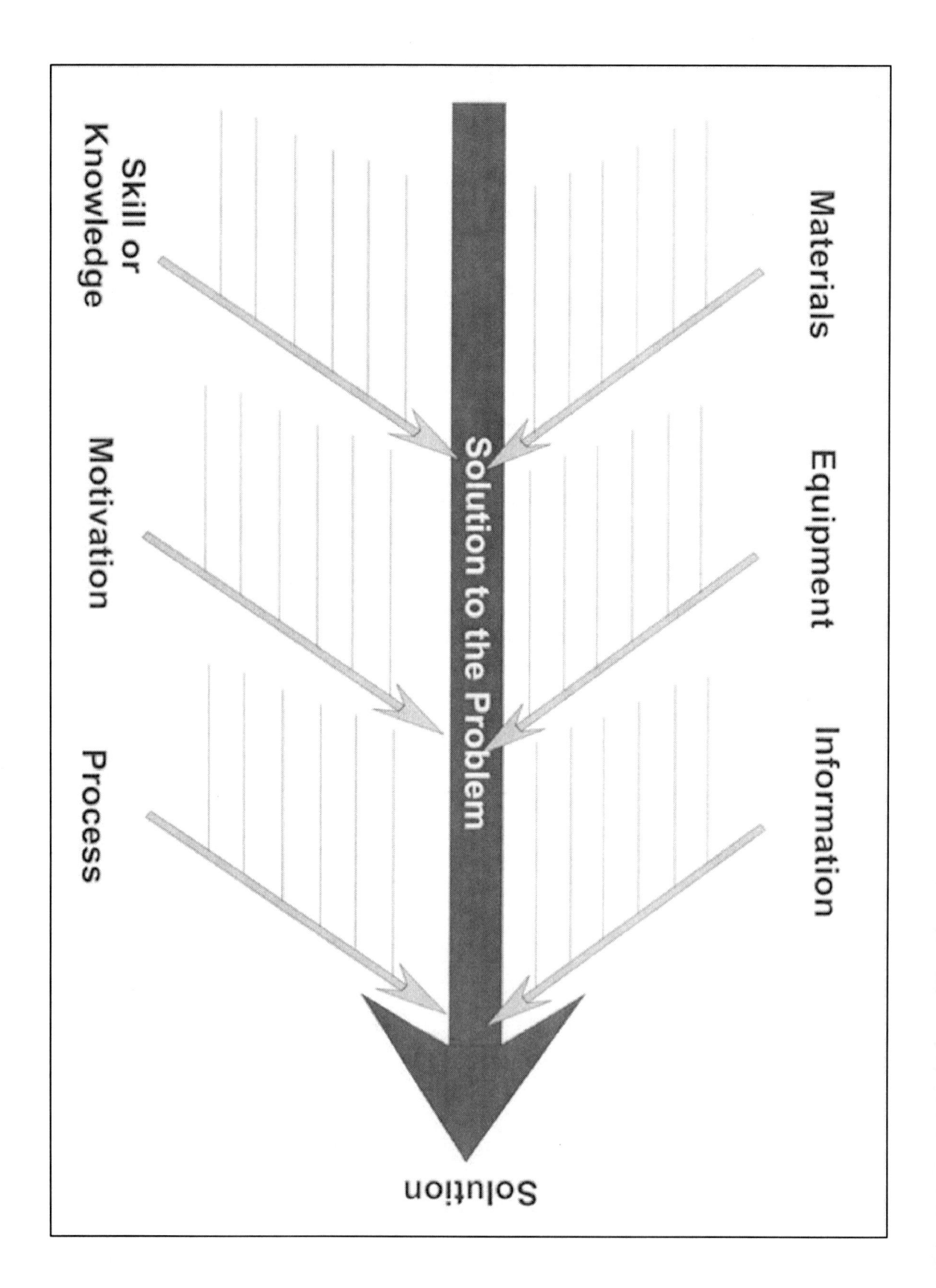

# Solution to the Problem

**Inputs (arrows into spine):**
- Skill or Knowledge
- Motivation
- Process
- Materials
- Equipment
- Information

→ **Solution**

## 7. ACTION PLANNING – TAKE ACTION

Now you have to be a manager. You have to manage the implementation of solutions. This is not difficult, but it requires a disciplined approach. On the following page you will find an Action Planning Worksheet that will be helpful.

Every action plan should include the following simple elements:

**What** Action Needs to be Taken: Make a list of the specific actions that need to be taken to implement your chosen solution. Be as specific as possible when listing these action steps. List them in the order you think they need to occur.

**Who** will take the action: It is very helpful to put this simple action planning sheet on a flip chart at the front of the room as you develop the action plan. As you write down each action step that is agreed to by the team, ask "Who will do this?" It isn't going to happen if no one commits to taking responsibility for action. Write down the name or initials of the person who commits to act.

**When** will the action be completed? The person who agreed to take the action should now commit to a completion date.

**Status:** Following the development of this action plan, it should be reviewed at each meeting of the team. If you have the action plan on a flip chart page, it is a good idea to bring that and put it on the wall. The knowledge that this will be on the wall and that it will be reviewed is the best form of accountability. When we know that we are going to be held accountable for our commitments, we think seriously about them and hold ourselves accountable for getting the action completed.

## 8. CONTROL FOR RESULTS AND REVIEW

Control simply means to continue measuring your process and results. This is why you have a scorecard. You should now see changes on your graphs. If not, then why not?

Solving problems almost always requires repeated analysis and brainstorming solutions. You should never feel like a failure when you do not get the results you hoped for. Be a scientist. Learn from your results, experiment again, watch the results again, and you will discover the best solution.

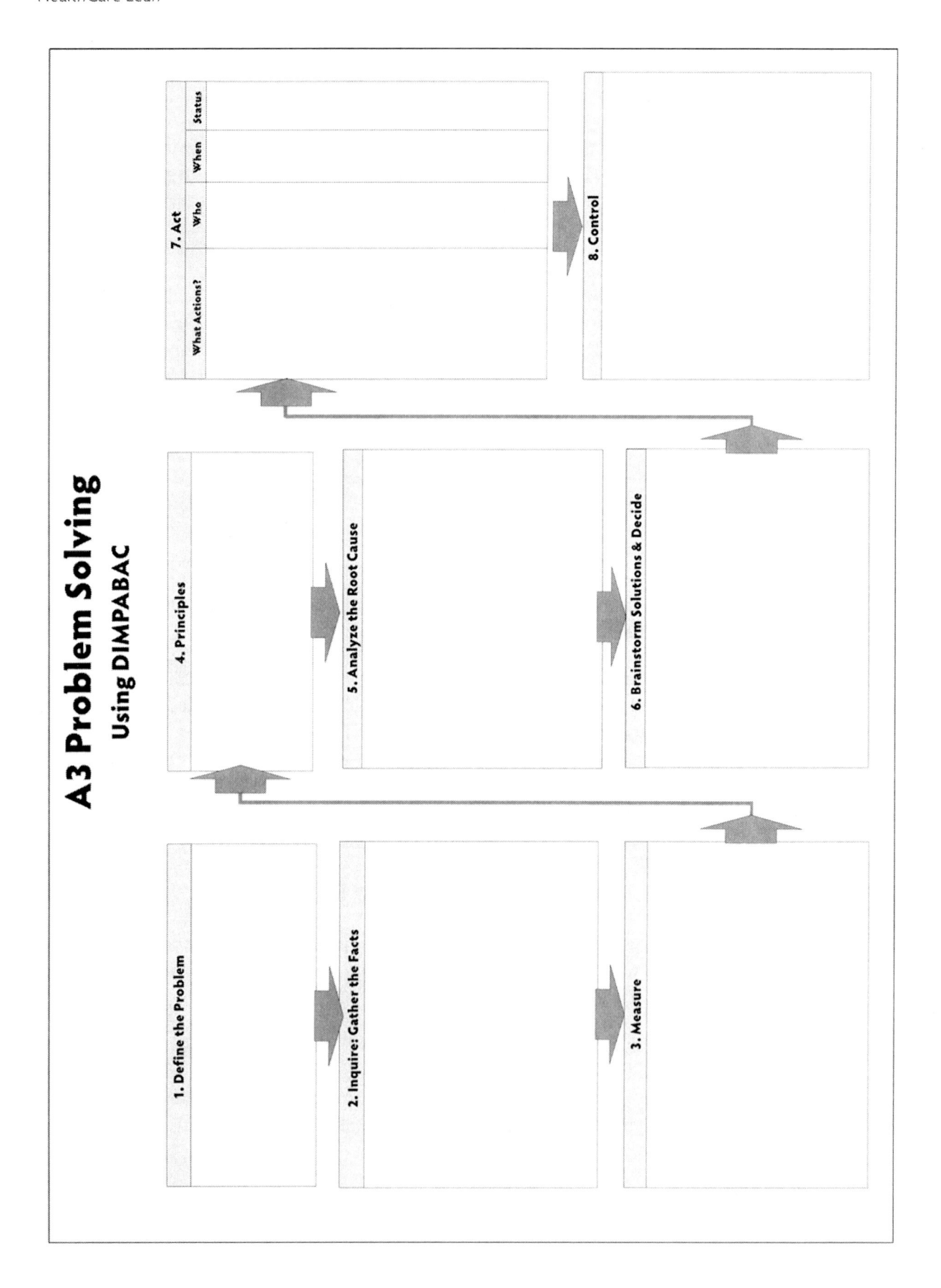

HealthCare Lean

# A3 Problem Solving
## Using DIMPABAC

1. Define the Problem

2. Inquire: Gather the Facts

3. Measure

4. Principles

5. Analyze the Root Cause

6. Brainstorm Solutions & Decide

7. Act

| What Actions? | Who | When | Status |
|---|---|---|---|
| | | | |

8. Control

Page 140

# A3 Problem Solving
## Using DIMPABAC

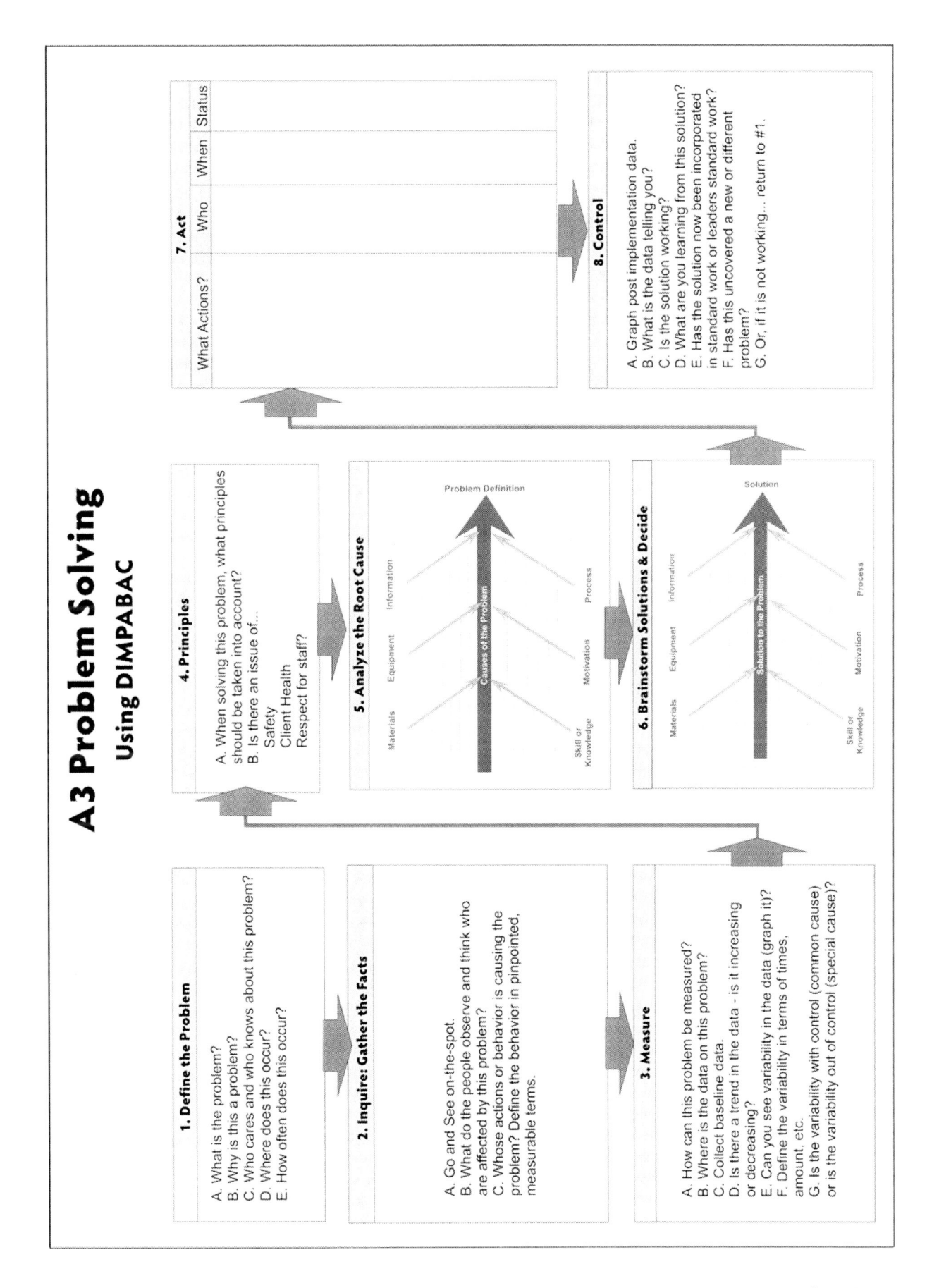

### 1. Define the Problem

A. What is the problem?
B. Why is this a problem?
C. Who cares and who knows about this problem?
D. Where does this occur?
E. How often does this occur?

### 2. Inquire: Gather the Facts

A. Go and See on-the-spot.
B. What do the people observe and think who are affected by this problem?
C. Whose actions or behavior is causing the problem? Define the behavior in pinpointed, measurable terms.

### 3. Measure

A. How can this problem be measured?
B. Where is the data on this problem?
C. Collect baseline data.
D. Is there a trend in the data - is it increasing or decreasing?
E. Can you see variability in the data (graph it)?
F. Define the variability in terms of times, amount, etc.
G. Is the variability with control (common cause) or is the variability out of control (special cause)?

### 4. Principles

A. When solving this problem, what principles should be taken into account?
B. Is there an issue of....
   Safety
   Client Health
   Respect for staff?

### 5. Analyze the Root Cause

Problem Definition

Causes of the Problem: Materials, Equipment, Information, Skill or Knowledge, Motivation, Process

### 6. Brainstorm Solutions & Decide

Solution

Solution to the Problem: Materials, Equipment, Information, Skill or Knowledge, Motivation, Process

### 7. Act

| What Actions? | Who | When | Status |
|---|---|---|---|
| | | | |

### 8. Control

A. Graph post implementation data.
B. What is the data telling you?
C. Is the solution working?
D. What are you learning from this solution?
E. Has the solution now been incorporated in standard work or leaders standard work?
F. Has this uncovered a new or different problem?
G. Or, if it is not working... return to #1.

# Action Plan

**Problem:**

**Solution:**

| Action-What? | Who Will Act? | When? | Status |
|---|---|---|---|
|  |  |  |  |

# Chapter 12

# Motivation and Human Performance

The purpose of this chapter is to help the team and the individual members manage their own motivation and that of their fellow team members.

## Objectives

1. To provide models of motivation that will assist the team members in their understanding of their own level of motivation.
2. To help the team manage the human side of the team's performance.
3. To learn to use positive reinforcement effectively.
4. To learn a model of analyzing and solving human performance problems.

Those who choose to come to work in healthcare are most likely motivated by a desire to serve and care for others. It is what we do. It is our mission as a charitable organization. However, even in a healthcare or other charitable organization, individuals and teams can encounter performance problems. Sometimes these performance problems are due to the lack of information or skills. And, sometimes they are due to a lack of appreciation by others in the organization.

You want to develop a culture of shared appreciation, a culture in which we love coming to work both because of the intrinsic satisfaction of serving our clients, but also because of the support and appreciation we receive from our colleagues.

Human motivation is a subject on which there have been more theories developed and more books written than almost any other. Debates about the source of motivation go back to the Greek philosophers, Plato and Aristotle. Much of the debate about motivation has been about whether motivation comes from within or is the result of outside forces in the environment. Entire schools of psychology have grown up around these two ideas.

It is safe to say that human motivation is complicated and there are a lot of individual and cultural differences in how we are motivated. But there are also some universal motivations although they may appear different in different cultures. One way to understand motivation is to consider that there are three levels of motivation: the *spiritual*, the *social* and the *situational*.

## MOTIVATIONS OF THE HUMAN SPIRIT

The spiritual level of motivation refers to those things that are very deep personal beliefs and values. Your religious faith, your family, and your country may all be sources of motivation at this spiritual level. Motives at this level are almost always focused on the very long term. You will sacrifice for achieving a goal in the afterlife. You will sacrifice much of your own pleasure for the well-being of your family. And many have willingly sacrificed their own lives for their country and their faith.

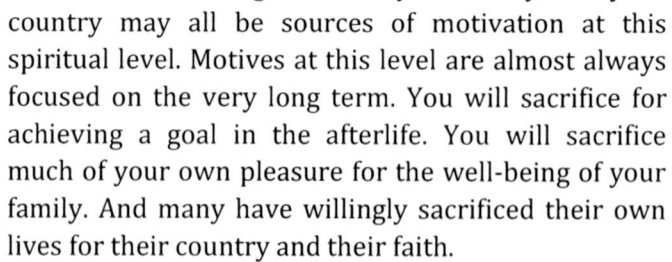

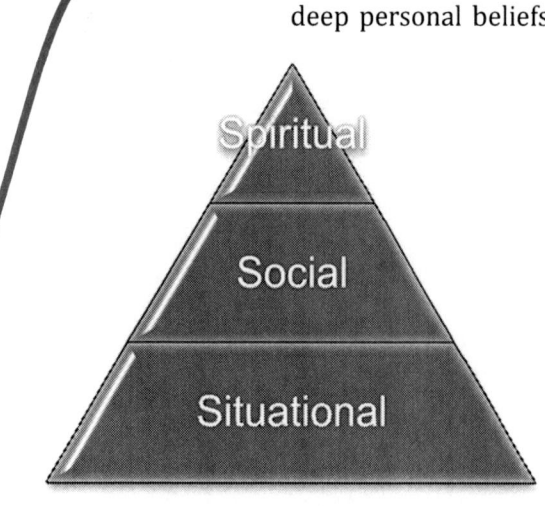

While no one at work will ask you to sacrifice your life, there are still spiritual motivations in the world of work organization. Knowing that your organization has a worthy purpose, is doing something worthy for society, and is creating a positive legacy is important. It is not something that you will see reported in this month's scorecard, but it is something that will cause people to make sacrifices for the organization. We all want to know that we work for a worthy organization that does important work.

## SOCIAL MOTIVATIONS

One of the intentions of the team process is to increase the motivation that comes from working with a group of fellow care providers. Social motivations are those that define who you are in relation to other people. It is innate in the human species to seek friendship, family, association, and a respected status among those whom we value. There are not many among us who would want to go live on a mountain top by ourselves as a hermit. It may seem like an interesting escape for a short time, but most of us could not stand the loneliness and isolation for long.

Just as the family farm and craft shop were a strong source of social support one hundred years ago, the work or management team, as well as the larger social network in our organization, can serve as a system of needed social support. A healthy social system tends to make individuals psychologically healthy. A dysfunctional social system creates personal dysfunction. This rule can easily be seen in the social system of the family. We all know of examples of dysfunctional families producing dysfunctional individuals.

Take some time to think about healthy families and their parallel in the work place.


Why do healthy families tend to produce healthy individuals? What are the important elements of this social system?

_____

_____

_____


How do these characteristics relate to teams in your area? Is there anything that your team could do to strengthen the social support system at work?

_____

_____

## SITUATIONAL MOTIVATION

Situational motivations are those that occur from our environment. Management systems tend to focus on these sources of motivation because they are most easy to modify.

Behavioral psychology, or behavior analysis, is the study of how the environment affects human behavior. There is a great deal of research that clearly demonstrates that you can increase (or decrease) performance by controlling those events that come before and after behavior. This is not a new revelation, nor is it complicated.

One simple way of remembering this model is to think about the "A-B-C" Model. The "A" is for antecedents. An antecedent is something that comes before and acts as a *prompt* or *cue* for behavior. It triggers the behavior. Red light, green light, stop sign and a thousand other things that we see every day are antecedents for behavior. They are intended to serve as cues or prompts for a specific behavior. The "B" is for the desired behavior, such as taking your foot off the gas and putting it on the brake at a stop sign. The "C" is for consequences. When you stop for a stop light, the consequence may or may not happen, but the chance that you will have an accident or receive a traffic ticket if you don't stop is sufficient to control our behavior. It is clear that the antecedent and the consequences in this case serve as motivation for the behavior of stopping your car.

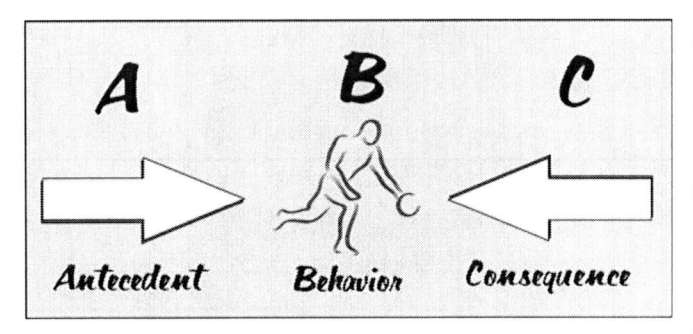

If you have children, it is easy to think of examples of antecedents and consequences that affect their behavior. Think about the children cleaning their rooms. Have you ever had difficulty getting your children to keep their rooms clean? What antecedents and consequences might have an effect on this behavior?

**Antecedent** ⟹ **Behavior** ⟸ **Consequence**

_____

_____

_____

Discuss with your team which antecedents may have a positive effect and which may not. Why would an antecedent not have an effect?

Antecedents are conditioned, in other words we *learn* to respond to an antecedent. What does this mean? The traffic sign on the freeway says 100KPH. How fast is the traffic going? Probably 120KPH. Why? Because you know that if you are going 120KPH there is no consequence. Actually, there is a positive consequence for going faster than 100KPH. It is pleasurable. And you enjoy passing others more than you enjoy being passed by others. In your experience, you have learned that you are not likely to get a speeding ticket unless you are going more than 120KPH. Therefore, the antecedent that says "100KPH" actually means 120KPH in terms of behavior. That is what you have been taught. But what would happen if tomorrow, on the same highway, you suddenly were stopped by a policeman and given a ticket for traveling at 120KPH? You would be shocked and angry. Yes, you know the speed limit is 100, but this isn't fair! It isn't "fair" because it is a change in the consequences. If every driver, every day, were given a ticket for traveling even 105 KPH, how long would it take for all the traffic to slow down to 100KPH? Only a couple days.

Now, what antecedents may work to promote studying by your child? One very powerful antecedent would be if one parent sat down with the child and read a book and suggested that they sit and read together. You do your homework, while the child does hers. Another antecedent would be saying, "OK, its homework time" and turning off the television.

But these will become effective if the child studies and then the parents provide a meaningful consequence, a positive consequence that the child will then associate with the antecedent. In other words, you sit and read with your child, and after fifteen minutes you say to the child, "I really like sitting here with you while we both read."

Imagine this situation, which is unfortunately too often typical. Mom, Dad, and their son are sitting after dinner watching *The Simpsons* on television. Ten minutes into the show Dad looks at his watch and says to his son, "Hey, Junior isn't it time for you get upstairs and do your homework?" (Prompt #1) His son does not answer and both keep watching the TV.

Ten minutes later a commercial comes on and Dad realizes that his son is still sitting there. "Hey, I thought I said it's time to get upstairs and do your homework," he says, a bit more aggravated this time. (Prompt #2) The son says, "OK, OK, I'm going; the shows almost over."

They both go back to watching TV. Ten minutes later the show is over and they are both sitting there watching the promos for the next show. Then Dad says to his son, "Hey, UPSTAIRS, NOW!" (Prompt #3) while pointing to the stairs. The son gets up and says, also in an aggravated voice "OK, OK, I'm going."

The way Dad is managing behavior in this situation is designed to teach his son NOT to respond to Prompts #1 and 2. He is teaching, but he doesn't realize what he is teaching. He is teaching his son that the only antecedent that he really needs to respond to is Prompt #3. Unfortunately, this teaches disrespect for authority, rather than respect. It teaches the son to wait for yelling and then respond with an angry tone of voice. This entire situation is completely unnecessary.

Your job is to redesign this behavior management situation. Your job is to create a situation in which the son learns, and it will take a few trials, to respond obediently to one prompt that is stated in a calm and dignified manner. Describe this new situation in terms of the ABC model. Be sure to make this a teaching experience by using positive reinforcement. Remember that you want him to learn to enjoy, to love, reading and learning. Discuss with your team why you think this will work.

**Antecedent** ⟹ **Behavior** ⟸ **Consequence**

_____

_____

_____

Let's do some analysis of prompts, cues, or antecedents in your own work setting. Just look around, and I am sure you can see some. There are probably some as you walk into the building. Ask yourself whether or not these are effective. Why are they, or why are they not, effective?

When you think about the antecedents in your work environment, think about the graphs, charts, and process maps that may be visible. Do these serve to prompt the desired behavior? Do you think that the size and color of these may have any effect? How could you maximize their effect?

| **Antecedent** ⟹ | **Behavior** ⟸ | **Consequence** |
|---|---|---|
| _____ |||
| _____ |||
| _____ |||
| _____ |||
| _____ |||

As you can see from your analysis of those things that come before a performance, the consequences to behavior are critical. As a child you probably remember experiencing some consequences that were intended to change your behavior. As a parent, you deliver consequences to your children every day, whether intentional or not. You will be able to solve performance problems, whether in the home or at work, if you are effective in managing consequences.

## Reinforcing Values

How values are transmitted is very easily seen by understanding the ABC model. If you want your children to value reading and education, how do you transmit this as a value that will impact their behavior? Of course, you model reading behavior yourself (an antecedent). And, you praise and reinforce your child for doing the same.

If you look at the next two pages, think about how we develop our values today and how we could tomorrow. Today, what are the antecedents that prompt the behavior to occur and what are the consequences (what happens) after the behavior has occurred. In the future if we want to reinforce positive behaviors what antecedents do we need to put in place and what consequences do we need to happen to make sure the positive behaviors get repeated?

| How We Do Reinforce Values Today |||
|---|---|---|
| **Antecedent** | **Behavior** | **Consequence** |
| Value 1: |||
| | | |
| | | |
| | | |
| | | |
| Value 2: |||
| | | |
| | | |
| | | |
| | | |
| Value 3: |||
| | | |
| | | |
| | | |
| | | |
| Value 4: |||
| | | |
| | | |
| | | |
| | | |

## How We Could Reinforce Values Tomorrow

| Antecedent | Behavior | Consequence |
|---|---|---|
| **Value 1:** | | |
| | | |
| | | |
| | | |
| | | |
| **Value 2:** | | |
| | | |
| | | |
| | | |
| | | |
| **Value 3:** | | |
| | | |
| | | |
| | | |
| | | |
| **Value 4:** | | |
| | | |
| | | |
| | | |
| | | |

## INTRINSIC AND EXTRINSIC REINFORCEMENT

There are several different ways to understand the different types of consequences that impact behavior. One way is to understand that some motivation comes intrinsically from the work itself. If you enjoy playing the piano or playing tennis, it isn't work. You don't need to be paid for this activity because it is intrinsically reinforcing. The pleasure comes from the activity itself. Much of the work that needs to get done in this world is not sufficiently intrinsically motivating and requires extrinsic motivation.

In a hospital or other healthcare setting much of the work we do does provide intrinsic motivation. Of course, there is also the extrinsic motivation of compensation. Consider some of the activities of a care provider and consider what intrinsic and extrinsic reinforcement strengthens or maintains these activities.

| Care Provider Behavior | Intrinsic Reinforcement | Extrinsic Reinforcement |
|---|---|---|
| Participating in Care Provider team meetings. | | |
| Following safety guidelines such as safe cell phone use. | | |
| Show empathy and concern toward clients. | | |
| Completing client service reports. | | |
| Learning and conforming to the College of Nurses standards of practice. | | |

Then ask yourself "do these behaviors occur sufficiently, or do they need to be strengthened?" If they need to be strengthened, how could you accomplish that? Is there a way to increase intrinsic reinforcement or would you have to call upon extrinsic motivators?

## Types of Consequences

There are three types of consequences to behavior. The first is positive reinforcement. The word "positive" doesn't refer to something you like. It refers to the *presentation*, rather than the *removal* of a reinforcing event. There is "negative" reinforcement, which does not mean punishment. It means the withdrawal of a stimulus that increases a performance. In all cases the word "reinforcement" is empirically defined by the increased frequency of a behavior. If there is no change in behavior, you cannot correctly say that you "reinforced" someone's behavior. Similarly, you cannot say that you have "taught" someone if they have not learned. You can say "I tried to teach them," but whether they were taught or reinforced is determined by whether their behavior changed.

This empirical definition, determined by an actual change in frequency of behavior, may seem like an academic difference. But it is actually very important. It is part of becoming *fact based* in how we manage.

Positive reinforcement can be of many kinds. It can be social ("Thank you, I really appreciate your doing that for me!"); it can be material (a gift or money); it can be intrinsic.

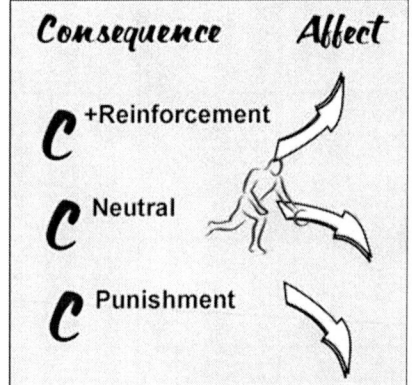

There are also neutral consequences. This is when nothing happens. But nothing happening is a consequence in itself. Imagine that you have worked very hard on a report for your manager. You were told that this was an important study, so you worked at night and on the weekend to get it done. You believe that you did a great job, and you are very proud of the work you did. You then bring the report to your manager. He isn't in, but you lay it on his desk where he can't possibly miss it. A day goes by, and you hear nothing. A week goes by, and you hear nothing. A month goes by, and you hear nothing. What will be the effect on your behavior? This neutral consequence will de-motivate you. The rate of behavior will decline. The next time you are asked to do a similar job, you will be less excited, and it is likely that you will put in less effort. Your performance has gone down. This is the effect of neutral consequences.

We are all familiar with punishment. Punishment is the presentation of an event that reduces the rate or frequency of a behavior. Just as reinforcement is empirically defined by a change in the frequency of behavior, punishment is also empirically defined. Punishment is only punishment if the behavior occurs less frequently. It is very, very, common for parents to behave in a way that they think is punishing when it is actually doing nothing or even reinforcing a behavior. This can happen in the workplace also.

## Understanding the System of Consequences

In all organizations, there is a system of reinforcement or appreciation. In the society, there is a similar system. Why does government constantly change the tax code to provide a deduction for investments in oil drilling, or research, or education? Because tax deductions are a form of reinforcement, and the government uses this to strengthen effort in that direction.

Every school has a system of reinforcing good academic performance. Every sport has a scorekeeping system and a system to reinforce good performance in many ways. There is a Rookie of the Year Award, an award for the best lineman, the best quarterback, and the best special team player. There are hundreds of different types of reinforcers that are designed to reward many different kinds of behavior.

Choose a sport and ask yourself these questions:

How many different types of positive reinforcement can we name in either a college or professional sport (such as soccer, baseball, football, or basketball)? Make a list. What behavior is each designed to increase?

| Reinforcement | Behavior |
| --- | --- |
| _____ | _____ |
| _____ | _____ |
| _____ | _____ |
| _____ | _____ |
| _____ | _____ |

Why has it proven effective to have so many different types of positive reinforcement? Why not just rely on one?

The answer is that people are different. In sports you have different positions in which players are able to perform in different ways. A defensive lineman can do different things than the quarterback or a wide receiver. So to motivate all of them, there must be different kinds of measurement and different kinds of awards. Notice also in our sport that some of the awards are individual and some are team. Why is this important? If every player were only thinking about how he could win an individual award, this might work contrary to good teamwork. Similarly, in your own team environment you should have both individual and team recognition or reinforcement.

As a group exercise, it will be a good idea to share what you have come up with among your team members. Now ask yourself the question, what performance do we want to increase, and what types of reinforcement could be added that would improve that performance.

## THE BALANCE OF CONSEQUENCES

The idea of a balance of consequences is that for every decision or behavior, there are likely to be consequences, both positive and negative, on both sides of the equation. Deciding to take job A or to take job B involves assessing the balance of consequences, potential rewards and potential negative events for either choice. Sometimes only a slight shift in the balance of consequences will tip the scale.

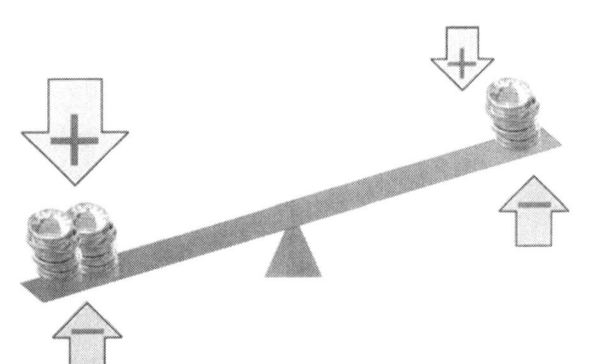

You can probably think of some behavior of your own, deciding to make an extra client visit in a day, or deciding to do something extra for your client, that only required a slight tipping of the scales to cause you to do it, or not to.

When we think about improving the performance of a team or an individual we can think about increasing some positive consequence for the desired behavior, or reducing some negative consequence, without feeling that we have to change all of the consequences. Whether we eat that pie and ice cream tonight will not be determined by eliminating all positive consequences. After all, it does taste good and that is reinforcing!! But, if we can add some reinforcement on the other side of the balance, for eating well and deferring gratification, we can change the behavior.

# Making Reinforcement Effective

What are the keys to the effective use of positive reinforcement to improve individual or team performance?

## Shape Behavior:

We don't learn a new language all at once. We learn it in small bites, each bite getting a bit larger and more complex than the previous one. We learn virtually everything, at least everything that is complex, by taking small steps that get larger and larger.

Reinforcing gradual improvement is called "shaping" behavior. Like a statue being made out of clay, it takes shape gradually, with repeated encouragement.

I remember when my second daughter was taking "keyboard" lessons and she called me into her room and said, "Daddy listen to this." It was Three Blind Mice, or something, but I couldn't really tell. It was an effort, but it was not exactly a concert performance. I could have said, "Well, that is not what I was hoping to get when I paid for those lessons. Call me when you can play something well!" If I had, this would have been the end of those lessons and probably any motivation for her to learn music. No! Daddy knows his job. Of course I said, "That's wonderful; it sounds like you are really learning some good songs!" and she smiled.

All parents know that you must reinforce approximations (shaping) toward a goal performance if you are going to motivate a child to learn. We are all the same. You and I need reinforcement for our efforts, for making improvement, for trying. A team will not instantly achieve its goals. But, it should be recognized for making improvement and for making the effort to improve. If it keeps trying to find improvement it will succeed.

## Do It Immediately and Frequently:

There is a lot of research that proves that the longer the delay, the less impact the reinforcement will have on strengthening a behavior it follows. If you reinforce immediately, the value of the reinforcement is greatest. Have you ever handed in work and waited months for feedback? When it came, you probably didn't feel any great joy.

Because immediacy matters, we need systems and habits of reinforcement that provide many opportunities for earning recognition or rewards. If there is only the monthly paycheck and an annual bonus or review, there are simply not enough opportunities to provide frequent and immediate reinforcement. Motivation depends on the immediacy and frequency of reinforcement.

### Personalize It:

What may be experienced as reinforcing by one person may not be by another. Some individuals may love to be recognized and applauded in a public gathering, while that same recognition may make others feel extremely uncomfortable. Some may consider time off from work a great reward while others would rather be rewarded with an additional assignment. Just as you think about the personal interests when buying a birthday present for someone, consider the personal interests of the individual you are encouraging in the work setting.

### Use Variety:

We love variety in most aspects of our lives. If the same thing, words or events, are used repeatedly, they will become less meaningful. The best reinforcement is the surprise, delivered when least expected or spontaneously. Simply varying the schedule on which reinforcement is delivered can greatly increase overall performance with no additional costs.

You can vary both the type of reinforcement (what) and the schedule (when). The knowledge to vary both will significantly raise the effectiveness of your performance improvement efforts.

### Be Consistent:

A sense of fairness and justice results from the consistency with which reinforcement is delivered. Inconsistent use of reinforcement creates disunity. Consistency does not mean not varying reinforcement. It means providing equality of reinforcement to different people or at different times. Just as parents teach values by consistently approving behavior, managers teach values by the consistency in their expressions of appreciation. By rewarding improvement consistently, managers give members of the organization confidence in the values represented by that appreciation. With consistency come confidence and the elimination of fear. If employees can see that you are consistent in your approval or disapproval, they will come to trust that value.

## STRENGTHENING BEHAVIOR WITHIN OUR TEAM

Let's try to apply the idea of positive reinforcement to improving behavior that we think is important.

| TEAM BEHAVIOR ||||
|---|---|---|---|
| WHAT BEHAVIOR MATTERS? | DOES IT NEED TO BE STRENGTHENED OR WEAKENED? | WHAT ARE THE CURRENT CONSEQUENCES? | WHAT REINFORCEMENT CAN BE STRENGTHENED? |
|  |  |  |  |
|  |  |  |  |
|  |  |  |  |
|  |  |  |  |
|  |  |  |  |

## ANALYZING HUMAN PERFORMANCE PROBLEMS

Many years ago, Robert Mager devised a model for analyzing performance problems, performance analysis, that is still extremely useful.[21] Whenever you observe a human performance problem, you can use this model to analyze the problem and define a solution.

The model essentially begins by asking the question – "Is it a ***can't do*** or ***won't do*** problem?" You will know this if you ask, "If his/her life depended on it, could he/she do it now?" If you ask me to sing opera, or play concert piano and you told me my life depended on it, I am dead! It isn't a "want to" issue. I just cannot do those things. It does not matter how big the reward or how big the threat, I simply don't have the skills. Maybe I could have developed these skills if my parents had trained me to sing or play golf at an early age, but it is unlikely even with training. I wasn't genetically endowed with the ability to sing opera. These are "can't do" rather than "won't do" problems.

In the work setting, most "can't do" performance problems, problems of knowledge or skill, are not like singing opera. They don't require unusual

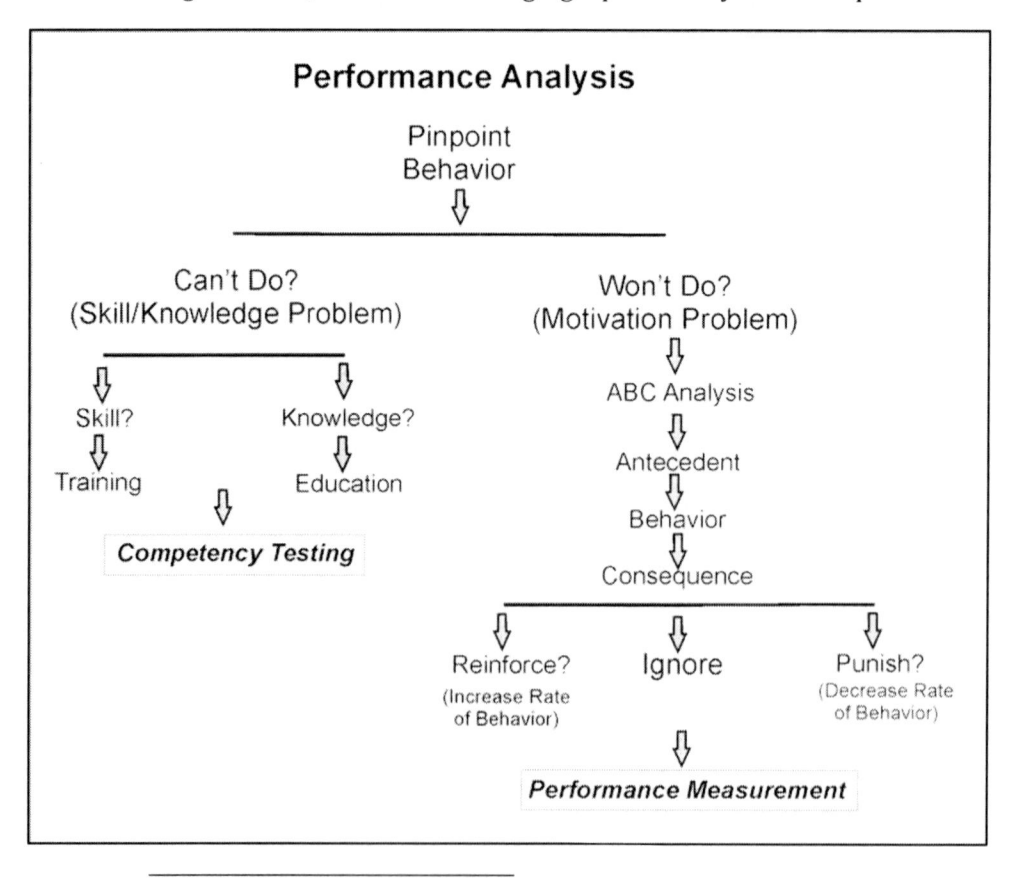

### Performance Analysis

Pinpoint Behavior

**Can't Do?** (Skill/Knowledge Problem)
- Skill? → Training
- Knowledge? → Education
- Competency Testing

**Won't Do?** (Motivation Problem)
- ABC Analysis
  - Antecedent
  - Behavior
  - Consequence
- Reinforce? (Increase Rate of Behavior)
- Ignore
- Punish? (Decrease Rate of Behavior)
- Performance Measurement

---

[21] Mager, Robert F. and Pipe, Peter. *Analyzing Performance Problems or You Really Oughta Wanna.* Atlanta, CEP Press, 1997.

genetic material, and they don't have to be developed in early childhood. They simply require training. This is true for most nursing and home support skills.

Many of the performance problems in a work setting are within the capability of employees; they just haven't been "made to matter" in a way that creates the necessary motivation.

If a problem is a "can't do" problem, it then requires the development of new skills through training, rather than motivation. If the problem is "won't do," a motivation problem, then the techniques of positive appreciation or positive reinforcement can strengthen that performance.

## EXERCISE

With your team members, select one human performance problem. Work through the performance analysis model, and develop a solution to this problem. First work through a 'can't do' problem, be specific about what you would do, then work on a 'won't do' problem and again be specific about what you would do. Share your solutions and get feedback from other team members.

# CHAPTER 13

# MAPPING YOUR VALUE STREAM

In this chapter your team will be guided to identify their "core" and "enabling" processes, map the value stream of those processes, and, initiate continuous improvement. Every team should be expert in their process and should be able to visualize the map of that process. This mapping is also at the heart of any kaizen event.

## OBJECTIVES

1. To identify the work processes that is your team's responsibility.
2. To provide methods for mapping the value stream of those work processes.
3. To learn methods of analyzing work processes to improve cycle time, reduce costs, and increase reliability and productivity.

## The Value is in the Flow

Healthcare Lean is about the flow of the work, from suppliers to clients and customers, and creating the ideal flow that will add the most value for your clients and customers and contain the least possible waste. The ideal process is so lacking in interruptions that it feels natural - it *flows*.

High performing teams or individuals appear *natural* when their performance flows with seemingly little effort. Athletes experience *flow*, or what they may call, "being in the zone." A musician may say she is in "the groove." Flow for an individual is complete focus, absorption in a task, when all energies move with ease and without interruption. Rather than feeling like great exertion, the work feels natural and exhilarating. Mihaly Csikszentmihalyi described flow as the psychology of optimal experience. *"It is what the sailor holding a tight course feels when the wind whips through her hair, when the boat lunges through the waves like a colt – sail, hull, wind, and sea humming in a harmony that vibrates in the sailor's veins. It is what the painter feels when the colors on the canvas begin to set up a magnetic tension with each other, and a new thing, a living form, takes shape in front of the astonished creator."*[22]

If you have ever watched a great basketball team run the court on a fast break with each player having perfect confidence in the other, looking one

---

[22] Csikszentmihalyi, Mihaly. Flow: The Psychology of Optimal Experience. New York. Harper Perennial, 1990. p. 3.

way, and passing the ball another with certainty that the teammate will be there, and three quick passes around and over defenders ends in what looks like an effortless dunk through the hoop, you have observed flow.

Can a home support or nursing team experience flow? What would that look and feel like? What prevents a health care team from experiencing this type of flow?

_____

_____

_____

Processes at work rarely provide a similar sense of exhilaration. Notice that processes that are exhilarating are without interruption, have an efficiency of no unnecessary steps, and those who are engaged in the process are in control.

Think about these two elements of flow: a) no unnecessary steps, and b) the players being in control. Do you feel that the process that you perform within every day incorporates these two elements?

_____

_____

_____

In a high performance organization, the organization is designed to facilitate the process. Teams and structures are formed around the process to enable the process Clients and customers pay for the output of the process, not any artificial requirement of vertical approvals or orders issued *up the line*. Why shouldn't the organization be ordered to serve the needs of the flow of the process, to support and enable the process, rather than the other way around?

Teams are formed and designed to optimize the ability of team members to control and manage their process. As the primary care teams at VON Canada were designed, the idea was to enable them to manage their process.

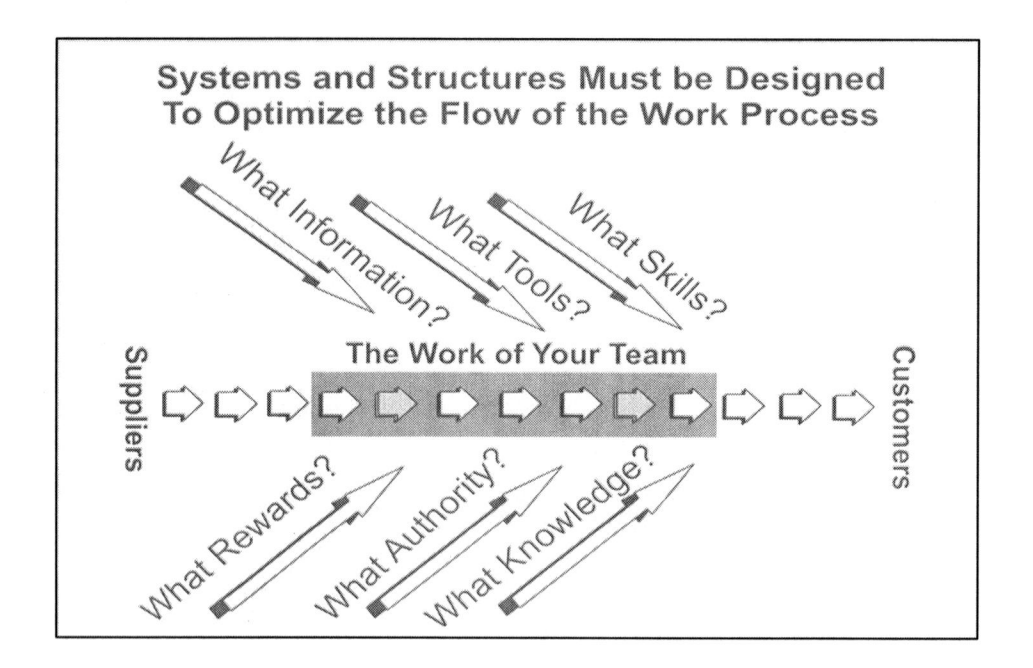

**Systems and Structures Must be Designed To Optimize the Flow of the Work Process**

*What Information? What Tools? What Skills?*

Suppliers → The Work of Your Team → Customers

*What Rewards? What Authority? What Knowledge?*

## DEATH BY PROCESS!

Processes can kill you and sometimes do. I don't know how many coroners' reports have said "Death by Process," but many should have.

My consultants and I were working with a large healthcare provider in the Midwest and had been given the assignment to "re-engineer" the core process in the organization. Of course, the core process was providing health care solutions to individuals in both clinics and hospitals. A design team was formed to study the core process and develop an improved solution to eliminate many well-known problems. The seriousness of those problems was sometimes buried under the routine of daily work.

The design team, after several months of work analyzing the process and developing a solution, made a presentation to the senior Executive Committee that included the company president. Because they were about to propose some fairly radical solutions, they were concerned that they get the executives' attention in a dramatic way. So, they dramatized a patient experience. They role-played a scenario in which one of their client members develops an unexplained stomach pain.

Her first stop is to her general practitioner and after filling out forms and sitting for an hour in the waiting room, she is told that she needs to see a specialist and is given a list of several specialists whom she could then call.

Of course, she has taken off from work for her appointment.

She goes home and gets on the phone. It will be a month before any of the specialists can see her. She makes an appointment.

She shows up a month later at the specialist's office. The specialist immediately tells her that he wants her to take a series of tests and she is referred to a clinic that provides the necessary tests. She calls and makes an appointment for two weeks later.

When she shows up at the clinic, she is informed that she has to get pre-approval from her insurance provider before they can administer these tests.

She goes home and calls the insurance provider.

You get the picture. The story was detailed and frustrating just listening to it, let alone if you had to go through it. The story ends, after months of wrong appointments, delays, and re-routing, in the doctor's office where she finds out that she has cancer and the doctor informs her that treatment could have been much more successful if she had come in sooner. She dies. In effect, *the process* murdered her.

The leader of the design team, to lighten up the somewhat somber mood in the meeting with the executives said, "Of course that story may be a bit exaggerated. Perhaps we don't kill people, but people do suffer through our system."

With that the president of the company, a doctor and healthcare executive for many years, interrupts. "Excuse me, but there is nothing exaggerated about that. That was my mother! That is exactly what happened to my mother."

A long and tense silence followed as everyone tried to figure out how to respond to that revelation. The president broke the silence and said, "Well, let's fix it!" Not surprisingly, they approved implementation of the redesigned process.

Isn't it odd that we handle packages with more efficiency and care than we handle patients? And that is because package delivery companies have become much more focused on eliminating waste from their processes and assuring that their process meets their client's requirements. Your team should be like the package delivery company.

> **The Attitudes of Process Improvement:**
>
> - MOST PROBLEMS ARE IN THE PROCESS, NOT THE PERSON!
> - DON'T BLAME THE PERSON - FIX THE PROCESS.
> - EVERY PROCESS CAN BE IMPROVED – FOREVER!
> - PROBLEMS ARE NORMAL – EACH AN OPPORTUNITY TO LEARN.
> - MEASUREMENT OF PROCESSES LEADS TO IMPROVEMENT.
> - EVERY PROCESS MUST HAVE A "PROCESS OWNER" OR TEAM RESPONSIBLE FOR ITS EXECUTION AND IMPROVEMENT.
> - WE "KNOW WHAT WE ARE DOING" BY KNOWING THE PROCESS.

## LEAN PROCESS IS OPTIMUM FLOW

Managers today are a hundred times more aware of their processes than they were twenty years ago. The Toyota Production System, what we now like to call lean management, is an innovation in process. It is not an innovation in either product or service. It is all about the effectiveness of the process of making cars that led to tremendous competitive advantage for Toyota and other car companies. Now, this same efficiency in process is rapidly coming to health care.

Process thinking becomes a way of life. Process thinking is learning to look horizontally through the organization as work flows. Those who are trained in lean processes can walk through a work setting and immediately see piles that signify process delays, interruptions in the form of pallets or in-boxes on the desk, or hear questions about "who owns the problem," all of which indicate process problems. You should work on developing your automatic, habitual thoughts about process. Developing this competence will serve you well. Think flow!

## DIFFERENT TYPES OF PROCESSES MAPS

A process is a set of related activities that together result in a desired output for a customer or client. That set of activities can simply be listed on a sheet of paper. However, we have all heard the saying that a picture is worth a thousand words. It is true. If you have ever downloaded directions on MapQuest, you received a list of turns and highways. You then also see the map of the suggested route. The map is much more helpful. Human beings were created as visual creatures. We like to see pictures, and we find it easier to understand a picture than a list of words.

You will have to decide the most useful way to map your process. It will be helpful to look at a number of different process maps and see how each may be useful in different situations.

## Macro Maps

Let's start with a very high level map. Think of "macro maps" as looking at your organization from an airplane thirty thousand feet in the air. They give you the big picture.

The following is macro map of the core and enabling process for a large organization. This is an administrative organization of a major university. Their core processes are the enabling processes for others in the organization, such as the academic departments. In this case you can see that they identified each of the major steps within their core processes. This became the map of the work of the senior team of this support organization. They organized the senior around these processes, with each process owner a member of the senior team.

### University Campus and Hospital Center Business Services

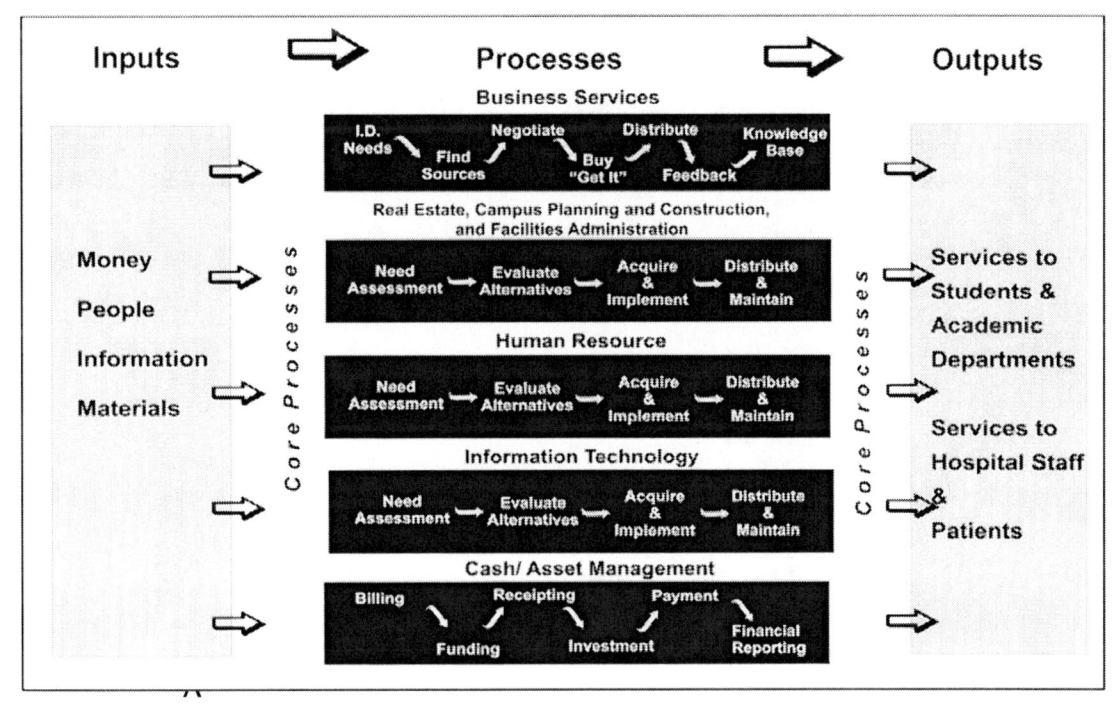

| Inputs | Processes | Outputs |
|---|---|---|
| Money | Business Services: I.D. Needs → Find Sources → Negotiate → Buy "Get It" → Distribute → Feedback → Knowledge Base | Services to Students & Academic Departments |
| People | Real Estate, Campus Planning and Construction, and Facilities Administration: Need Assessment → Evaluate Alternatives → Acquire & Implement → Distribute & Maintain | |
| Information | Human Resource: Need Assessment → Evaluate Alternatives → Acquire & Implement → Distribute & Maintain | Services to Hospital Staff & Patients |
| Materials | Information Technology: Need Assessment → Evaluate Alternatives → Acquire & Implement → Distribute & Maintain | |
| | Cash/Asset Management: Billing → Receipting → Payment → Funding → Investment → Financial Reporting | |

PS

Your team is more likely to be concerned with a more detailed description of how you do your daily work. A map that describes the work we do is a work process map. Again, there are many different ways to map work processes, so it will help to look at a few examples.

The Health care Delivery Design Team mapped out the details of how the work would flow from the time a CCAC called with a referral through to the billing process. You should review and be familiar with these maps, or any revisions of those maps that may be more up-to-date.

The following is a very simple map created by a team responsible for managing a conference. You will see that they have identified the major core activities across the top. This was their first map of their process. Then, they decided that more detail would be needed so they "drilled down" and mapped the detailed steps within each of the original general steps. You can see that under "define clients and customers, needs and goals" they have mapped the five steps for getting that job done. Of course, they did this for each of the seven steps.

## Conference Planning Process

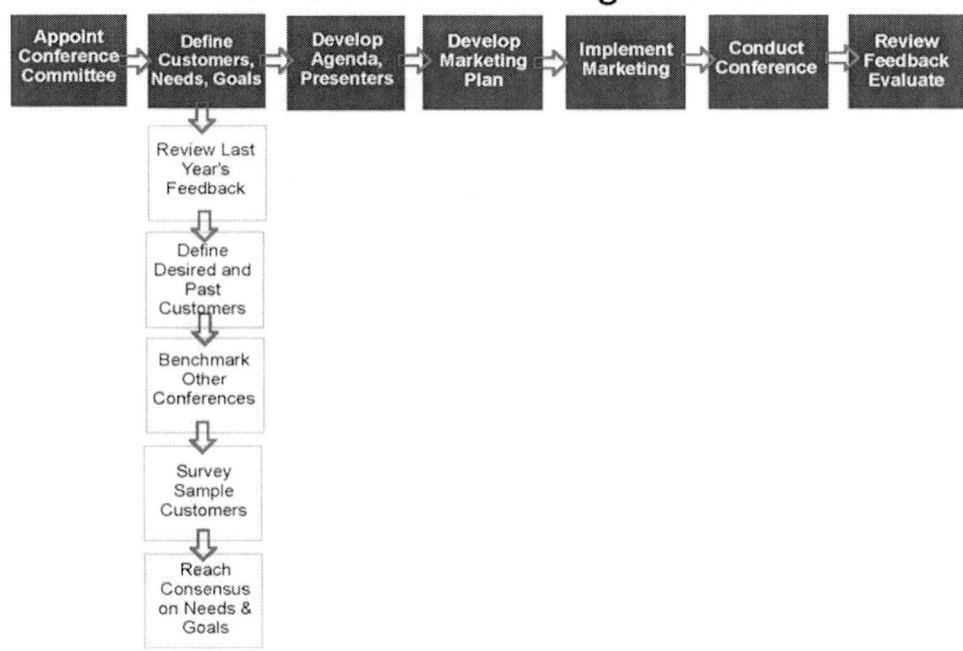

Appoint Conference Committee → Define Customers, Needs, Goals → Develop Agenda, Presenters → Develop Marketing Plan → Implement Marketing → Conduct Conference → Review Feedback Evaluate

Under "Define Customers, Needs, Goals":
- Review Last Year's Feedback
- Define Desired and Past Customers
- Benchmark Other Conferences
- Survey Sample Customers
- Reach Consensus on Needs & Goals

One of the advantages of doing this is that this team plans and manages a conference each year. In the past, every time they had to plan a conference, they would have new members who had not done it before. So the learning would begin again with little or no memory of the lessons of previous years. Now, at the beginning of their planning for the conference they take out the planning map and review the steps from last year. They decided whether these steps still make sense this year, and they assign responsibility for each of the steps. Then, after that conference is completed, they have a learning-reflection meeting. They review what went well and what did not go well. They look at the map again and make changes so the team next year can avoid any mistake they made. In this way, each annual team is able to improve the process and maintain some "corporate memory." This is a form of knowledge management that is often lacking in organizations.

## IDENTIFYING THE "VALUE" IN THE PROCESS STREAM

Another name for process mapping is value stream mapping. What is the meaning of "value?" Value is created when there is a transformation in the material, information, or other input, and that transformation is necessary to satisfy the client or customer. Anything that does not add value is waste. Sitting still is waste. Re-doing is waste. Any time spent that is not directly creating the desired transformations is waste. The job of the team studying a process is to identify exactly which time, materials, motions, etc., are adding value and which are waste.

Value adding and non-value adding activity can be identified on your process map by using data boxes. Below you will see an example. These data boxes illustrate three measures of value: CT, the actual cycle time from beginning to the end of that process step; VCT, the value adding cycle time; and CTVR the ratio of value adding to total cycle time.

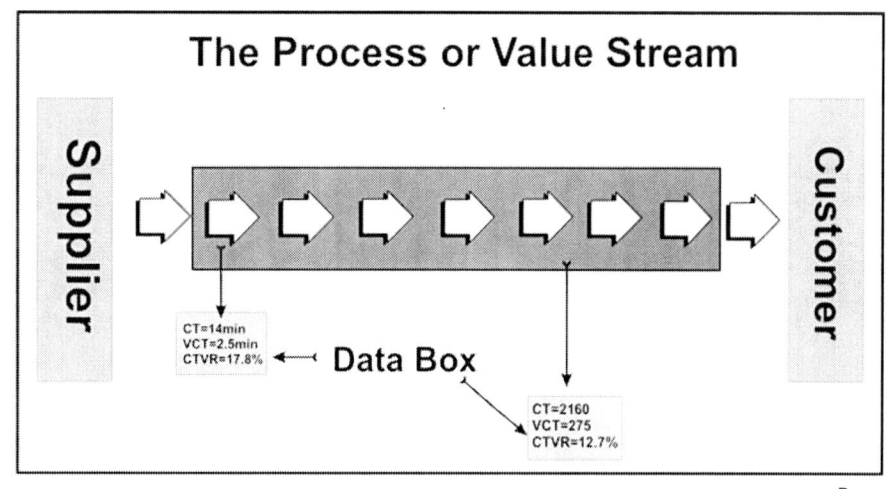

Identifying the actual cycle time and the value adding time requires discipline, doing your homework. You should not guess. Go and see! Go and measure! Get the data. Often, it will surprise you.

Below you will see a completed analysis of cycle time for one process. The total and value-adding cycle time of each step has been identified, as well as the totals for the overall process. The percent of value adding time is

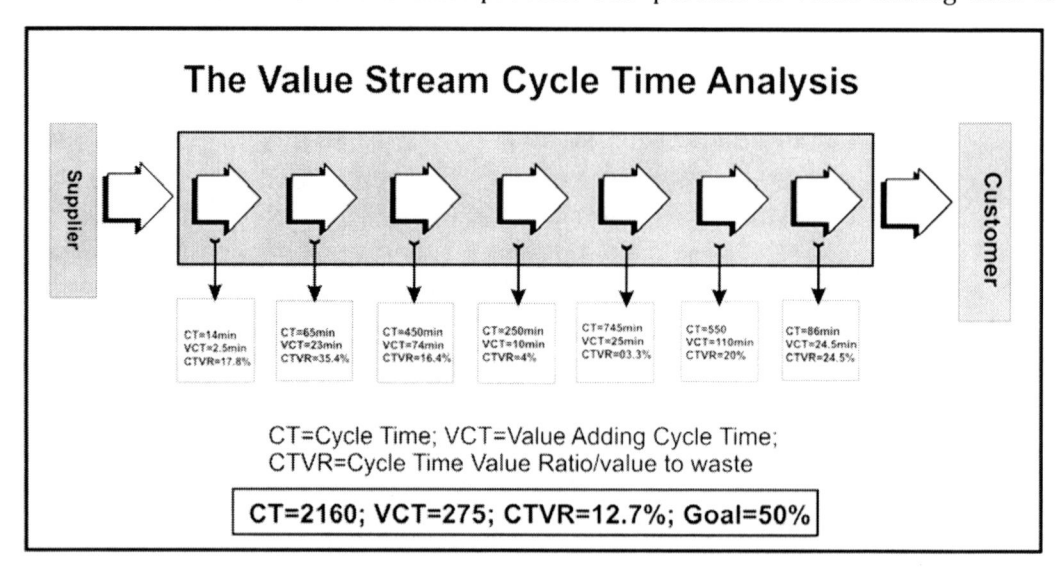

## The Value Stream Cycle Time Analysis

| Step | CT | VCT | CTVR |
|---|---|---|---|
| 1 | 14 min | 2.5 min | 17.8% |
| 2 | 65 min | 23 min | 35.4% |
| 3 | 450 min | 74 min | 16.4% |
| 4 | 250 min | 10 min | 4% |
| 5 | 745 min | 25 min | 03.3% |
| 6 | 550 | 110 min | 20% |
| 7 | 86 min | 24.5 min | 24.5% |

CT=Cycle Time; VCT=Value Adding Cycle Time; CTVR=Cycle Time Value Ratio/value to waste

**CT=2160; VCT=275; CTVR=12.7%; Goal=50%**

12.7%. This is not an unusual ratio when processes are studied carefully. You will see that this team has set an ambitious goal of getting to 50% value adding time. This will mean eliminating a lot of non-value adding activity, delays, re-do loops, or other interruptions in the process.

Which value measures you decide to use when analyzing your process will be dependent on the nature of the work and the output of the work. Beginning with cycle time, analysis is one of the most certain ways to get started.

## COMMON PROCESS OR VALUE MEASURES

- CT = Cycle Time
- VCT=Value Adding Cycle Time
- CTVR=Ratio of Value Adding to Total Cycle Time
- CO=Change Over Time
- No.O=Number of Separate Operations
- WT=Work Time (actual value adding work)
- TT=Total Time Worked or Assigned to an Operation
- SC=Scrap
- SCR=Scrap rate (ratio of scrap to total)
- I=Inventory

**Problems tend to be found "Down-Stream" and "Caused Up-Stream"**

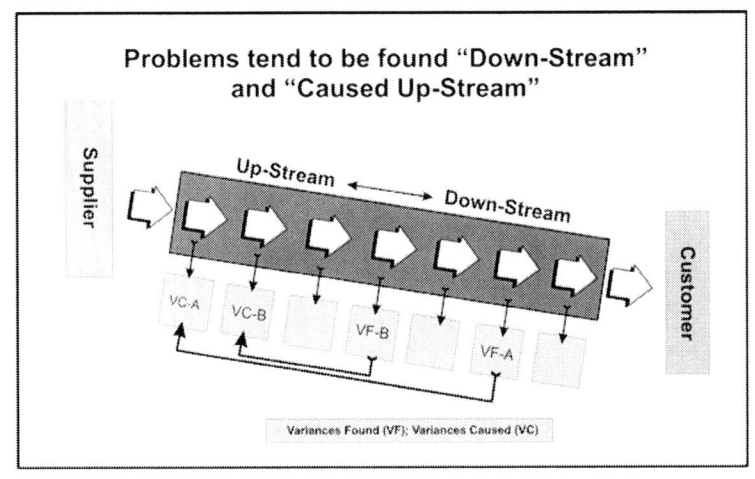

*Variances Found (VF); Variances Caused (VC)*

BUT YOU decide what process measures are most important for your process!!!

Another useful question to ask when analyzing processes is, "where are problems found, and where are they caused?" It is normal that problems are caused in one place, but discovered in another place. This almost always means that they are caused "upstream" and found "downstream." For example, imagine that you are making chairs. One department cuts and prepares legs for assembly. A "downstream" department does the actual assembly. It is important that the legs are exactly the same length. Hopefully, those who are cutting the legs are conducting their own self-inspection. However, it will not be surprising if those who are assembling the chair find that some of the legs are irregular and cause the chair to wobble. In such cases it is important that there be a clear feedback loop established whereby the assembly team can immediately provide feedback upstream to the team that caused the problem. This feedback loop should be almost instantaneous to avoid the production of off-specification parts. Any delay in this feedback loop will increase waste of materials and time.

This is a very simple map. This is a process with which we are all familiar. It is a simple work process: making a meal. If you are a good cook (like me!) you know that the order in which you do things is very important. For example, if you are going to make a spaghetti dinner, you don't start your preparations by sticking the pasta in a pot of cold water, and then thinking about how to prepare the sauce. You begin preparing the sauce long before putting water on to boil for the spaghetti. Order is important in most work processes. It is one of the reasons why you should map your processes. Problems often occur

1. Invite guests to dinner.
2. Decide on the menu.
3. Go shopping.
4. Cut the onions and brown.
5. Add and brown meat.
6. Cut and add green pepper and mushrooms.
7. Add tomato sauce.
8. Add spices.
9. Simmer for two hours.
10. Make salad.
11. Cook vegetable.
12. Warm water to boil.
13. Set table.
14. Add spaghetti to water.
15. Rinse spaghetti.
16. Serve above.
17. Eat.
18. Clean table.
19. Wash dishes.

because the order is wrong. Or you have missed a step or have unnecessary steps.

While this process map is useful, it is also lacking a lot of very helpful information. Who is doing what? Why is one person doing something and not other people? Does one person bear too much responsibility or not enough?

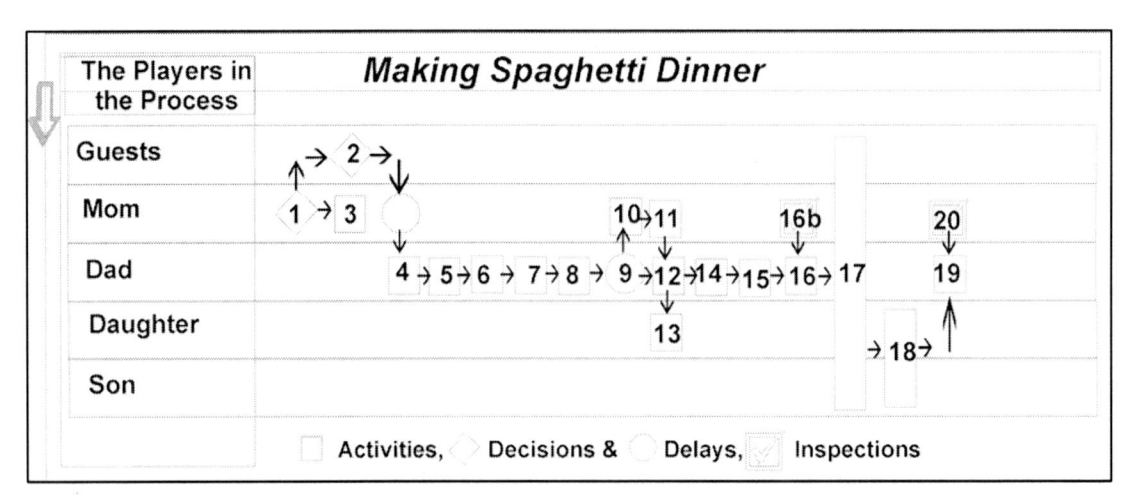

| The Players in the Process | *Making Spaghetti Dinner* |
|---|---|
| Guests | ↑→ 2 →↓ |
| Mom | 1 → 3    10→11    16b    20 |
| Dad | 4→5→6→7→8→9→12→14→15→16→17    19 |
| Daughter | 13    →18→ |
| Son | |

☐ Activities, ◇ Decisions & ○ Delays, ☑ Inspections

It is much easier to find answers to these questions in a "relationship map." The following map contains exactly the same steps; it is the same process, as the previous one. But, now you have who is doing what. You can see that Dad is doing the majority of the work. Maybe he wants it this way, or maybe he doesn't, but it certainly raises some questions that should be asked. You can see that relationship problems are often created by how we do things, the relationships reflected in the process. What problems do you think this process might lead to? You might try reversing the roles of Mom and Dad. Do you like it better or worse that way? Why?

☐ Work Activity
◇ Decision
○ Delay
⬇ Transport
☑ Inspection

Before you start mapping your processes it is important to agree on what symbols you will use. There is no rule or religion to this. The following is a set of symbols you can use, but you can choose others also. Just agree on them. That is what is important. You may find it helpful to use symbols that you find in a software program. The most recent version of MS Word includes symbols for process mapping.

# How to Turn Processes into Flow

Here are some simple steps to follow to create a process map.

## 1. Clarify Purpose and Goals

The purpose and goals of every process should be clear. You have may have already done this. Just review them here. The purpose should make clear why the process is important and to whom. The goals should not be detailed scorecard goals, but the general goal of the process.

## 2. Agree on Responsibility

Is the process the responsibility of the entire team, more than one team, or just a few members of the team? The process should be defined by those who "own" the process. Who owns this process?

## 3. Define Inputs & Outputs

If you have completed the work in the previous chapters, you have already done much the necessary work to be ready to work on process improvement. You should have answers to the following questions

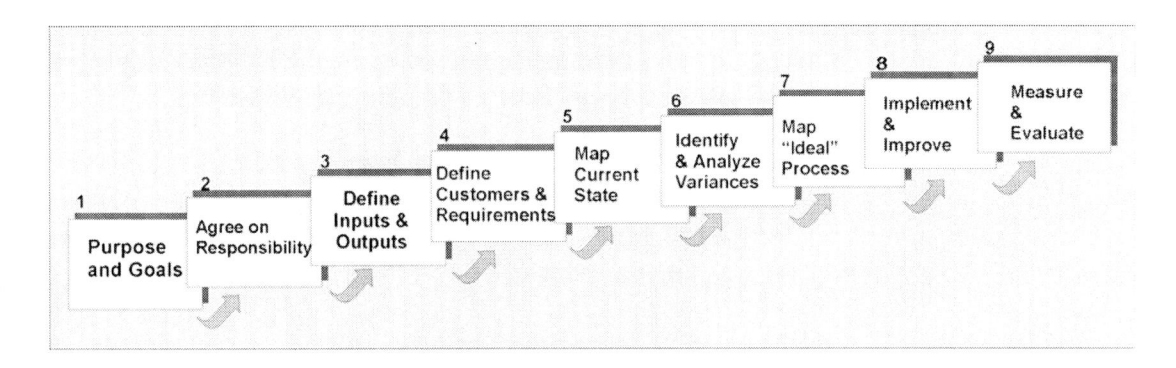

- What are the inputs to your work process (include materials, information, capital, people)? What are the requirements for each of these inputs?
- Who are the suppliers who provide input? What capabilities are needed on the part of suppliers in order to meet these requirements?
- What are the feedback loops from your team to your suppliers, and how do they function (speed, quality of information)?
- What are the outputs of your work system?

- Given the above, what are the requirements for your work process?
- What are the feedback loops that inform us of client or customer satisfaction, and how do they function (speed, quality of information)?

## 4. Define Client or customer Requirement

If you followed the guidance in the previous chapters, you have this. It is helpful to just put this on a flip chart so the team can see and refer to these requirements as they begin mapping the process.

## 5. Map the Current State

It is a mistake to start mapping how you think things should be until you have mapped how things actually get done today. This is the "current state" of the process.

It is often true that even people doing the job don't know how the whole process gets done. People only understand their very narrow piece of the work. You can't analyze how things can be improved or study the causes of variances if you don't know how things are currently done. First, map the current state of the process.

It may be helpful to imagine a meeting in which a team is going to map their process. Let's go through how that meeting might flow:

- ✓ First, let's check to see that we have the right people in the room. Are the team members in this room the "world's greatest experts" in this process? Is there anyone else we should invite to participate in mapping the process?

- ✓ Now let's define the process. Do we agree on the process boundaries? Where does this process begin and where does it end?

- ✓ Now we will make a list of the inputs and outputs and client or customer requirements for this process. We will also make a list of any other specifications for the output of this process.

- ✓ Now let's map the current state steps in the process. Let's start this by brainstorming without worrying about whether we have the steps in exactly the right order. It is very helpful to have Post-It-Notes, especially the 3x5 kind. Have the team members write down steps in the process and put those on the wall. It is very helpful to have a roll of brown paper that you can spread across the wall. Give yourself lots of room.

- ✓ Some process steps are work activities; some are decisions. If you can, use a different color for these. Or you can indicate in some way that these are symbols. Agree on another kind of note for delays.

- ✓ Give everyone a chance to get all of the steps up on the wall and then ask, "Who are the Players in the process?" Make a note for each individual who participates in the work of this process. Now put these players in a vertical column to the left of your paper. If you can, draw a horizontal line across the paper, representing the occasions when that player may be involved.

- ✓ Now order the steps. Arrange each of the work steps and decisions on your map going from left to right. They should be in chronological order. If two things are happening at the same time, they can be on top of each other. If they happen after one another, then they should be to the right of the previous step.

- ✓ Ask yourself how these happen in time. Are there delays between steps? If these delays are for any significant amount of time, put a post-it-note up for that delay.

- ✓ Now create a timeline from left to right. It may be that the process is not the same every time. Take a typical process cycle for the sake of your studying the process. On the left, when the process begins, put a zero at the beginning of your timeline. Then, at the end of the process put the amount of time a typical cycle takes, whether it is one hour or one month. Then, try to put time marks from left to right as the steps occur. This will give you some idea where the delays are occurring and how much time is involved in each step of the process. This may raise some questions when you analyze the process for speed or cycle time improvement.

- ✓ This is probably enough work for one meeting. Getting to this point may have taken one to several hours. When a team is assigned to work on a complex process that flows through the organization, just mapping the current state may involve many meetings over a period of weeks. It may also be necessary to go and interview other people who are working in the process in order to have knowledge of those steps.

- ✓ It is sometimes desirable at this point to invite others into the meeting, perhaps some managers, perhaps members of other teams and ask them if they agree that this is how things currently work. They may have some insights that your team may have missed.

✓ It will probably be in another meeting that you begin to analyze the variances in the process. Below is an introduction to the analysis of variances. This will be explored in more detail in the following chapter.

## 6. IDENTIFY AND ANALYZE VARIANCES:

A variance is anything in a process that varies from the way things should ideally be done or a result that varies from client or customer requirements. The next chapter will deal in more depth with analyzing variances.

For now, you should be aware that your process may include any single one, or a combination of at least five different kinds of problems or variances. You have "waste" in the form of unnecessary steps, unnecessary motions within a step, or waste in the form of delays that could be eliminated. Any step that doesn't add value to the process is also "waste."

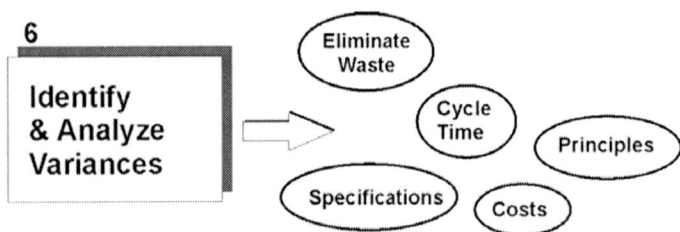

You may also have a cycle time variance from what may be an ideal cycle time. Speed is an important factor in almost all competition these days. Think about the pit stop in an auto race. Speed matters, and anything that slows down the movement from input to output should be questioned.

Probably the most obvious variance will be a variance from specifications. Your team should be able to measure conformance to specifications at each step in the process and at the end of the process.

Work teams and management teams are managing a business. Imagine that your team is actually a separate company with its own revenue and its own costs. You are now responsible for managing the business. If it was your business, you would seek to eliminate any unnecessary costs and costs that do not add value to the output of the team.

And, finally, you will want to ask yourself whether or not your process conforms to your principles. Look back on the principles you established in a previous chapter. If you have a principle to be client and client or customer focused, is your process genuinely client and client or customer focused? If you have principles to make decisions at the lowest possible level in the organization, does your process conform to that principle?

### 7. Map the "Ideal" Process

There is no such thing as an ideal process. There is only the most ideal process we can imagine at this time. That ideal will change as we experiment and learn more about our process. But for now, map what you regard to be the ideal process. Start where input comes into the organization, and the first step is taken. Go through all the steps you would recommend for a future process. Be sure not to add back in waste or sources of variance that you have eliminated.

### 8. Implement and Improve

If you have followed all of the steps above, it is now time to implement your new and improved process. However, you may feel that you have more work to do to analyze problems in the process. If this is the case, the next couple of chapters will help you find and make those improvements. Finding improvement and implementing those improvements should be an ongoing process, something you do many times in a year. By finding and implementing improvements to your process, you are doing your job as a high performance team.

### 9. Measure and Evaluate

If you have developed your team scorecard, you have identified measures of your work process. These are measures that you should be graphing and monitoring on a daily or weekly basis. The improvements you have made in your process should be reflected in these scores.

# CHAPTER 14

# ANALYZING VARIANCES

A variance is a problem. It is something that varies from either the standard way of doing things, or from performance that meets the client's or customer's expectations. In other words, it is a problem. The purpose of this chapter is to analyze your work process to eliminate waste and discover causes of quality, productivity and cost problems.

## OBJECTIVES:

1. To understand the costs and causes of variation.
2. To study variation within our own health care service delivery and management processes and seek to reduce variation.

If your are to become a truly lean organization it must become processed focused and must continually seek to reduce or eliminate variances.

There is statistical variation and there is a variance from how things could ideally be done. Both are problems within a process, and both need to be the focus of attention by your team. For example, there is an average, mean, time you spend in a home visit with a client. It is not the same every time. Therefore, it varies. The time it takes you to get from point A to point B is not the same every time. It varies.

Statistical variation is the variability around a mean for any performance. There is always some variation around a mean. The question is when is that a problem?

To understand variability it will help to understand a simple example. You may have a gun that you aim at a target. Let's assume that you are one hundred meters away from that target. Let's also assume that there is no wind and the gun is in a vice-grip so it will not move. Will every bullet land in exactly the same spot, assuming that the gun itself is perfectly stable? They will not all fall in the same place. If you fire fifty shots from the gun, you will see a pattern. That pattern can be described as statistical variation, the variability around a mean. The average bullet may fall at or very close to the target, but the pattern will be in a circle around that point. Depending on the gun, the pattern may be a few centimeters wide or a few meters. This pattern will describe the capability of this system in its current state.

Knowing *system capability* and normal *system performance* is important knowledge for anyone managing any system.

## COMMON AND SPECIAL CAUSES OF VARIATION

The concept of special and common cause no doubt has more utility in manufacturing than it does in health care. However, the basic understanding of how statistics point to different types of problems will help you to analyze problems.

Dr. Deming described the important distinction between what he called *"common cause"* and *"special cause"* of variation. In the example of the bullets hitting a target, if you fire fifty or one hundred shots, you will see that all of the shots fall within some circle. This variation from the mean, the center of the circle, is *common cause*. In other words, it is inherent in the nature of the system. The gun is a system with inputs, a process, and an output. The variability, under stable conditions (the gun is clean, it is not moving, etc.) that results from this system is common cause. Within the normal performance of this system, the only explanation for each variation is simple randomness.

There is always random variability around a mean. Every system produces variation that describes the capability of that system. You can and should expect it. If you want to reduce this variation, reduce the size of the circle made by the bullets, you will have to change the system. You could add a longer barrel on the gun and that would probably reduce the variation.

This is an important understanding because if you know what normal performance for a system is, you won't blame the person operating within that system. In almost any healthcare provider there have been problems in the design of the health care delivery system. Blaming individuals is useless. The system has to be redesigned.

But, there is another kind of variation and this is not the result of the inherent properties of the system. A *special cause* is the result of something "being wrong" in the operation of the system. In other words, if the circle on the target is normally a radius of twelve centimeters, this is "system" performance. However, if suddenly a bullet falls two meters away from the

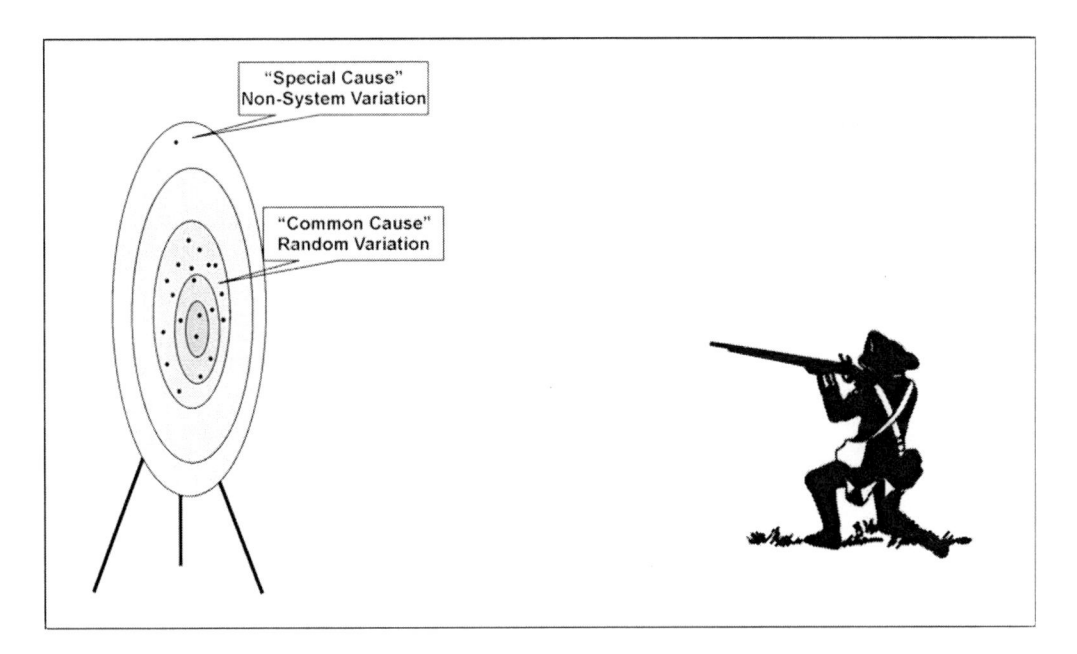

center, you know that this is not normal for this system. You only know this because you already have data on system performance. You immediately say "Hey, something is wrong here!" And what you mean is that "Hey, this is not a common cause; this is a special cause of variation." This is caused by some abnormality in the system or abnormal input. Now you can brainstorm the possible causes of this defect. The cause may be a bad bullet. Or something may have knocked and moved the gun. The gun may be getting dirty. There may be many possible reasons for a special cause.

The important point of this distinction is that you will do different things depending on whether the variation is a special or common cause variation. If you seek to improve the normal variation produced by a system, common cause, you will have to redesign that system. On the other hand, if you are witnessing a special cause, you would be making a serious mistake to redesign the system. This would cause even more variation. You need to track down the reason you have experienced a special cause.

| What Performance Demonstrates Statistical Variability |||
|---|---|---|
| What is the Performance? | What is Normal System Performance? | What are Examples of Common and Special Cause |
|  |  |  |
|  |  |  |
|  |  |  |
|  |  |  |

## THE COST OF VARIATION

There is a cost to variation. For example, when you drive to work each day it may take an average of thirty minutes to make the drive from home to work. But, it is rarely exactly thirty minutes. It may vary ten minutes on either side. If the weather and traffic are good, you may get to work in twenty minutes. But if there is an accident, it could take a lot more than thirty minutes. Let us assume that you live in an area where there is a lot of road construction and there tend to be a lot of accidents. When there is no traffic and no construction, the process of driving from home to work is

# Analyzing Variances

"interruption free." But, in your situation, during a normal drive to work, there is a fair likelihood of an interruption, something that will cause a deviation from the mean.

Now let's also assume that there are some consequences for being either late or early. Your team cannot start work until you get there. If one person is late by thirty minutes, that is the equivalent of all ten members of the team being late. The consequence is that there are three hundred minutes of lost work time. Being on time is so important that it is a factor in your performance reviews. If you are late too many times, that may result in not achieving a merit increase in pay. This is a risk that you do not want to take. On the other hand, if you are thirty minutes early, the door is locked and you can't enter. This means standing out in the cold. These are the costs of variation in the process. Variation almost always has costs even if we fail to see or understand them. We often behave on the assumption of variability in a process and we therefore consider it "just the way things are."

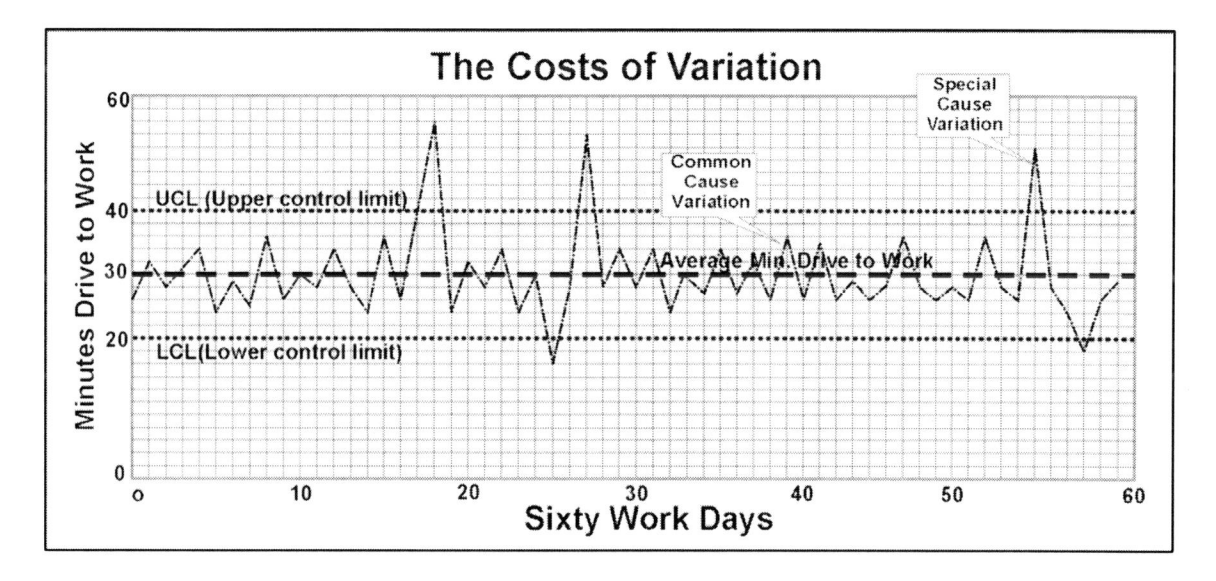

If you look at the above graph, you can see this variation illustrated. You have measured the time it takes you to drive to work for sixty days. The average is thirty minutes, but on three occasions it took about fifty minutes. On two occasions it took less than twenty minutes. Now that you know about the consequences of extreme variation (defining extreme as above or below the control limits), would you alter your behavior? What are the costs associated with this variation?

_____

_____

_____

_____

Now think about your own work process. Look at your most important three or four measures of performance. Do you know how these measures vary from day to day or by any other time frame? Make a graph of this variation? What are the costs of this variation? What are the causes?

_____

_____

_____

_____

_____

_____

You are probably familiar with cause-and-effect or fishbone diagrams. These serve the simple purpose of stimulating brainstorming. It is important that your team look at variation in your process and seek to understand the causes of that variation. It would be a good idea to place this diagram on a flip chart and brainstorm the causes of variation in your work process. The points on the diagram are simply suggestions. You may have other, or more important, major causes.

# Costs of Variation

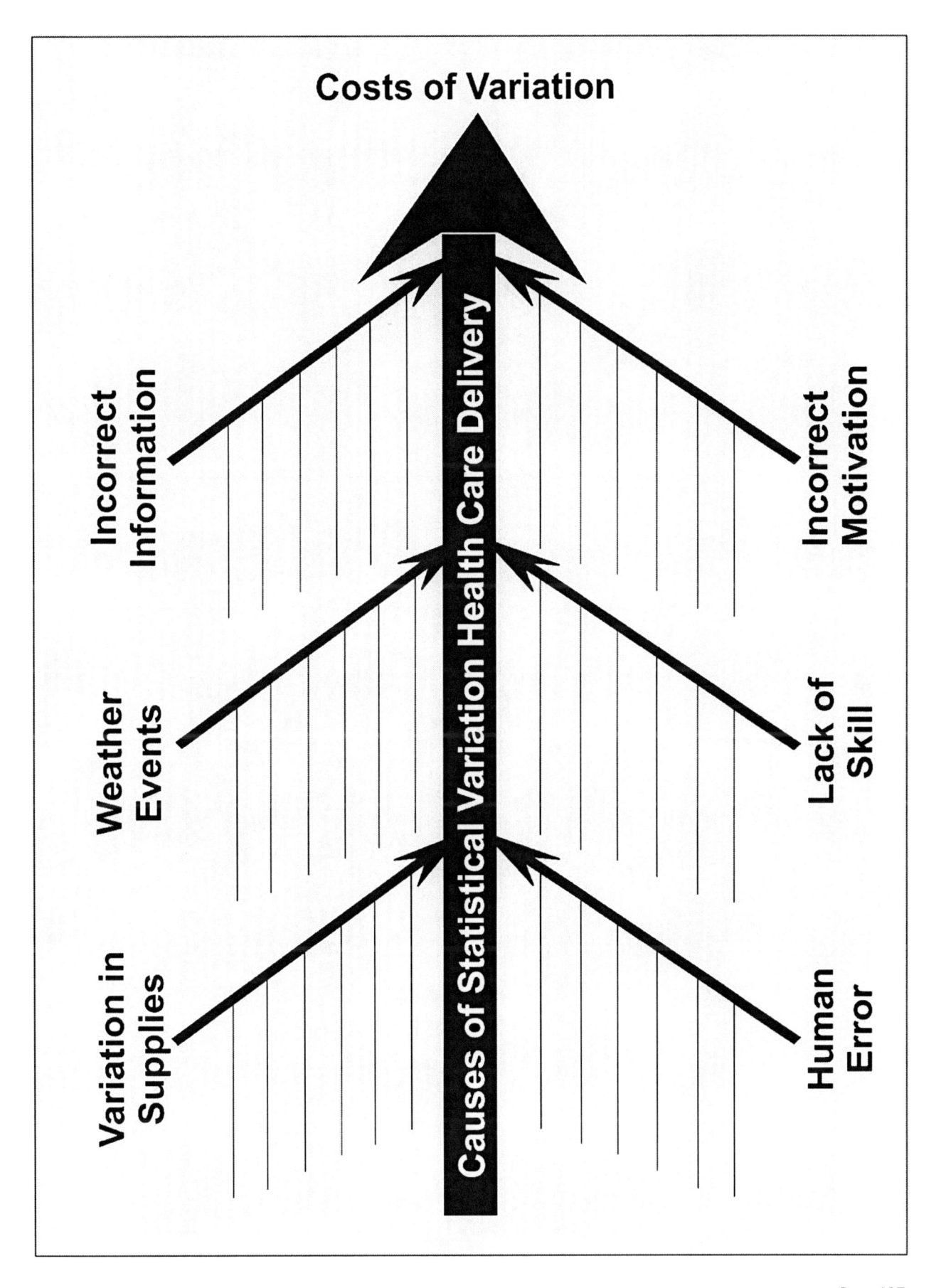

**Causes of Statistical Variation Health Care Delivery**

- Incorrect Information
- Incorrect Motivation
- Weather Events
- Lack of Skill
- Variation in Supplies
- Human Error

Analyzing Variances

# Variance Analysis Worksheet

| Key Variance | Cause | Where it's Found | Who Controls | Solutions: Change Process, Supply, Tools, Human Performance |
|---|---|---|---|---|
|  |  |  |  |  |

## VARIATION WITHIN HUMAN PERFORMANCE

The examples given above are oriented to the manufacturing setting. Many teams using this manual will not be making "things" but will be involved in a service delivery process. In what is often called "knowledge work," the rate and process of work is much more independently controlled by the individual. For example, if you are creating advertising, you cannot define exactly how each creative process is going to proceed as if it was a repetitive process such as one on an assembly line. It may be that the best creative work may be watching television or taking a walk around the block to get ideas. If you are writing grant proposals, each proposal will require some different information and will require unique research and writing. When one understands the actual work involved, one is in a better position to judge the nature of the variation.

Variation is often a result of interaction with the uncontrollable events in the environment. Imagine a football team. Even if the team played the same opponent with the same players every game, there would still be some variation in performance. The quarterback would not throw the same number of completed passes each game. But in the real world, every opponent is different, with different defensive schemes, and this will cause variation in the play of the quarterback. You can think of the job of the defense as doing everything they can to create "variances" in the play of the quarterback.

Much of our work is like this, continually adjusting to the client or customer, the economic conditions, and competitors. The trick is to learn what forces are influencing performance, seek to control those we can control, and adjust to those we cannot control.

Selling is also a human performance process that is very much under the control of the individual, but also continually interacts with forces in the environment. How does the idea of variation apply to these types of human performance?

In the chart below you will see the annual performance for a team of new car salesman in a group of auto dealerships. This is a "cumulative" graph. That means that each data point is added to the previous data points, so it never goes down. You will see that for the year the sales team will sell approximately one thousand automobiles. That does not mean that each month they will sell exactly one twelfth of this number. If they sold exactly the same amount each month, all end of month sales points would be on the line that is on the slope from zero to one thousand. You will also notice that within each month there is a pattern. Sales vary from the first week of the month to the last week. In fact, in every case, the last week of the month has much stronger sales than the first week of the month. If you were the manager of this organization, it would probably benefit you to know why there is this variation in performance. What do you think is causing this end of month increase in sales?

You will also notice that if you take the maximum slope that occurs during the last week of the month and project this line, it is a significantly greater rate of performance than the average performance for the year.

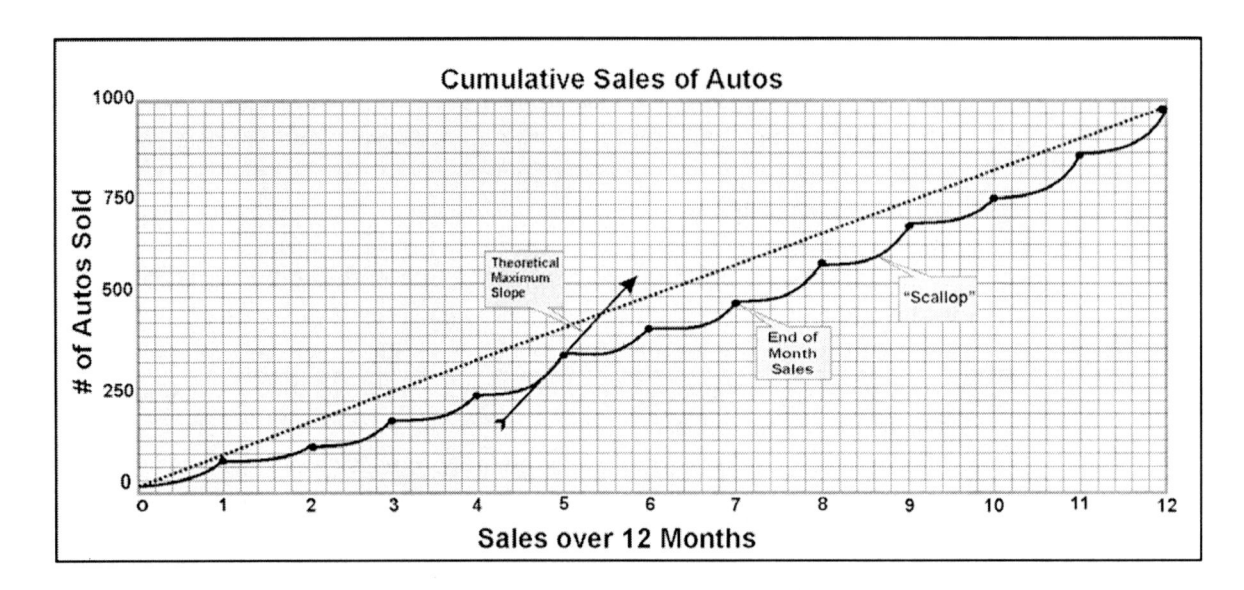

**Cumulative Sales of Autos**
*Sales over 12 Months*

The curve of performance within each month is what is known as a "scallop." It is very familiar to experimental psychologists who study the science of human behavior, particularly what are called "schedules of reinforcement." The sales people in this organization are very clearly on what is called a fixed-interval schedule of reinforcement. What this simply means is the rewards are delivered at the end of each month. After the end of each month, these salespeople experience what is known as a "post-reinforcement-pause." These sales people receive a monthly bonus check for their sales during the previous month. They receive this on the first day of the month. They do what most people do: as the potential reward approaches, they work harder to get that reward. We have all done this. It is the same as cramming the night before for the test in school. Congress passes the largest number of bills just before they achieve the reward of going home at the end of the session.

If you are a client or customer, what does this tell you about when is the best time to buy a car? When are you likely to get the best deal? Of course, during the last few days of the month. The incentive system conditions the sales people, and the sales people condition the clients and client or customers to buy at the end of the month.

Understanding this pattern of variability and its cause can be extremely valuable to the organization. How could the reward system be modified to reduce the variability and increase the total sales? The answer is in shifting from a fixed-interval (once a month on the last day of the month) reward schedule, to one that varies and has the element of surprise, like all gambling that maintains strong and consistent rates of behavior.

What are processes and performance that are more the result of human motivation than the design of the process?

_____

_____

If you plot that performance on a graph, what variation will you see?

_____

_____

What are the causes of this variation?

_____

_____

# Chapter 15

# Finding and Eliminating Waste

The purpose of this chapter is to engage in systematic and continuous efforts to eliminate all non-value adding activity, materials, time or costs from your processes. Eliminating waste has been a cornerstone of the Toyota Production System and whether in manufacturing, in health care delivery, or in management processes, we should continually be looking for and eliminating waste. We should also appreciate waste from the perspective of the customer. Time spent filling out forms, in waiting rooms, or other delays, are all waste to the customer.

## Objectives:

1. To understand and identify the seven forms of waste in your work and organization.

2. To practice and implement waste elimination from your processes.

Just off the top of your head – what activities, time, or materials have you seen wasted in your organization? Make a quick list of the types of waste you have observed and what you think may be the causes of that waste.

| Identify Waste ||
|---|---|
| **Types of Waste** | **Causes of Waste** |
|  |  |
|  |  |
|  |  |
|  |  |
|  |  |
|  |  |

For more than forty years, Toyota has worked to improve the process of designing and building cars by focusing on the elimination of waste. They are still doing it today. For how long have you been eliminating waste from your processes? When will you be done?

Contrary to the understanding of many, the primary focus of improvement in lean organizations has not been making more money or managing quality, although both have been the result. The primary driver for improvement has been the elimination of waste. It is not the same as cost reduction!

Most companies cut costs, which usually means cutting people, and they leave the waste. The waste is in the process, not the person. If you eliminate the waste in the process, you can then redeploy the person and other assets to "value-adding" work and thereby increase value to clients or customers. Company after company has gone out of business cutting costs, which results in worse products, worse service, fearful employees who lose their creativity, and the inevitable loss of clients and customers. You stay in business by maximizing value to clients and customers.

## WHAT IS WASTE?

Any activity that does not directly contribute to providing excellent health or health care delivery is waste.

The founders of Lean Manufacturing were Taichi Ohno and Dr. Shigeo Shingo. They focused on seven types of waste:

1. **Inventory:** Any "piles" are waste. Anything that is standing still and not in motion is waste, whether it is in a warehouse or in bins or on pallets in the production area. Inventory consumes space (waste), requires employees to move and manage (waste), inventory requires accounting (waste), and instead of having one mistake that is caught immediately, you will have a large pile of defects... big waste! Just-in-time is the process of arranging the supply chain and production process so that each input arrives at the process just in time, and each output goes directly to the next stage of the process, just in time.

2. **Motion:** Motion is a key variable addressed by industrial engineering. Teams in lean processes constantly study their motions to determine how motions can be eliminated or made easier by placement of fax machines and filing cabinets.

3. **Transportation:** If steps in the process are separated by physical space, forklifts, trucks, dollies, or other mechanisms of transportation are required. All of this is waste. The production process should be designed to minimize transportation.

4. **Defects:** Every defective product is waste. The time, effort, and supply that went into producing it are waste. Re-working errors is

necessary, but waste is not, because if it had been done right the first time, the re-work would not be needed. It is the job of the team to use problem-solving methods to study and eliminate waste.

5. **Waiting time:** Kanban and other methods in lean production are designed to eliminate waiting time. People should be flexible, trained, and assigned to move from one job to another in a production area so they can smooth the flow of production elements to prevent waiting for someone else to do something that only he or she can do.

6. **Overproduction:** Overproduction produces the need for storage, big piles rather than small piles.

7. **Processing:** By processing Shingo is referring to inefficiencies within a process – things done the wrong way, lack of training, etc.

Norman Bodek tells a Shingo story that may help us understand the attitude of eliminating waste in his excellent book Kaikaku.[23] Norman used to put on "Productivity" conferences at which I spoke for many years. These should have been called Lean conferences, but that term had not been invented yet. His conferences usually include talks by one of the masters of lean manufacturing and Quality Management, as well as lesser folks like me. Norman made trips to Japan and made it his mission to translate and bring to the United States the lessons from these innovators.

This story is from one of the trips to the U.S. he arranged for Dr. Shingo.

> On Dr. Shingo's first visit to America I took him to a Dresser, Inc. manufacturing plant, where they were producing gasoline fuel dispensing systems. After first meeting the management team we walked around the plant floor with a small group of engineers and managers.
>
> Dr. Shingo stopped in front of a punch press. He asked us all to look at the operation and to tell us the percentage of *value adding time*. He then took out his stopwatch to time the operation.
>
> We watched two workers in front of the punch press bend down and pick up a large sheet of thin stainless steel from the left side of the press. They placed the steel into the bed of the press. Then they removed their hands to press buttons outside the press, which indicated that their hands were out and clear of the press. The

---

[23] Bodek, Norman. Kaikaku: The Power and Magic of Lean. PCS Press, Vancouver Washington, 2004.

large press came down and formed the metal into a side of a gasoline pump. Then the two workers reached into the press, removed the formed sheet and placed the formed sheet at the right side of the press.

Dr. Shingo asked, "What was the value adding percentage?"

One engineer said "100%; the workers never stopped working."

Another engineer said "75%," and another said "50%."

Dr. Shingo laughed and looked at his stop watch. "Only 12% of the time was the process adding value. Adding value is only when the dies are pressing against the metal to create a formed sheet. The rest of the time is waste."

Dr. Shingo then asked, "What can be done to increase the percent of value adding time?"

An engineer immediately said, "You can place a table over here and put the raw inventory sheets on top of the table. This would help the workers. They wouldn't need to bend down. They could just slide the sheets directly into the press."

Another engineer said, "We could install a leveler to automatically raise the sheet metal to keep it at a constant height, similar to what you might see in a cafeteria when you reach for a dinner plate."

A third engineer said, "We could put a spring into the back of the punch press to force the formed metal to leap forward after the stamping."

Dr. Shingo laughed and said, "Yes, you all know what to do, so do it!"

An important point to notice in this story is that Dr. Shingo did not TELL them anything to do. He merely asked the right questions and defined things as they really are. He knew waste when he saw it. This is the primary characteristics of managers in lean operations. They ask the right questions. They constantly seek to improve by eliminating waste. Also notice that Shingo never suggested that there was anything wrong with the workers or that they weren't working hard enough. He did not blame the person; he assumed the problem was in the process.

How do the seven forms of waste appear in a typical hospital? They are generally described in terms of making a product. But think creatively and try to identify examples of each of these forms of waste in the service delivery or other processes at your organization.

| The Seven Forms of Waste ||
|---|---|
| **Inventory** | |
| **Motion** | |
| **Transportation** | |
| **Defects** | |
| **Waiting Time** | |
| **Over Production** | |
| **Processing** | |

The concept of "value-adding" is important. It is the activity and time that actually adds value to the client or customer. The client or customer doesn't care how many motions the workers go through, how much they have to move stuff, store stuff, or rework stuff. That all just adds cost. If your manager told you to go run around the building five times, you might do it. You might get paid during that time, and you might call it "work." But what value did it add for the client or customer? None!

## ELIMINATE MANAGEMENT WASTE

One of the core ideas of Lean Management is the elimination of waste. This usually means eliminating unnecessary tasks, motions, inventory, rework, etc. However, the new challenge for lean management is to improve the efficiency of management itself. Much management activity is waste. This waste is just as destructive, or more so, than waste among front line health care employees.

What does this waste look like? I have identified six forms of management waste. Feel free to add to the list.

**Management Waste # 1:** Sucking decisions up due to the lack of empowerment, education and encouragement at lower levels. Management thinks they are busy because they are doing other people's work and they do this because they have not structured the organization, established the training and systems to create competent problem-solving and decisions at lower levels.

**Management Waste #2:** Displaying contradictory models. If you want to teach your children not to smoke, drink or swear, but you walk around the house smoking, drinking and swearing, your efforts are going to be little more than waste. Management, leaders, must model the behavior they desire of others. The failure to do so cripples any change effort. Millions of dollars in consulting and training have become waste because management didn't walk the talk.

**Management Waste #3:** Failure to define and manage your own processes. There are processes that are owned by the senior management team. Every team, at every level, should have a SIPOC that defines input, output, and value adding processes owned by that team. They don't own any process? Than the entire team is waste! Tell them to go home. MOST management teams do not know what there processes are, and reinvent them in a random or annual manner. Developing strategy is a senior management value-adding process. Where is the map that visualizes how they develop strategy? When they did it last year, did they study the process and what did they learn? Unfortunately, they probably learned nothing and are not themselves engaged in continuous improvement. Therefore, they don't understand it and do not set the model.

**Management Waste #4:** Failure of decision-making: I have coached dozens of senior management teams. One would think, logically, that the higher you go in the company, the more skilled would be the decision makers and decision-making process. The value of decisions made at the top, should be of greatest value. Errors made at the top are the most expensive. The truth is that in most companies, the decision-making process at the top is terrible.

Many years ago I was doing a socio-tech redesign of a major financial organization on Wall Street. The only room the design team could find to meet in was THE BOARD ROOM!! Very expensive furniture, huge table, mahogany paneled walls, etc. After a day or two the design team had half the wall area covered with flip chart sheets. In stormed the official keeper of the room with steam spurting out of his ears. He yelled, "Take that down immediately! No one has ever put anything on these walls!" I asked, "Really? No one has ever brainstormed or put flip charts on the walls in here?" "Absolutely Not!" He yelled back. Poor fellow. He had never seen a room in which people were actually solving problems, brainstorming, reaching consensus, developing action plans, etc. It tells you a lot about how senior management teams fail to employ disciplined decision processes.

**Management Waste #5:** Wasted space and resources. That board room was used once a quarter. It sat empty and unused most of the time. Why do managers need larger offices as they move up the ladder. Do they get fatter? Do they have bigger computers or more books? What is that about? It is about waste. It is the waste of ego. The time spent at resorts doing annual strategic planning that could be done in their own conference room, or in someone's home, is also waste. Apply the same disciplined standards of waste and resource utilization at the executive and management level as you apply to the factory floor.

**Management Waste #6:** The failure of trust. An effective management team, like any team, is a social system built on trust. That trust enables members to share, to ask questions, to offer suggestions, and to listen well to each other. On MOST management teams there is a failure of trust among its members that inhibits their ability to solve problems and make effective decisions.

The solution to these forms of waste, which is the opposite of lean management, is not only training, but coaching and feedback. They need hands on help in order to change their behavior, their habits. It is these habits that define the culture.

# Waste Elimination Worksheet

Process:

| Steps | Time for Step | Value adding time | % |
|---|---|---|---|
| | | | |
| | | | |
| | | | |
| | | | |
| | | | |
| | | | |
| | | | |
| | | | |
| | | | |
| | | | |
| | | | |
| | | | |
| | | | |
| | | | |
| | | | |
| | | | |
| | | | |

# Improvement Worksheet

**Process:**

| Improvements to Steps: (Inventory, Motion, Transportation, Defects, Waiting Time, Overproduction, Processing) | New Time for Step | Value adding time | % |
|---|---|---|---|
| | | | |
| | | | |
| | | | |
| | | | |
| | | | |
| | | | |
| | | | |
| | | | |
| | | | |
| | | | |
| | | | |
| | | | |
| | | | |
| | | | |
| | | | |
| | | | |
| | | | |

# PART THREE
# IMPROVING TEAMWORK

# CHAPTER 16

# LEADING EFFECTIVE MEETINGS

The success of any team is in large part a function of the process by which it makes decisions, solves problems, and the degree to which members communicate well with each other. This requires effective facilitation. The purpose of this chapter is to present the basic skills of facilitation. The next chapter on listening skills will enhance facilitation and teamwork by all members.

## OBJECTIVES:

1. To develop a standard agenda that will lead to effective meetings.
2. To introduce the basic skills of facilitation.
3. To gain understanding that these skills need to be employed not only by the formal facilitator of each meeting, but by all team members.

As you implements lean management a significant component of that will be developing effective meetings. These meetings will sometimes be telephone conferences between members of a primary care team or they may be meetings of district managers who are spread over a wide area and need to consult together by phone; or, it may be a face-to-face get together. No matter where the meeting is conducted, it may be efficient or it may be inefficient. We have all experienced meetings that are chaotic and frustrating. By following the simple guidance in this chapter you can do a lot to make your meetings rewarding and productive.

## Planning the Agenda

The agenda is the plan, the roadmap for every meeting. Without a roadmap, a group can wander around looking lost for a long time. It is important to plan the agenda in advance and have the team quickly discuss and agree on the agenda as soon as the meeting begins. This gets everyone in agreement about where we are, where we are going, and how we are going to get there.

It is desirable to have the agenda visible. If meeting face-to-face this may be projected on a screen using an Excel agenda template. However, it is not necessary to have it on a computer. It could be on a flip chart or on paper distributed to each member either before the meeting or when the meeting starts. Being able to visualize where we are in our progress is important to the comfort level of the group. As soon as members of a group begin to feel lost, they feel uncomfortable and anxious, and that may be expressed as frustration.

The agenda should either have been planned at the end of the last meeting or someone should be given the authority, by the group, to plan the agenda for the next meeting. This is a tentative agenda. The final agenda should always be agreed upon by the team as the first item of business.

Here is a possible standard agenda that you might use as a starting point with a brief explanation of each item:

> **Standard Team Agenda**
>
> 1. Approve/Agree on Agenda
> 2. Health and Safety
> 3. Recognition
> 4. Review action plans
> 5. Review Scorecard
> 6. Information sharing
> 7. Problem-solving
> 8. Action Planning
> 9. Next Agenda
> 10. Self Critique

## 1. Approve/Agree on Agenda:

This should also include agreeing on the amount of time required for each item. This should be quick. It is a common error that when a group starts discussing the agenda individuals want to start explaining why one item is important, and then someone replies to that, and quickly you are actually discussing the item, rather than agreeing that it is on the agenda. The facilitator needs to be active and maintain pretty tight control during this quick period of agreeing on the agenda.

If the agenda is somewhat complicated or will not follow an established pattern, the facilitator may wish to go to a flip chart and list the items for consideration as they are offered by the group. It will then be important to prioritize them. Simply ask the group if they can agree on the one or two most important items. You could ask "Which items are 'A' priorities?" You could then ask for "B's" or "C's" and the ask how much time will each require and construct the agenda starting with the highest priority items to be sure these are covered.

## 2. Health and Safety:

In any health care setting there are issues that are critical to the health and safety of team members. It is often a good idea to simply ask the question "are there any health or safety issues that we should discuss?" Or, "Does anyone have any health or safety tips they have learned or issues they have observed in the past week?" This opportunity to discuss these issues can bring healthy and safe behavior to the forefront the each team members mind and possibly prevent some unfortunate incident.

## 3. Recognition:

It is part of our culture to focus on the problems, and most of us are pretty good at pointing out the errors, flaws and failings of our team members, management, family members and politicians. Pointing to our failures probably doesn't need to be on the agenda because it comes so naturally for most of us. Recognizing positive contributions is another matter. This does not come naturally to many of us, and it is a big factor in the motivation of the team.

We want to develop a culture of positive recognition. We are all here to serve our clients and customers and it is very reasonable to assume that everyone is well intentioned. But, if we fail to recognize those good intentions and good behavior, the lack of appreciation can diminish those efforts.

Some teams, and often the higher you go in organizations the more true this is, there is a discomfort, anxiety, around offering recognition or praise. This is a good thing to overcome. It is a bad habit of a bad culture.

## 4. Review Action Plans:

One of the surest signs of poor team meetings is the failure to follow-up on action plans agreed to in previous meetings.

It is a good idea to record action plans either on an Excel spreadsheet or other electronic form and distribute it to all team members immediately after or during the meeting. Or, you can simply do it on paper. But, it is important that it be shared for all members to see and to take with them. The action plan from the last meeting should be displayed for all to see at the following meeting.

The facilitator simply goes through each item –the *What, Who,* and *When*, and asks the *who* "how did it go?" The person responsible for that item then reports that it was completed or gives some other explanation. If it was not completed, then the facilitator simply asks "What would we like to do about this now?" Generally the person who was responsible offers to get it done by a new date and the group either agrees that this is acceptable or comes up with another alternative.

This is accountability. However, it is a participative, shared, non-authoritarian accountability. When the group agrees to an action plan, they are acting together as the manager. This is "self-management," and it will have the effect of training the group members to follow through on their commitments to the team.

Here is an Action Planning form you can use. Electronic versions of this and other action planning forms are available from your coaches.

## Action Plan

**Problem:**

**Solution:**

| Action-What? | Who Will Act? | When? | Status |
|---|---|---|---|
|  |  |  |  |

## 5. Review the Scorecard:

An important aspect of lean management is becoming a "scientist;" in other words, developing a respect for the facts, the empirical evidence that something is working or not working. Watching your scorecard is the key to becoming a fact based team.

A team is a team because it keeps score. In a later chapter we will discuss the development of your balanced scorecard. A scorecard is useless unless it is reviewed regularly. Your scorecard should be reviewed regularly. It should be reviewed either weekly or monthly depending on your circumstance. Hopefully, your team will have identified the few key data variables that best reflect the performance of the team. These should be graphed, and the graphs should be on the wall for visual display at each team meeting. The review of the scorecard should include a discussion of "how are we doing?" on our measures. This should be a background for the team's problem-solving.

## 6. Information sharing:

In most meetings there is a time for information sharing. For example your team lead may have information from funders that is important to pass on. Or there may be new health alerts or other information related to providing excellent care that can be passed on at this point in the meeting.

## 7. Problem-solving and Decision-Making:

This will often be the largest block of time in a meeting. This is when you dig into problems that have been identified while you were looking at your scorecard. How do we improve performance? What are the major constraints or problems in achieving your performance targets on your scorecard?

## 8. Action Planning:

Many meetings end with everyone in apparent agreement, yet nothing happens as a result. There is no action, no follow-up, and no accountability. The meeting begins in words and ends in words. The value of most meetings is not only in the sharing of information or discussion, but in the actions that follow. Too often we fail to make clear who is going to do what to whom, and when. Every meeting should end with a clear action plan, written down, with the names of individuals who are agreeing to act and dates by which they will act.

Use the action plan form given above or some other way to record your decisions to take action with the *What, Who* and *When* clearly stated.

### 9. PLAN NEXT AGENDA:

Every meeting should include at least a brief discussion of the next meeting's agenda. There are almost always items that are carried over, or individuals may express their desire for something to be placed on the agenda.

### 10.  SELF CRITIQUE

Lean management is about continuous improvement. Everything can be improved. We can all improve, every day. At the end of each meeting is desirable for the facilitator to simply as the question, "How did we do today?" Or, "What went well in our meeting today, or what could we improve?" This gives members the opportunity to make suggestions for improvements in a painless way. Without asking these questions members may have dissatisfactions that do not get aired until they reach some point of frustration. It is much wiser to seek continuous improvement than to wait for frustrations to rise.

Periodically the team might want to do a more in depth self-assessment based on their charter or their principles of how they work together, both of these documents can form the basis of a quick survey, ask your team coach for more details when you are ready to take this step.

The above items are suggested as a beginning point for your team to agree on a standard agenda. These items have worked for hundreds of teams, however; you should feel free to add other standard items you feel are important.

## THE SKILLS OF FACILITATING

To facilitate is to make easier, to help bring about some result. We will provide the best possible care to our clients if we make things easier for each other. We have to help facilitate each other's work. In meetings we all have to help each other voice their opinions, think together in constructive ways, and reach decisions that will be helpful to all.

It may be useful to first clarify what the facilitator is not. The facilitator is not the person in charge. She is not the boss, the manager, or the formal leader of the group. It may be in some meetings that the manager of the group also serves as the facilitator. However, these are entirely different functions. The formal manager might also serve as the scribe or the timekeeper, but this has nothing to do with her being the formal manager of the group.

The following are the basic skills, the behavior, that a facilitator employs to assist the individuals and the group in their effort to make decisions or solve problems.

## 1. Organizing:

All groups want both order and the opportunity for participation. They want control, but they don't want an excess of control. The first type of order that a facilitator brings to a group is to create and gain agreement to an agenda. Where are we beginning and where are we trying to go, and where are we in the journey? These are the questions that all members want to know, and it is the job of the facilitator to be sure that the journey is clear. But the agenda is only the plan. Keeping the group and individuals on the agenda with simple questions like "does that address our topic?" or restating the topic occasionally, just reminding the group what we are trying to accomplish, are acts of facilitation that a group will find helpful.

## 2. Establish the Topic

No one comes to meetings to be entertained. Most people are busy and want to know that their time will be well used. Tell them why you are here. Make it important. If the facilitator doesn't feel that it is important, he or she will never convince the members of the group that it is important.

Importance equals energy. Energy drives the ability of the group to achieve goals. When one speaks to a group, it is useful to imagine the audience saying "So what?" This question is not simply irreverent. It is perfectly legitimate. They are asking why? Why am I listening to you? Why am I spending my valuable time here? What difference will this make? Give them a good reason to spend their valuable time. Give them purpose.

**Tips for Clarifying the Topic**

- State the Topic and Gain Commitment: The facilitator should clearly state what he or she believes to be the topic, look around at the members of the group and ask them if this is their understanding. The act of asking for their commitment will help them to stick to the topic during conversation.

- Write the Topic on a Flip Chart: The ability to see, in writing, a topic or decision helps the group members focus, understand, and create unity of thought and action.

- Discuss Outcomes: At the beginning of a meeting it is helpful to both state the purpose and discuss possible outcomes, actions, next steps that might follow the meeting.

- Share Expectations: Ask the group to share their expectations and objectives for the session. They came for a reason. Ask them to share that reason and what they feel would be a successful outcome for them.

### 3. Clarifying:

Very often we are not clear in our communications. Many of those who participate on teams are not entirely comfortable expressing their ideas or feelings to the group. This is particularly true when the topic is one that involves emotions on the part of that member.

It is very helpful, and encourages members to participate, when the facilitator says something like "It sounds like you are concerned about...." or, "I hear you saying that it would be helpful to you if we....." These are examples of good listening skills discussed in the next chapter and they help clarify their own thoughts.

A key job of the facilitator is to clarify where we are in the discussion. "Have we identified the facts that matter in this case?" "Have we discussed the causes of a problem?" "Are we in agreement?" "Are we ready to move on to solutions?" "Have we now all agreed on a solution?" "It sounds like we have agreement." Each of these questions or statements helps to clarify where we are in the process of getting to a decision.

### 4. Reflecting:

Reflecting is to put the conversation in perspective. "Let me share where I think we are in this conversation. It feels to me that everyone has voiced their opinion, and I think there are basically two approaches being discussed...." This is a statement that reflects on where we are and it is very helpful to the group by giving them a view of where we are on our journey. This then makes clear where we need to go from here. This reflection will also give them an opportunity to share their understanding of where we are in the process. This may be different than yours.

### 5. Motivating:

Both individuals and groups need encouragement. It is important that the facilitator be someone with an essentially positive outlook, someone who recognizes the progress, the contributions and the hopes about the outcome of our journey. Motivation is infectious, as is discouragement.

Simple things make good facilitation. Saying "Thank you" after someone has made a contribution, particularly if it was difficult for that person, can be very helpful. Nodding your head forward and back, signaling that you understand what the person is saying, is encouraging. Smiling can be a sign of encouragement. Just saying, "good" after someone has spoken is the simplest form of recognition, and it can help motivate members to contribute.

Sometimes the group needs more serious motivation. The group may be stuck on a very difficult point, and it may be helpful for the facilitator to reflect on the group's progress and point out the things they have accomplished, the progress they have made, and then assure them that they will overcome this obstacle as well.

Another aspect of motivation is having fun. Every group should laugh, take time to do things, go somewhere together, and tell jokes, just for the sake of having fun. Teams at work, just like families who have fun together, are more likely to solve problems and trust each other. Having fun is not trivial. It is an important part of what leads to the effectiveness of a team. The facilitator should be thinking about each of these aspects of motivation and thinking about how he can contribute to the motivation of each member of the team.

## 6. COMFORTING:

If you have spent a lot of time in group meetings, you are probably comfortable making contributions. However, many teams at work are comprised of individuals who are not experienced. The lack of experience leads to discomfort or anxiety. Difficult topics, topics concerning the behavior of members of the group, or issues that may threaten our position in the group or in our job rightfully cause us anxiety.

What does a facilitator do to help create comfort in a group when some members have these anxieties? One important skill of a facilitator is to express empathy. Empathy statements usually begin with the following:

"I can understand that... (the reason for their concern)....may cause you to feel.(a word like 'worried', or 'upset') "

"It sounds like you feel...(a feeling word like 'upset')...because...(the reason)."

"It must be … (feeling work like "difficult, or painful")…when … (the circumstance causing the difficulty).

## 7. Resolving Conflicts:

In almost any group there will be times when conflicts arise among members of the group. These conflicts can be simple matters of disagreement on a topic, or they can be more severe conflicts between two people who don't trust each other, or one may have been offended by the other.

Your best tools to resolve conflicts are your listening skills that are discussed in the next chapter. Your ability to demonstrate genuine understanding of the position and feelings of both parties helps to reduce their frustration or anger.

There is another critical skill in resolving conflicts and that is the thought process of looking for points of unity. When two people are in conflict, for example, over a course of action to solve a problem, it is helpful to point to their agreement, or point of unity. For example you might say "It's great that you are both concerned about solving this problem." Or, you can look for the elements of their solutions that are in agreement – "It sounds like you both agree that this is a priority and you also both feel that we should …" (then add the parts of the solution on which they agree).

It is then helpful to clarify the points of disagreement in a clear and objective way. That objectivity may have been lost in their passion to express their views. It may be helpful then to turn to other members of the group and ask them to identify the pros and cons of each alternative.

Here are a few things you may do to create unity from differences.

### Recognize the Validity of Experience

It may be easy to facilitate a group of ten white male accountants who graduated from the same school, have been through the same training courses, and work for the same company. Of course, they are likely to think in very similar ways. But we often have team members with totally different backgrounds and experiences, and they may arrive at different understandings of the same events.

As a facilitator it is helpful to think that everyone is "right" from his or her point of view. Based on their experience, as they understand the issue, given the facts they know, what they say is right to them. The difficulty is that no one else has the exact same experience. Many disagreements are simply based on the different "data" that we each possess. The facilitator can simply ask, "There are two very different views here. What do you think might be the different experiences that result in these different views?" Asking the question in this manner transforms the issue from who is right or wrong to how and why diverse backgrounds result in diverse views.

## IT IS NOT ALWAYS EITHER-OR

A facilitator was assisting the Board of Directors and the staff of a school to develop their vision and strategic plan. There had been a history of tension at the school between those who felt that the most important thing was for children to enjoy learning, to develop love of learning, and those who felt it was important to develop competence, knowledge of reading, writing, and arithmetic. The conflict was categorized as the liberals versus the conservatives, the soft approach versus the hard approach.

The facilitator could see the participants in the room lining up behind each of these views' arguments. It appeared that there was a fundamental difference in what was viewed as important in education.

The facilitator, seeking to resolve this conflict, drew this matrix on a flip chart and explained that there are two dimensions being discussed, and they are both good and important. But are they necessarily contrary? Isn't it possible to do a great job of imparting knowledge and, at the same time, do a great job of causing children to love the process of learning? He also asked those who thought knowledge was most important how parents viewed the school. They felt the school was high on creating love, and low on creating knowledge. In other words, the knowledge people thought the school was North-West on the matrix. He then asked the love of learning group how they viewed the school today. They viewed it has being South-East, low on love and high on knowledge.

You can image how the poor staff felt. Bombarded and not appreciated by either group. The staff felt the school was in the North-East quadrant. After much discussion they all agreed that what was important was for the school to be North-East. Neither group felt the other group's concern was unimportant. They both wanted the same thing.

This is an example of how a matrix, a simple tool for looking at two different qualities at the same time, can help resolve conflicts and create unity.

### OK, WE SEE IT DIFFERENTLY

Finally, the facilitator may not be able to reconcile two different points of view. It may be useful to simply acknowledge the differences and accept them.

I like blue and you like red. Do we have to resolve that? There are many different points of view, preferences, and interpretations of events that do not need to be resolved. They need to be left behind.

When resolving conflicts between two members of the team try the following:

- ✓ Clarify the points on which the parties agree.

- ✓ Clarify the disagreement and the reason for that disagreement. Check this out with them.

- ✓ Express empathy or understanding of both of their views so that they feel "heard."

- ✓ Ask the rest of the group if they have other alternatives, or ask them to discuss the pros and cons of the different solutions.

- ✓ Ask the group for criteria, what is important, in solving this problem.

- ✓ Ask the group if there is a way to take the best parts of each solution and combine them.

- ✓ Ask the group if there is then a consensus point of view, or ask the group to vote on a solution.

### 8. CONTROLLING – PLAYING "COP":

Every group gets "out-of-control" from time to time. In fact, it is a sign of a healthy comfort level that the group will drift into social periods where members are talking about their children or the weekend baseball came and be "off-task." This is when the facilitator, perhaps after letting the group enjoy some "play-time," will have to get the group back "on-task."

It is important to do this in a way that is not punitive or bossy. Some facilitators have a little bell they ring, or tapping on a glass or cup, can get everyone's attention and you can just say "Let's get back on-task, folks!" or, "Time-out, we need to go back to work!" Or, you may need to remind the group of their time constraints, which there always are.

A good facilitator has a comfortable sense of how and when to exert control. It is important that the group doesn't come to feel that the facilitator is excessively controlling or they may rebel. A good facilitator knows how much "play-time" to allow the group before calling for control.

## Exercise:

Consider a meeting you have attended that was both highly productive and which had a spirit of unity. How did the facilitator behave that encouraged this environment? How did other members behave to help create this environment? What did the facilitator do to make all feel welcome?

_____

_____

_____

Recall a meeting that was tense, anxiety provoking, and lacking unity and harmony. Again, how did the facilitator or other members of the group behave that resulted in this feeling?

_____

_____

_____

When considering these two meetings, what are the implications for facilitation skills? How did listening contribute to these conditions? How could effective listening have improved these meetings?

_____

_____

# GROUP PROCESS SELF-ASSESSMENT

This is an assessment to identify how you can improve your group problem-solving and decision-making. This may be used by any group that has responsibility for making team decisions and implementing those decisions. It should not be used to judge that we are "good" or "bad" or to criticize. Rather, it is to be used to say "exactly what is it that we can improve?" and, "are we doing better now than before?"

This self-assessment should be scored by all the members of the team, the scores added up, and then you can ask a) "which items do we feel good about?" and, b) "which items do we most need to improve?" Identify specific actions you can take to improve and then review the progress on those at future meetings.

On each of the following items indicate the degree to which you agree with the statement.

|   |   | Disagree | | Somewhat Agree | | Agree |
|---|---|---|---|---|---|---|
| 1. | My group has a clear purpose that all the members understand. | 0 | 2.5 | 5 | 7.5 | 10 |
| 2. | My group meets at a regular time and location. | 0 | 2.5 | 5 | 7.5 | 10 |
| 3. | The location where we meet is free of distractions and is comfortable. | 0 | 2.5 | 5 | 7.5 | 10 |
| 4. | We have flip chart or white board to use in problem-solving and decision-making. | 0 | 2.5 | 5 | 7.5 | 10 |
| 5. | We prepare ourselves before the meeting by reviewing information that has been distributed. | 0 | 2.5 | 5 | 7.5 | 10 |
| 6. | When we meet the topic is clarified by the chairperson/facilitator. | 0 | 2.5 | 5 | 7.5 | 10 |
| 7. | The members are good at staying focused on the topic. | 0 | 2.5 | 5 | 7.5 | 10 |
| 8. | The chairperson/facilitator provides the opportunity for all to participate. | 0 | 2.5 | 5 | 7.5 | 10 |
| 9. | The members of the group are sensitive to, and respectful of, cultural differences and styles of participation. | 0 | 2.5 | 5 | 7.5 | 10 |

|  | Disagree | | Somewhat Agree | | Agree |
|---|---|---|---|---|---|
| 10. When we consult on an issue we discuss the principles that underlie or are important to this issue. | 0 | 2.5 | 5 | 7.5 | 10 |
| 11. Before suggesting possible solutions, we gather and examine the facts pertaining to this issue. | 0 | 2.5 | 5 | 7.5 | 10 |
| 12. When discussing possible solutions or courses of action we allow time for brainstorming, free thinking without judgment, to allow for creative ideas. | 0 | 2.5 | 5 | 7.5 | 10 |
| 13. We use a flip chart or white board so everyone can see and reflect on previous ideas, helping to create unity of thought. | 0 | 2.5 | 5 | 7.5 | 10 |
| 14. When new ideas are presented the members consider the ideas without prejudice (who they come from) or bias (holding to previous ideas). | 0 | 2.5 | 5 | 7.5 | 10 |
| 15. When discussing problems we tend not to blame individuals, but study and improve the process. | 0 | 2.5 | 5 | 7.5 | 10 |
| 16. We reach consensus by considering all the ideas that have been presented, considering their pros and cons, and narrowing them to a critical few. | 0 | 2.5 | 5 | 7.5 | 10 |
| 17. When we reach a decision the chairperson or facilitator clarifies the decision and gains commitment from all members of the group. | 0 | 2.5 | 5 | 7.5 | 10 |
| 18. Decisions are written down so all can see and review the decision. | 0 | 2.5 | 5 | 7.5 | 10 |
| 19. Each decision is followed by an Action Plan, which specifies *Who* will do *What* by *When*. | 0 | 2.5 | 5 | 7.5 | 10 |
| 20. At each meeting, the prior action plans are reviewed and revised as needed. | 0 | 2.5 | 5 | 7.5 | 10 |

# CHAPTER 17

# EFFECTIVE LISTENING SKILLS

The ability to listen well to others, to not only hear, but to understand, is an essential skill for all team members. This chapter is intended both to present the skills of effective listening and to practice those skills within the team.

## OBJECTIVES:

1. To gain understanding of the critical skills of listening to others.
2. To practice and develop this skill.

Those of us who enter the health care profession most likely have a desire to give care to others. We are predisposed to empathetic with our clients. Empathy or caring is expressed in many ways. It is expressed in body language. It is expressed in showing up on-time, every time. It is expressed in thoughtful actions toward you client. But, perhaps most often, we demonstrate caring with our language.

Members of the entire clinical, service or support team should be skilled at caring because that is what we do as an organization. And, that caring must extend not only to our clients and customers, but to our associates, or team members, in every function and at every level of the organization. The key skill of demonstrating caring to others is effective listening.

Effective listening skills are the most essential skills of a good facilitator. Listening does not mean simply not talking and waiting for the other person to finish. Listening is the process of gaining understanding, checking your understanding with the other person, and encouraging the other person to express herself fully and frankly. Effective listening skills are also the most important skills in the process of creating unity within a group. If we truly listen to each other, rather than quickly reacting to what we think the other person said, we will cause unity and harmony to be achieved.

Effective listening skills are comprised of five component skills. These are *asking questions*, *expressing empathy*, *rephrasing*, *acknowledging*, and the use of *silence*. We will consider and practice each of these. They are also important skills in one-to-one communication in the family, at work, or in any other setting. Without a doubt, the best communicators are the best listeners. The worst communicators talk endlessly.

Please take note that these skills are not ONLY for the formal facilitator. Every member of the team has a responsibility to help facilitate, to help make it easier for other members to give their best contribution to the team.

## A. Asking Open-Ended Questions

The act of asking questions demonstrates interest in the other person, opens the opportunity for the other person to voice their views and feelings, and leads to understanding. Facilitating a team is one part speaking and ten parts asking questions and listening.

Different types of questions lead to different results. The skilled listener knows when to use different types of questions. There are two types of questions: open-ended and closed-ended questions.

Imagine that you are meeting with your team members. You can see that one of your associates is just staring off into the distance. You can see that her eyes are beginning to tear and her head turns down avoiding the gaze of others.

In a quivering voice she says "This is very hard for me. I'm not sure I can do this." Everyone is silent as they wait for her to continue.

"It happened last night" she continues in sobbing voice. "I had just arrived home from work. I didn't think I had done anything wrong. I can't image what I did to cause this. I was totally unprepared for this." Again she looks down and is overcome by sobbing. It is almost too difficult for her to continue.

You start to imagine what horrible thing must have happened. You say to her, "Take your time, Jane. We will do whatever we can to be helpful." She still seems too grieved to continue.

Harold, one of the team members asks, "Jane, does this have to do with your children? Is there a problem with one of your dear children?"

Jane looks up, appearing somewhat surprised and says "Oh, no, my children are fine."

Another team member, Bob, then asks, "Jane is there a problem between you and your husband. Maybe we can help you. You know several of us have faced our own marriage issues. I know your husband and he is a good person even if he does have some faults."

Jane looks up again and looks somewhat puzzled. Jane says, "I don't think there is a problem with my husband. Actually, I am sorry to say, but, it's my dog. He died last night?"

The members of the group then look at each other surprised and embarrassed. Jane then looks at Bob and asks, "What faults do you think my husband has?"

What could have been done by members of the group to handle this situation better?

_____

_____

_____

The key in this situation is in the types of questions that were asked. "Is there something wrong with your children?" is a closed-ended question. It can be answered with a "yes" or "no." Any question that can be answered "yes" or "no" is a closed-ended question. It is, essentially, a guess. "Is there a problem with one of your children" is a closed-ended question. You can guess a lot of things before asking the right closed-ended question. And, as you can see, some of those guesses could get you in trouble.

Closed-ended questions do not elicit conversation from the other person. In this case, they did not elicit Jane's own ideas or feelings. If you ask a series of closed-ended questions, it feels like you are playing Twenty-Questions, trying to guess the right question. In the scene described above, how many questions of this type would the group members have had to ask to finally arrive at the question "Did your dog die?" - Probably hundreds!

An open-ended question usually begins with what, where, why or how.

- *How can we help you?*
- *What seems to be the problem?*
- *What happened last night?*
- *Why are you upset?*
- *Where were you when you first felt this way?*

These are all open-ended questions. Notice that none of them can be answered with a "yes" or "no." You can see why all good conversationalists have the habit of asking open-ended questions.

How you ask questions is often a matter of habit. To develop the habit of asking open-ended questions, let's practice. First, here are several statements that might be made in a meeting. Don't respond with a statement or argument. Respond with a question. Write down several open-ended questions that you might use in response to these statements:

"I am so tired of those clients changing their schedules. Don't they realize how difficult it makes my life?"

_____

_____

_____

"These meetings are a waste of time! We never decide anything. Why doesn't management just tell us what to do and let us do our work?"

_____

_____

_____

"I am doing my job. I just wish everyone else on this team would do their job. Then I wouldn't have to waste my time listening to y'all just yap about this being wrong and that being wrong!"

_____

_____

_____

Open-ended questions can be useful in a number of situations:

- ✓ To Start A Discussion: "What do you think about the new marketing plan?" Or, "How did you feel about our performance?"

- ✓ To Include A Member of the Group: "John, how do you feel about this issue?" "Serena, what is your experience on this issue?"

- ✓ To Bring a Conversation Back to Topic: "What other information do we need to make this decision?" Or, "On the subject of how we should plan this project, what other steps should we take?"

- ✓ To Make a Transition from One Agenda Item to the Next: "Before we summarize our decision, what other thoughts do you have on this subject?"

## EXERCISE:

Now form groups of three. Have one member present a problem or concern related to your work. This can be entirely fictitious or real. State this problem in one brief sentence. A second member of the group now asks at least three open-ended questions that cause the first person to reveal more about the concern. The third person will serve as a coach and give the person asking the questions feedback or help if they get stuck. Rotate roles until each person has practiced each role.

How did it feel to be asked these open-ended questions? How would it have felt if the questions were closed-ended? Did you find that asking these types of questions was natural or difficult?

_____

_____

_____

### B. Expressing Empathy

With an empathy statement you express how you think the other person feels and why. Showing empathy towards another person helps that person feel like a part of the group, is a cause of unity between the group members, and reduces any tendency to respond negatively or defensively. We all have a strong need to know that our feelings are understood.

It takes courage to express personal feelings in a group. Those feelings are often an important component of group problem-solving. Problem-solving that includes all of the facts, but none of the feelings, is not likely to lead to unified action.

Here are some models for empathy statements:

***"It sounds as if you feel...** (..add in a feeling word) ... **because...** (reason)."*

For example: "It sounds as if you feel upset that we don't have the resources for this project because everyone is too busy."

Or, "It sounds as if you feel anxious because you have to make that presentation tomorrow."

***"It must be**...(feeling word)...**when**...(reason)."*

For example: "It must be frustrating to work so hard on a project when no one else appears to recognize that work."

Or, "It must be annoying when it seems that no one is listening to your point of view."

*"I can understand that...(reason)...would make you...(feeling word)."*

For example: "I can understand that the amount of time it took us to make a decision would make you upset."

Or, "I can understand that getting appointed to this new job would be very exciting for you."

Each of these statements demonstrates that you are at least attempting to understand how the other person feels. These empathy statements can defuse emotions that might get in the way of progress, and they can allow the other person to clarify her own feelings if your understanding is not exactly correct. These are all helpful outcomes.

A facilitator may use empathy statements...

- ✓ To help reduce strong emotions that may prevent rational thinking and conversation. Making an empathy statement to someone who is expressing pain or anger can diffuse those feelings. Empathy is like someone holding your hand, letting you know that they understand. For example, "I can see that you are really hurt that you were embarrassed in front of your friends."

- ✓ To encourage other people to listen. If others feel that you are genuinely recognizing the emotions of a member of the group, they will recognize this model, and they are more likely to feel empathy and listen to the other person.

- ✓ To relieve anxiety about discussing a problem publicly. In a team setting it is difficult for many people to express their own feelings. Many of us are "private people." A statement such as "I can understand that you are concerned about...." relieves some of the anxiety and makes communication easier.

## EXERCISE:

Form small groups and practice making empathy statements. One person should present a situation that caused some emotion and the other person should listen, and then express empathy with the other person, using one of the models above. Switch roles until each person has an opportunity to practice expressing empathy.

How did you feel when the listener expressed empathy for your situation?

_____

_____

_____

How did you feel expressing empathy for others?

_____

_____

_____

### C. Rephrasing or Reflective Listening

Rephrasing, or reflective listening, is a way of checking out your understanding of what you think the other person meant to say. Conveying emotions or deep thoughts on any matter is a difficult thing. When we speak, we make an effort to convey our *meaning*, our intended thought or feeling. However, what we *meant* and what the other person *receives* or understands are often not the same thing.

For example, during a meeting of nurses responsible for health and safety a member says, "I've had it! I just can't do this anymore. I am tired of trying to get people to wash their hands."

Another member then says, "So, I hear you saying you don't want to be on the health and safety committee anymore."

"No, no, no! I mean I am tired of having to remind these people, saying the same thing over and over again. There's never any consequence to them."

You can see that her first communication in which she says "I just can't do this anymore!" she is expressing an emotion, and the words can be interpreted in several different ways. If the listener assumed that he knew what she meant by those words, rather than checking out what he heard, there would have been a misunderstanding.

Often, when we hear someone express a thought or emotion our impulse is to respond, react, answer or even argue. We want to act on what we think we hear. In doing so we often create more of a problem because we are reacting to what we think we hear, not what the other person intends to communicate. In this manner two people can be talking right past each other.

Let's replay the conversation above.

She says, "I've had it! I just can't do this anymore. I am tired of trying to get people to wash their hands."

Another member says, "Well, you can quit if you want, but I was appointed to this committee and its part of my job and I'm doing my job whether you do or not!"

"Oh, please!" she responds, "stop playing holier than thou."

"Excuse me. But I don't think doing your duty should be taken lightly."

What just happened here?

Did this create more understanding or misunderstanding? Was the cause of unity served or was disunity created?

If we react to what we think we heard, we often increase the gap in understanding between us and the other person. With all good intentions, we may create hurt feelings and damage the motivation of the other person. If we check out, reflect, rephrase what we think we heard, and give the other person the opportunity to clarify, we can often create understanding and harmony rather than dissonance.

Rephrasing implies and conveys a sense of humility. It conveys that you are not sure that you understood the other person, and you would like them to clarify so you can improve your understanding. This humility tends to defuse emotions and serves the cause of unity.

Rephrasing statements start with phrases such as:

***What I'm hearing is...***

***So, in other words you (think, feel that)...***

***So, it sounds as if...***

***Let me make sure I've got this right, you...***

A facilitator may use rephrasing...

- ✓ **To clarify a group member's statements**. "It sounds as if you are ready to move on to the next subject."

- ✓ **To resolve conflicts between two group members.** "I hear you saying that we need to emphasize this at our next meeting, and I heard John say that he also felt this was very important."

- ✓ **To help someone express their emotions.** "What I hear you saying is that you feel very strongly about this and it has caused you considerable pain."

- ✓ **To get at a deeper understanding of the issue than may have been expressed.** "So, it sounds like this is not merely about what time and place we meet, but about what we value, what is most important to us."

## EXERCISE:

Try rephrasing each of the following statements in your own words. Use one of the above lead off phrases to express, in your own words, what you think the other person means.

"I think we should ask Mary to lead the effort to deal with the supplier problems because she never stops talking about that!"

_____

_____

_____

"I'm sorry, but I don't care if I am the oldest nurse here, I simply can't stand in front of new employees and teach a class on the history of this hospital! I just can't do that!"

_____

_____

_____

"I am not sure I can keep working here. There have been so many changes and so much uncertainty; it really drives me crazy!"

_____

_____

_____

Share your rephrasing with other members of your group and listen to how they reflected their understanding of these statements. Discuss how you think the speaker would have reacted to each of these different statements. You will probably find that different people heard different meaning in these statements. That's why it's a good idea to reflect and seek clarification.

## D. Acknowledging

Sometimes an effective listening skill is so simple and subtle that it is easy not to notice. For example, eye contact. If you are talking and the listener's eyes are wandering around the room, it would be easy to feel that he was not really listening. Good listeners acknowledge that they are listening by simply looking at the speaker.

Body language, particularly head movement, may convey that you are listening and have understood the other person. When facilitating a team meeting someone may raise their hand and start asking a question that has a negative tone, as if they feel that you have said something that is not correct. By looking at them and gently nodding your head forward and aft, you are conveying that you hear them and consider the point they are making to have worth. This tends to defuse the situation and makes everyone, including you, more comfortable.

When a member of the group offers an idea or suggestion you may simply say, "right" or "I can understand that" or "good point." These are all simple responses that let the other person know that they have been heard.

## E. Using Silence

As the facilitator of a group, is it necessary that you respond to every comment made by a member of the group?

No. Sometimes it is best to simply let a comment digest; allow time for quiet reflection or meditation on a comment. You might then ask the group "How do the rest of you feel about that?"

This may be particularly useful if someone has expressed anger or a very negative emotion. Rather than confront, or attempt to empathize, it may work well to simply let the remark sit there for ten, twenty seconds. Then you might say "That's an interesting point of view. It sounds like this has been bothering you for quite a while. Does anyone have any thoughts as to how we might resolve that?"

As a facilitator remember that it is not your responsibility to have an answer or solution to every issue or emotion. It is your responsibility to facilitate learning and to create unity. Sometimes, if you try too hard to resolve every issue, you may find that you are working too hard and actually creating anxiety in the group. And, remember that the entire group has a responsibility to assist in the facilitation and make it easier for all members to contribute.

You can see that the use of each of these listening skills requires practice and good judgment. This comes only with experience and reflection on your own facilitation. Practice using these skills with your health care clients, your children, your spouse, as well as with team members. They are skills that will serve you well throughout your life.

# Chapter 18

# Giving and Receiving Feedback

The purpose of this chapter is to convey and develop the skills of effectively giving feedback to others and receiving feedback in a way that leads to learning and improvement.

## Objectives:

1. To learn and to practice giving feedback to others in a manner that will facilitate learning by the other person.
2. To learn and practice the skill of receiving feedback in a manner that will improve your own ability to learn from others.

## The Road To Abilene

What happens when members of a team fail to use straight talk, fail to express how they really think or feel about a matter?

Jerry Harvey, in The Abilene Paradox[24], tells a wonderful story about his family, when he was young, sitting on the porch one evening in the sweltering heat of west Texas and someone asks "What's for dinner?" Someone then mentions a restaurant down the road in Abilene. Somehow they end up in the car, with no air conditioning, the dust blowing through the windows and everyone miserable, when Ma asks Pa, "Why the hell are you dragging us to Abilene anyway?" To which Pa says, "I ain't draggin' you anywhere, you wanted to go to Abilene." "Did not" replies Ma. And the question comes, how did they end up on the road to Abilene when no one wanted to go in the first place?

As Jerry Harvey, a college professor, tells it, he was sitting in his office one day when an attractive young woman student came into his office sat down and looked rather depressed. Dr. Harvey, concerned, asked "What's wrong, you look rather depressed?" And, she replied, "Well, you'd be depressed too if next weekend you were marrying someone you didn't love." To which he naturally responded, "Well, why are you marrying someone you don't love." And she explained, "Well it was a moment of passion, and I couldn't say no; it would have broken his heart. And, he told his folks, and they called mine, and the wedding got planned, and I can't say no now. I just couldn't do that to him."

The next day Dr. Harvey was sitting in his office and a young man came in and sat down, looking rather depressed. The ever-empathetic Dr. Harvey asked, "What's wrong, you look rather depressed?" And, he replied, "Well, you'd be depressed too if next weekend you were marrying someone you didn't love." To which he naturally responded, "Well, why are you marrying someone you don't love?" And he explained, "Well it was a moment of passion, and I couldn't say no, I would have broken her heart. And, she told her folks, and they called mine, and the wedding got planned, and I can't say no now; I just couldn't do that to her."

Witness a young couple "on the road to Abilene." How does a group get on the road to Abilene? It is a simple matter of assuming someone else knows the answers or just failing to express your true feelings and opinions. It is often because the great "why" question isn't asked by anyone. It is a failure of

---

[24] Harvey, Jerry. *The Abilene Paradox and Other Meditations on Management.* Jossey-Bass Inc., Publishers, San Francisco, 1996.

honest inquiry. This is how major corporations, even entire industries, ended up in Abilene. And, it happens to teams every day.

### EXERCISE:

Has your team or organization ever been on the "road to Abilene?" Have you seen any other group of people going down this road? Describe how you think this happened?

_____

_____

_____

_____

What are the exact behaviors or lack of behavior that result in a group going down this road?

_____

_____

_____

## GIVING AND RECEIVING FEEDBACK

One of the most common reasons for poor performance and problems among team members is that members of the group fail to give each other honest feedback, what some call *straight talk*.

Why do we hold things inside and fail to share them with our team? We may say the following things to ourselves:

- "If I am the only one who feels this way, it must just be me."
- "If I raise this subject, it will start an argument, and I don't want to argue."
- "If I really say how I feel, I will hurt his feelings and make matters worse."

Each of these thoughts is a prescription for getting "on the road to Abilene." It is important that we know when to give feedback. There is no rule, but there are some thoughts that may be helpful.

- First, is the feedback I have to give intended to be genuinely helpful to the other person or group?
- Can I express it in a way that will point to positive action, rather than only expressing anger?
- Can I give the feedback in a way that does not demean the person, but rather focuses on specific behavior?

If your answer to these questions is yes, you should probably give the person or group the feedback you have.

## GUIDELINES FOR GIVING FEEDBACK

The following guidelines may be helpful when considering how to give another person, or the team, feedback.

1. Be sure that your intention is to be helpful to the other person or team.
2. Think it through. Be clear about what you want to say. Even if you are not sure about the reasons why you feel the way you do, you can share that uncertainty.
3. Emphasize the positive. You care about this person or group and you want to help them improve. Tell them why you care.
4. Be specific -- Avoid general comments or exaggerations. Don't say "You always..." This will cause the other person to be defensive. Be specific about what and when the person or group does something.
5. Focus on pinpointed behavior rather than the person. The person is good and worthy (why you care) but the behavior is what is bothering you, and it is also what the person can change.
6. Own the feedback -- Use 'I' statements to indicate that this is how "I feel and others may not experience the same thing."
7. Your manner and the feelings you express are important. Be direct, but be kind and helpful. Be sincere.

## GUIDELINES FOR RECEIVING FEEDBACK

We can all benefit from feedback... IF we listen well and seek to understand in a way that will promote our own learning and development. Here are some guidelines for receiving feedback from others:

1. Understand that the person giving you feedback is attempting to be helpful. Try to receive the feedback as a gift given to you by this person who wishes to help you succeed.
2. Listen for actionable feedback. Ask yourself "What can I do differently in the future based on this feedback?" Do not focus on the person giving you the feedback or how you feel about that individual.
3. Ask for clarification. Ask when or under what circumstances you do something. Ask for examples that can clarify the situation or behavior. Ask the other person what you might do as an alternative in that situation. Seek to understand.
4. Engage in problem-solving. Think together about the problem.
5. Summarize what you have heard. Reflect back to the person giving you feedback your understanding of what you have heard.
6. Take responsibility for your behavior and demonstrate a willingness to modify your own behavior.
7. Remember that this feedback is not an evaluation of how good a person you are, but how your behavior is perceived by others at certain times.

## A Model for Giving Feedback

This simple model may be helpful when giving another person or a group feedback:

- **Ask permission** ("I would like to share a feeling I have, if you don't mind."
- **When...** (Describe the circumstance, time, etc.)
- **What happens** (describe the specific behavior)
- **It makes me feel...** (why it is a problem for me and possibly for others)
- **A suggestion.** It is always best not to act as if you know for certain what the right course of action is, but it is helpful to have a possible or suggested course of action.

For example: "If you don't mind, I would like to share a concern I have. *(Permission)* When we get on a topic that everyone is interested in *(When)* we lose track of the time and our meetings go ten or fifteen minutes over time. *(What happens)* I have children that I need to pick up after our meetings and this makes me very anxious I am going to be late. *(How it makes me feel)* Could we have a timekeeper give us a ten minute warning, then a five minute warning, before our meeting are supposed to end?" *(Suggestion)*

The following are exercises and experiences that you may find helpful to improve the team dynamics in each of the five categories.

## Team Feedback Exercise

It will be helpful to practice using this model. Practice giving feedback to the entire team. The purpose of this exercise is to give every member of the team the opportunity to give the entire team some feedback that may be on their mind.

- The facilitator should instruct the team that the feedback they are going to give is for the entire team, not directed at any one person.
- Give the group fifteen minutes to write down the feedback they have using the model and guidelines described above.
- When the group is ready, tell them that we are going to go around the room and everyone will have a chance to give their feedback, but we are NOT going to stop to react or analyze each statement.
- After everyone has made their statement, ask the group the following questions:
    - What was most helpful in terms of how these statements were made?
    - What feelings did you have and what caused these feelings?
    - If we were just receiving any one of these at a time, how would we respond?
    - What does this experience tell us about what our team should do in the future?

## One-to-One Feedback Exercise

The purpose of this exercise is to practice giving and receiving feedback between team members.

**Directions:**

- The first stage of this exercise is to practice the skill of observing behavior. On the following page you will find a "Behavior Observation" sheet. You will ask each member of the team to use

- this sheet to observe behaviors that are both helpful and not helpful to the progress of the team.
- Pair up the team members so each member is paired with another.
- Ask every member of the team to observe the behavior of their partner over the next two team meetings. Ask them to observe both desirable and undesirable behavior and indicate the affect those behaviors have on other team members.
- At the third meeting of the team have the group break down into their pairs. Each partner should be in a chair directly facing the other.
- Review the guidelines for both giving and receiving feedback, above. Also review the model for giving feedback. Ask them to spend ten minutes planning how they will give the other feedback using the model and following the guidelines.
- Then ask them to share the feedback with each other, giving time for each of them to both give and receive feedback. This will take approximately fifteen minutes.
- Then ask them to share with each other how they felt receiving the feedback and share suggestions for how both giving and receiving feedback might be improved.

**Debrief:**

With the group back together, ask the following questions:

- What did you learn from this experience in terms of the process of giving and receiving feedback?
- If you were to give an employee feedback outside of the team, would this impact how you would do that?
- Do you think practicing giving and receiving feedback will increase or decrease your comfort in doing this in the future?
- What are the implications for how we work together as a team?

# CHAPTER 19

# DIALOGUE: THINKING TOGETHER

The quality of conversations within the team will determine the success of problem-solving and collaboration. It will also contribute to the bonds and unity between team members. The purpose of this chapter is to help the team examine those conversations and strive to move from a culture of debate to one of dialogue.

## OBJECTIVES

1. To assess the quality of conversation within the team.
2. To create awareness of the cultural patterns of discussion that are normal within the team and which may hinder the team's ability to solve problems.
3. To provide the key skills of dialogue to enhance the quality of conversation and increase the ability of the team to solve problems and to achieve unity of understanding and action.

All conversations are not equal. Have you ever sat down to talk with someone, perhaps someone who you never met before, and felt that they were completely understanding, completely aware of what you were saying, how you were feeling and the meaning behind your words? Do you remember how that made you feel to be so well understood?

Have you ever sat down and talked with someone and felt, no matter how hard you tried, that they just didn't get it? They just could not understand, or worse, seemed to misunderstand everything you said. Even worse, have you had the experience of speaking to someone and they just seemed to want to disagree with everything you said, no matter how simple and true your statements? Do you remember how you became frustrated, and perhaps argumentative in response?

The nature of conversation is, largely determined by culture. We learn to talk to each other in ways that become comfortable and acceptable to us. Native Americans may sit and talk with each other in very quiet voices and almost never look each other in the eye, a gesture they regard as a sign of disrespect. A group of old Jewish men in New York may sit on a park bench and to a stranger passing by, may appear angry and agitate, but in their minds are simply passing the day in friendly conversation. Native islanders in the South Pacific may sit in complete silence for a long time, thinking and then speaking only after they have thought about a matter in great depth. These cultural speech patterns are neither right nor wrong. They each represent a language of communication. But a team in the workplace is usually comprised of individuals with different cultural patterns as well as the personal patterns each member has learned from their family or other experience. These patterns of behavior can help or hinder the decision-making and unity of the group.

## THINKING TOGETHER VERSUS THINKING ALONE

One understanding of conversation in a group is to think about the group as a number of different people, individuals with different perspectives or ideas, each member of the group sharing his or her ideas and the group deciding which idea is the best and moving forward with that idea. With this understanding, each individual is thinking alone, forming his or her own ideas and opinions and then attempting to convince the others of the value of those ideas. The "locus" of thought is internal, focused on the self, and "my" ideas, "my" contribution, the acceptance of "my" views over those of another.

Another understanding of group conversation is to consider that the group is thinking as one system, one organism, or one collective mind. With this understanding, the individual members are not so focused on their own ideas or their own opinions. They are less focused on convincing others to accept their ideas. They are not trying to "win". They are just as interested in understanding the ideas of others, trying to find the best solution for the group, regardless of who it comes from. When thinking together, the members are interested in encouraging and supporting the ideas of others because those ideas become their own. The objective is to create "collective wisdom", to find the best answer for the group, with no concern for whose idea it is.

It may be useful to define our terms since we will use these terms as a reference throughout this chapter.

>**Conversation** will be used to describe all interaction among a group of people in their effort to reach a decision or understanding regardless of the quality or nature of that interaction.

>**Debate** is a conversation in which the parties assume opposing positions and view the goal of the conversation to be the victory of their position over that of their opponent.

>**Discussion** is a conversation in which the goal is to reach a decision that both parties can accept and which may represent a compromise or combination of positions previously held by the parties.

>**Dialogue** is a conversation that explores the meaning and nature of an issue in an effort to create insight and understanding on a deeper level. Dialogue seeks to gain the insight of all parties and create collective wisdom, unity, or a new way of looking at an issue.

## Exercise:

If you had to choose the most common style of conversation in your group, would you describe it as debate, discussion, or dialogue?

_____

_____

How does this style of conversation usually make you feel?

_____

_____

What effect does this style have on your behavior in the group?

_____

_____

Would you want to change this style of conversation? Why?

_____

_____

It may be helpful to visualize how we communicate with others. The following triangle illustrates the mental framework from which we engage in conversation. In most conversations, particularly those conditioned by current culture in Western societies, people are thinking about their own ideas and how to persuade the other person to accept their ideas. Unfortunately, the other person is doing the same. This defeats the opportunity for shared understanding and may result in conflict. When we are in our own corner, thinking alone, we are in a win-lose posture, searching for victory for our position at the cost of defeat for the other person.

Think of the shaded area of the triangle as the locus of thought, where you are thinking, or who is involved in your thinking. At the bottom of the triangle we are in our own corner, thinking alone. The bottom of the triangle represents debate, an all too common mode of discourse in our culture.

When we are trying to win a debate, to have our ideas victorious over the ideas of another, we listen to the other with an ear to exclude and label those ideas in a way that makes them unacceptable.

## WHEN TO PRACTICE DIALOGUE, DISCUSSION OR DEBATE

While this chapter presents dialogue as an ideal or desired style of conversation, does that mean that all conversation should be a dialogue? Imagine that you are driving in your car and your children shout "Mom, there's a McDonald's. Can we get a Happy Meal?" Should Mom now enter into a deep and meaningful dialogue about why they really want a Happy Meal, or the true understanding of a Happy Meal? I think not. Mom will probably, and correctly reply, "No, it is almost dinner time and we will be home soon." End of discussion -- and hopefully with no debate.

Our lives are filled with simple decisions, and our concern is often for efficiency and not depth of meaning. In team meetings, much of the time may be reviewing numbers, brainstorming a cause or solution of a specific problem, or deciding who will fill in for someone who will be absent next week These decisions do not require in-depth dialogue.

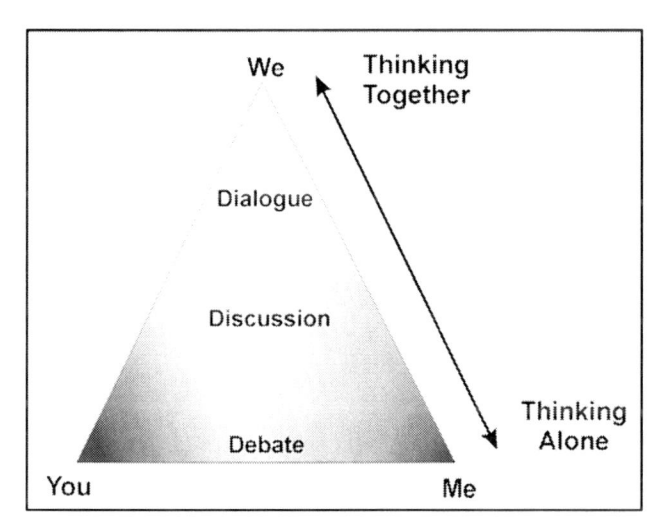

Dialogue helps us reach consensus decisions. It should be employed for questions of significance. Why are we organized the way we are? Are we genuinely meeting the current and future needs of our clients? Are we assisting each other in the development of our personal capacities? Are we doing the best we can to make this an enjoyable and fulfilling place to work? These are important questions, and they are not matters of just choosing "A" or "B." Rather, they are issues with several levels of meaning and possible action. These are the types of issues around which we should engage in genuine dialogue.

Dialogue can be a frame of reference. Once the team understands the potential of dialogue and its tools, a team member may recognize that we are engaged in a debate when we should be engaged in a dialogue. It is helpful to simply ask "shouldn't we have a dialogue on this issue for a while?" This will trigger a different thought pattern in all the members of the team.

## ACHIEVING THE VALUE OF "WE"

The concept of unity was integral to Native American culture, and the symbol of the circle had religious importance as a symbol of the oneness of the human family. When Europeans conquered the continent, they built square houses with square windows cut out, sat around a square, chopped up the land into square acres, and arranged their houses into square blocks. They even did square dancing, which is so unnatural that it requires a supervisor shouting directions to the dancers! A square has four equal sides, and each side has a distinct point of beginning and ending. The sides of a square are connected but individual and separate, four separate lines.

Native Americans tended to live in round tents or huts. They sat in circles when making decisions. They formed their tents into larger circles and danced in circles. Where does a circle begin or end? It can begin anywhere or end nowhere. It is one, a complete unity. Is this merely an interesting coincidence of symbols? Or does the square and circle represent some pattern of thought and behavior? Europeans were certainly better at engineering bridges and mechanical objects. But, perhaps Native Americans were better at understanding the profound nature of relationships, what they simply called human beings.

Among Native Americans it is disgraceful to raise one's head or voice above the group, to separate or distinguish oneself from the unity of the group. While this may hold down individual initiative, it also serves as a force for unity within the tribe.

Dialogue is like the circle. Dialogue is a conversation that seeks unity of thought, unity of understanding and unity of action. These are not achieved by a competition between you and me, but rather through the pursuit of a solution that represents the interests and harmony of "we."

## THE HIERARCHY OF PURPOSE: FOUNDATION OF DIALOGUE

Some years ago I attended a workshop on marriage. The presenters used a diagram to illustrate the relationship between husband and wife. At the top of the pyramid they placed God. At the two corners the husband and wife. The point of the triangle was to illustrate that the closer each partner came to God, the closer they came to each other. This simple device always impressed me as representing a profound truth. The closer two people are to a common purpose, a common set of values and beliefs, the closer they come to each other.

What is a comparable unifying force in your work place?

_____

_____

Shared purpose may be something as basic as helping to achieve the survival of your company. It may be a genuine dedication to serving your customers. It may be any mission to which you and your team members are dedicated. The degree to which we lack common purpose is the degree to which we are likely to remain at the bottom of the pyramid, focused on our self, in pursuit of our individual needs. If we are focused only on our personal needs our conversation will tend toward debate, and we will be motivated to win all we can.

As we achieve common purpose, the nature of our motivation and conversation changes. We move from simply trying to win or convince the other person to teaching, sharing, understanding, learning, and serving as we move up the pyramid to a condition of genuine dialogue.

Imagine a congress in which every representative had no self-interest, no concern about his or her election, no concern about winning any personal or party victory. Rather, every member was focused on only one purpose, the collective, shared good of the country. In a true attitude of service, they would seek deep understanding and meaning, striving to make decisions that would be in the best interests of the country. The entire spirit would be transformed, the quality of decision would accelerate, and the country would benefit.

## THE COST OF THINKING ALONE

Where in the organization are the most costly quality problems? Are they the defect caused on the factory floor? Are they the missed sales opportunity? Or, are they in conference rooms and offices where managers and executives make decisions? The choice to enter a different type of business, or the decision to select a new chief executive, or the decision to produce one product over another or to buy one type of equipment over another – the quality of these decisions, which will never appear on a Six Sigma project chart or process control graph, are the greatest opportunity for quality and cost improvement.

One of the more amazing realities of recent corporate history is the much discussed collapse of the Enron Corporation. This failure can be described in many ways - a failure of corporate ethics, poor strategic judgment, or outright stealing. But, how did this happen? The Board of Directors of Enron was highly regarded as a model of corporate Board composition. Only two insiders served on the Enron board. No corporation could have had a more financially competent and experienced board. The list included a former Stanford Dean of the Business School who was an accounting professor, the former CEO of an insurance company, the former CEO of an international bank, a hedge fund manager, a prominent Asian financier, and an economist who is the former head of the U.S. government's Commodity Futures Trading Commission. Yet the members of this board have claimed to have been confused by Enron's financial transactions.[25]

How could this group of experienced and respected individuals look over books of a corporation that were so complicated and confused that no analyst could figure out where the money was coming from or where it was going, and thousands of deals were being done that amounted to little more than a shell game of moving money and accounting entries around to give the appearance of profits where there were none?

Jeffrey A. Sonnenfeld writing in the Harvard Business Review[26] said "We need to consider not only how we structure the work of a board but also how we manage the social system a board actually is. We'll be fighting the wrong war if we simply tighten procedural rules for boards and ignore their more pressing need – to be strong, high-functioning work groups whose members trust and challenge one another and engage directly with senior managers on critical issues facing corporations."

Was the Board of Directors engaging in dialogue? Were they thinking deeply and understanding the meaning of the facts presented to them? Of course they were not. Rather there was a classic case of "group think" in which even the most analytic board members did not question the facts presented to them, did not dig deep to understand how and why the numbers presented could make sense. Perhaps it was the simple fact that each person around the table had so much respect for the others that they were saying to them "Well, if it makes sense to him, it must make sense." Perhaps this was a case in which a "court jester" was needed, someone to ask the absurd questions, someone who could display complete lack of respect and ask "why "or "how could that be" or request other members of the Board to explain where the money was coming from.

---

[25] "What Makes Great Boards Great", Jeffrey A. Sonnenfeld, Harvard Business Review, September, 2002, p.108.

[26] J. A. Sonnenfeld, Harvard Business Review, September, 2002, p.106.

Over and over again in corporate and government history, there are cases of major decisions being made that completely overlook some simple fact and lead to extremely costly decisions. One petroleum company admitted to me that they had invested approximately one billion dollars exploring for oil in a land-locked African country. When they finally found oil, someone asked the obvious question, "How are we going to get it out of the country?" Incredibly, there was no possible way to transport the oil to market. One billion dollars had been wasted because no one had asked an extremely obvious question. These were smart people. How does that happen?

It happens because they are engaged in group-think, acquiescing to someone else and failing to engage in dialogue.

# THE BEHAVIORAL CHARACTERISTICS OF DIALOGUE

There are eight key characteristics of groups engaged in a process of dialogue versus those engaged in a process of debate. There is no particular order in which they occur; rather they tend to be parts of a "whole-system" in which the parts reinforce each other.

The following eight characteristics are patterns of behavior of either open or closed human systems or cultures.

## 1. LISTENING VERSUS CONVINCING:

When you walk into a debate, your mind is set on convincing the judges or audience of the superiority of your point of view. You plan your "arguments," and a great debater voices those arguments in the most convincing manner possible. She speaks with the voice of certainty and authority. The debater has already planned her rebuttal to the expected arguments of the "opponent." This is the way the debate game is played and won. The purpose of a debate is not for the parties to engage in learning. Rather it is to convince the audience that one participant has a superior position and has most skillfully argued that position.

When the motive of conversation is convincing, there is little learning because altering your view would be a sign of weakness, almost an admission that your position is inferior. This would signal defeat. When the motive of a conversation is to listen and to learn, there can be no thought of winning or losing. There is no external audience to convince in a dialogue. You are the audience, the team is the audience, and the purpose is to gain knowledge, understanding, and meaning, and this does not result from authoritatively arguing pre-packaged positions. It derives from listening and thinking together.

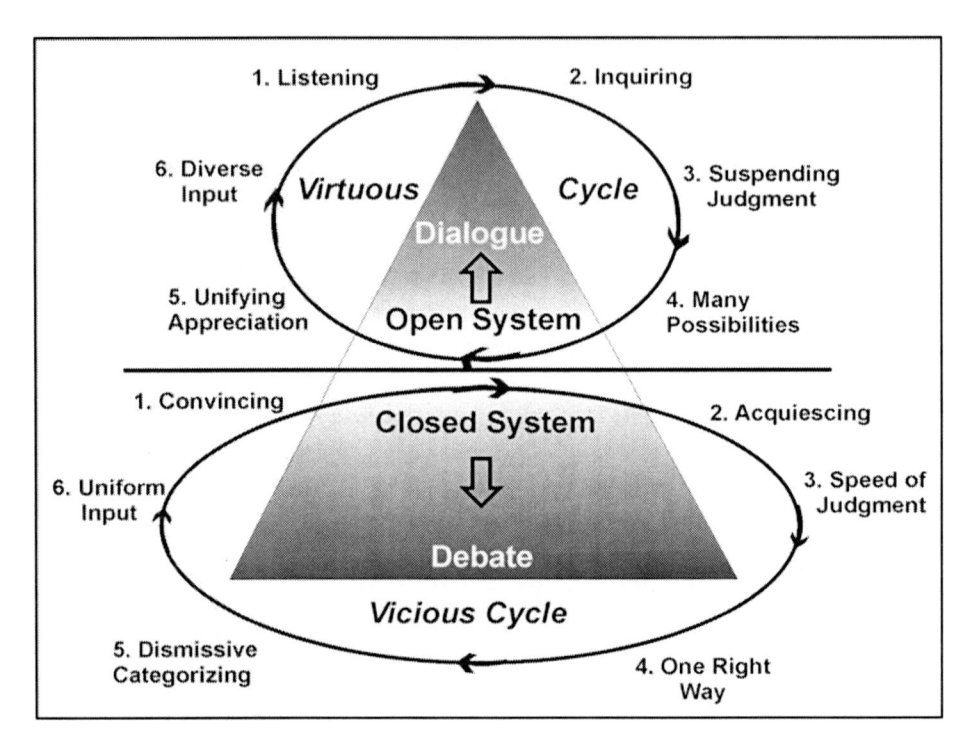

We have presidential debates. We don't have presidential dialogues. Which skill will be most relevant and useful to a president confronted with complex issues? Perhaps we should have presidential dialogues to help us select the best candidate.

Everyone has a story, a life history, a life of experiences and knowledge gained, that is different than our own. In dialogue you seek to understand the story of others.

## 2. Inquiring versus Acquiescing:

In health care an attitude of inquiry is essential. Simply acquiescing to the opinions or view of others, without asking "why" can lead to misdiagnosis and mistreatment.

Groups in a closed system are likely to be extremely accepting of the views of its members, particularly when those views are expressed by the person in power or expressed framed in the legitimacy of their ideology. This acquiescence avoids the intellectual inquiry, the asking of questions that are the fundamental tool of learning.

Groups who are not engaged in dialogue are highly likely to simply accept a position when legitimized by an accepted ideology, without considering the deep meaning or significance of the position. Good decision-making requires forward thinking, anticipation, considering steps two, three, and four going forward. A culture of debate, in which members of a group acquiesce to power or ideology, blinds the group to the consequences of their decisions.

Inquiry is the foundation of science. Without inquiry, asking questions, there would be no science or human progress. Inquiring minds, questioning minds, seek meaning, significance and underlying truths. The ability to ask questions, to ask the simple question "why?" is the first skill of acquiring wisdom. There is no more important member of a group than the person who recognizes when it is important to ask "why?" It is not at all unusual for groups to be headed off in a direction that no one questions, but neither can anyone explain why they are headed in this direction.

## 3. Suspending Judgment versus Speed of Judgment

A judgment is something that comes "down" at the end of a "trial." If a judge or jury entered a trial with a judgment already in their mind, we would demand that they be disqualified. We ask judges and juries to suspend judgments, to hear all sides, to reflect, and to consider alternative explanations

Healthcare professionals, perhaps more than others, should have a tendency to suspend judgment until they have sufficient data to support an hypothesis. When a patient walks into a hospital or clinic, he or she enters an area where data is quickly being gathered and judgments are being made. Hopefully, the process of dialogue within the clinic or diagnostic area will not be so hasty as to prevent alternative views to be considered and full data to be gathered.

Dialogue is intended to achieve profound understanding, to find new meaning, to explore new and creative solutions, and to create consensus among a group. In order to achieve these things, it is essential that we participate in a period of suspended judgment. We agree to withhold judgment.

In the dominant Western culture we have difficulty suspending judgment. But this is not true of all cultures. A friend of mine worked for a time with native people in the South Pacific Islands. She was a clinical psychologist who specialized in group therapy. She was very skilled at group dynamics, at least from the perspective of her culture. She went to work with a group of local island leaders, the elders of the people in that region. They came together and the topic that required discussion was put forth. There was then a long period of silence in which no one said anything. She felt like it was five minutes, but it was probably more like one minute. In a fast-talking culture like ours, time moves very slowly when there is silence in a group. After a while she put on her "facilitator's hat" and said "Well, why don't we talk about it. We could each share how we feel about this issue." The village elder raised his head and said softly to her "Here we first think about something. Then, once we have thought, we speak."

How often have you found yourself first speaking and then attempting to think about what you wish to say while your lips are already in motion? These native people, as a cultural norm, practiced suspending judgment.

## 4. One "Right Way" versus Open to Alternatives

One enters a debate with a position. One enters dialogue with questions. In debate one defends one's position and argues one's position. In dialogue one defends nothing and questions everything in a search for meaning and importance.

In an authoritarian culture there is little consideration of alternatives precisely because the more alternatives are considered, the more questioning must occur. The more questioning that occurs, the more one undermines the assumptions of authoritarian control – the leader knows and you obey. Hence, all democracies, to survive, must be open systems.

A group engaged in open-systems thinking will consider more alternatives because it is precisely from that consideration that learning will occur and creative, or previously impossible, alternatives will emerge. In the process of dialogue there is a joy in discovering new alternatives; like a child discovering a present under the Christmas tree, the group enjoys the thrill of discovery.

The more authoritarian and the more ideological the group, the lower the level of acceptance of diverse points of view will be, and therefore they are more likely to make major misjudgments. A belief in a "right way" can close our eyes to the possibilities of other courses of action. Dialogue implies keeping our minds open, like keeping our eyes and ears open to the sights and sounds in our environment.

## 5. Unifying Appreciation versus Dismissive Categorizing

Order makes sense out of things. We therefore seek order in conversation. Are we at the beginning or end? Is the conversation hostile or friendly, intelligent or dumb, interesting or boring? There are a hundred ways that we can categorize people, comments, or entire conversations. How we categorize contributions to conversation will have an impact on our ability to enter a meaningful dialogue.

When we hear a comment we do not like, one that differs from our understanding or point of view, we may have a tendency to place that in a category, or place the entire person in a category. This has become unfortunately common in recent years, and points of view are dismissed with "Oh, he is just one of those liberals (or conservatives)."

Imagine that you are in a team meeting and you are discussing how the process of learning and development can be improved. A young woman who has been employed for only a couple of months speaks up and says, "I thought people would be friendlier when I first came to work here. I thought people would help each other more." The manager of this group, somewhat uncomfortable with this expression of personal feelings and emotion thinks to himself, "Well, she just said that because she is young and inexperienced." By placing the young woman and her comment in the category of "young and inexperienced," he alleviates his need to deal with her comment in a meaningful way. He can now move on to listen to comments he may find more comfortable.

How else could the manager think about this remark? He could have thought to appreciate the truth in her comment. For example, he could have said, "I know that it is important when you first come to work that you feel that people want to help you succeed. And, I think you are making the point that we learn well when we help each other, whether we are new or old on the job." By acknowledge the truth or value in the young woman's comment he has created a unifying bond, the opposite of alienation. This appreciative comment will make her more comfortable and more likely to contribute in the future.

## 6. Uniform Input versus Diverse Input

In a culture of debate, the participants tend to welcome input that reinforces their view and reject or even disparage input that is from a diverse perspective. Each time this happens, the possibility of future diverse input is reduced.

Debate is usually between two people, but it can just as well be between groups. In companies debate can be between the marketing and manufacturing groups or between operating managers and staff managers. More than once I have sat in meetings when some request or suggestion came from that "other" group, the other corner of the triangle, and was rejected immediately, without any genuine consideration, simply because it was one of those "typical" comments by those other people.

A group of corporate decision makers who are all engineers, or all finance managers, or who all come from the same industry or corporate culture, are similarly likely to become a closed system, reinforcing each other's views. One of the advantages of the push for diverse boards and diverse management teams is simply that minorities or women, not conditioned to the same corporate culture and assumptions are more likely to ask the questions that force the group to think about the meaning of what they are doing.

One of the perceptions that causes members of a group to stay in the corners of the triangle is the perception that those who are unlike us have little to offer. If one is trained as an engineer and the primary work of the organization is engineering, it is normal to value the ideas of other engineers. On senior management teams there will typically be several operating managers who are trained and have risen from the area of core competence of the organization, such as engineering. But there will also be a finance manager, a human resource manager, possibly an attorney or others. The nature of conversation is often prejudiced by the value placed on these areas of expertise, independent of the actual merit of a contribution by a team member.

The assumption of dialogue is that the group is seeking the best understanding, the best solution, for the combined interests of the group. This can only happen if the members of the group can learn to look beyond their own filters that differentiate the contributions of one individual over another.

# Chapter 20

# Improving Team Dynamics

The purpose of this chapter is to develop relationships within the team that will allow open, honest, and trusting communications among team members.

## Objectives

1. To assess the patterns of communication among team members.
2. To build trust among team members.
3. To get to know team members as individuals with unique preferences, fears and desires.

# Team Dynamics Assessment

Complete the following team dynamics assessment and have your coach compile the results and feed them back to the team.

## Trust:

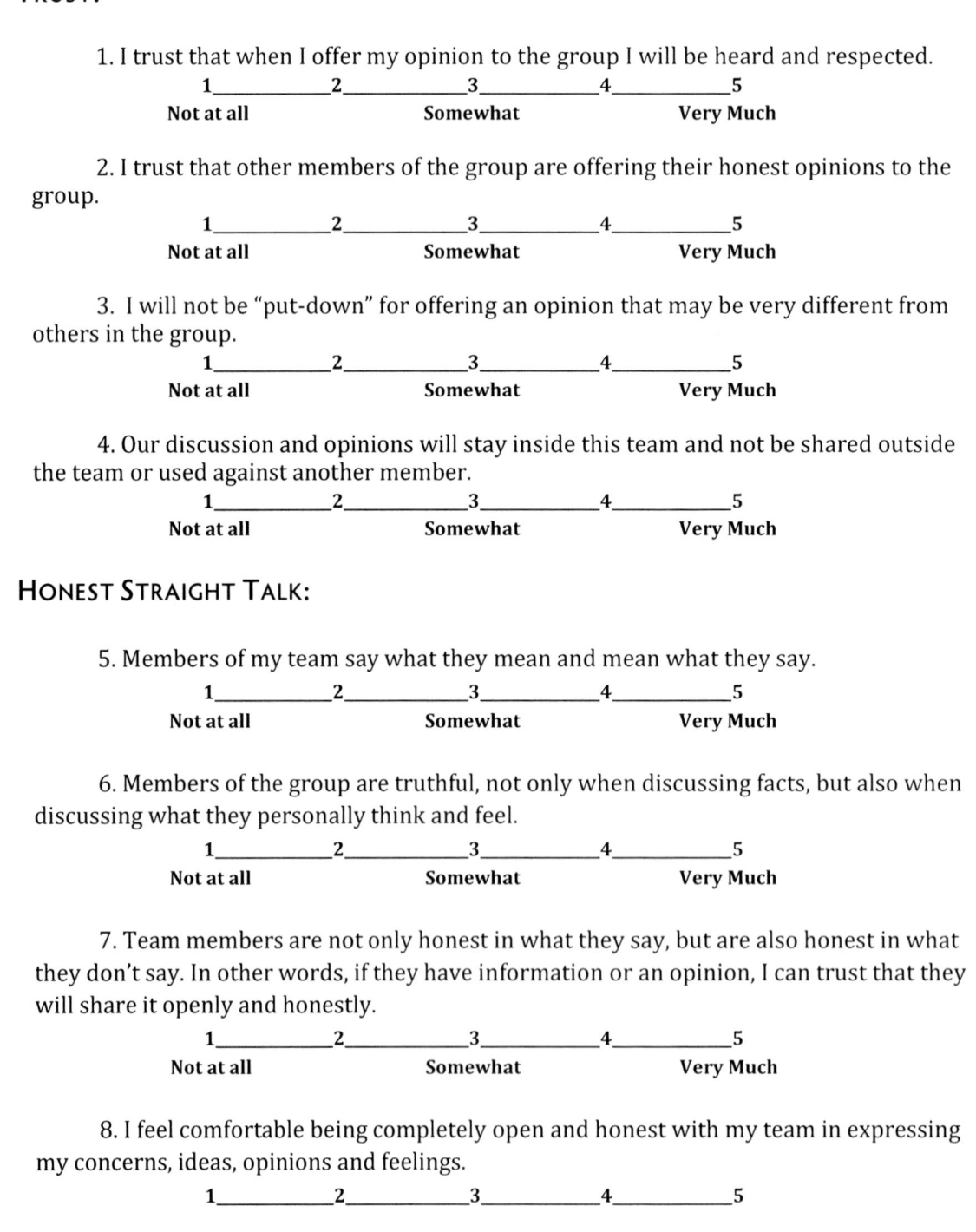

1. I trust that when I offer my opinion to the group I will be heard and respected.

   1_____2_____3_____4_____5
   Not at all              Somewhat              Very Much

2. I trust that other members of the group are offering their honest opinions to the group.

   1_____2_____3_____4_____5
   Not at all              Somewhat              Very Much

3. I will not be "put-down" for offering an opinion that may be very different from others in the group.

   1_____2_____3_____4_____5
   Not at all              Somewhat              Very Much

4. Our discussion and opinions will stay inside this team and not be shared outside the team or used against another member.

   1_____2_____3_____4_____5
   Not at all              Somewhat              Very Much

## Honest Straight Talk:

5. Members of my team say what they mean and mean what they say.

   1_____2_____3_____4_____5
   Not at all              Somewhat              Very Much

6. Members of the group are truthful, not only when discussing facts, but also when discussing what they personally think and feel.

   1_____2_____3_____4_____5
   Not at all              Somewhat              Very Much

7. Team members are not only honest in what they say, but are also honest in what they don't say. In other words, if they have information or an opinion, I can trust that they will share it openly and honestly.

   1_____2_____3_____4_____5
   Not at all              Somewhat              Very Much

8. I feel comfortable being completely open and honest with my team in expressing my concerns, ideas, opinions and feelings.

   1_____2_____3_____4_____5

|   Not at all   |   Somewhat   |   Very Much   |

## EMPATHY:

9. The last time I shared a personal concern or problem with my team I feel that they understood my feelings.

   1_____2_____3_____4_____5
   Not at all                  Somewhat                  Very Much

10. Members of this team genuinely care about the well-being of other members of the team.

    1_____2_____3_____4_____5
    Not at all                  Somewhat                  Very Much

11. If a member of the team shares a need for help, other members of the team will volunteer to provide that help.

    1_____2_____3_____4_____5
    Not at all                  Somewhat                  Very Much

12. Team members look out for each other, not just themselves.

    1_____2_____3_____4_____5
    Not at all                  Somewhat                  Very Much

## UNITY OF PURPOSE:

13. Members of my team share a common purpose and define "winning" in the same way.

    1_____2_____3_____4_____5
    Not at all                  Somewhat                  Very Much

14. When we meet we are working on the same agenda, and team members do not have hidden or personal agendas that interfere with the purpose of the group.

    1_____2_____3_____4_____5
    Not at all                  Somewhat                  Very Much

15. There is a high "sense of purpose" on the team, a desire to accomplish our mission.

    1_____2_____3_____4_____5
    Not at all                  Somewhat                  Very Much

16. Our team feels united, as if we are working together as one cohesive unit.

    1_____2_____3_____4_____5
    Not at all                  Somewhat                  Very Much

## APPRECIATION OF DIVERSITY:

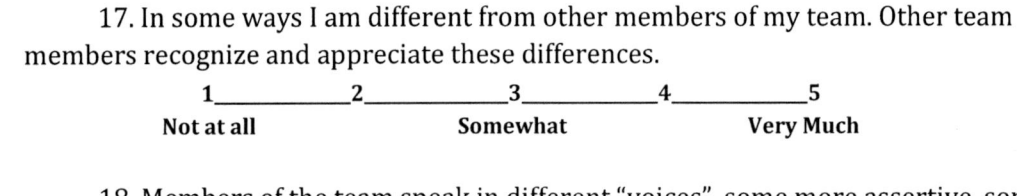

17. In some ways I am different from other members of my team. Other team members recognize and appreciate these differences.

| 1 | 2 | 3 | 4 | 5 |
|---|---|---|---|---|
| **Not at all** | | **Somewhat** | | **Very Much** |

18. Members of the team speak in different "voices", some more assertive, some more quiet or reserved. All members are heard equally for the content of what they have to say, rather than how loudly they speak.

| 1 | 2 | 3 | 4 | 5 |
|---|---|---|---|---|
| **Not at all** | | **Somewhat** | | **Very Much** |

19. In every group there is a dominant culture. There are usually individuals who represent a sub-culture or minority culture. Our team listens and respects the views of those representing these different cultures with respect and understanding.

| 1 | 2 | 3 | 4 | 5 |
|---|---|---|---|---|
| **Not at all** | | **Somewhat** | | **Very Much** |

20. Diversity of experience, perspectives and opinions is an asset to a team. It is the expression of this diversity that prevents "group-think." My team is diverse, and diverse views are expressed and well received by the team.

| 1 | 2 | 3 | 4 | 5 |
|---|---|---|---|---|
| **Not at all** | | **Somewhat** | | **Very Much** |

## How Did Your Team Score?

Compile the average scores for each item and for each category. There is a potential score of twenty for each category.

---

**TRUST**

1  2  3  4  5  6  7  8  9  10  11  12  13  14  15  16  17  18  19  20

**HONEST STRAIGHT TALK**

1  2  3  4  5  6  7  8  9  10  11  12  13  14  15  16  17  18  19  20

**EMPATHY**

1  2  3  4  5  6  7  8  9  10  11  12  13  14  15  16  17  18  19  20

**UNITY OF PURPOSE**

1  2  3  4  5  6  7  8  9  10  11  12  13  14  15  16  17  18  19  20

**APPRECIATION OF DIVERSITY**

1  2  3  4  5  6  7  8  9  10  11  12  13  14  15  16  17  18  19  20

---

## DEBRIEF:

In your team meeting, discuss the following questions and reach consensus on ways you can improve the inter-personal dynamics of your team. It is very important to keep in mind that EVERY team, every family, every community, every group of human beings, can improve how they deal with each other. The purpose is not to conclude that you are either good or bad. The purpose is to make continuous improvement in the human dynamics of your team.

When debriefing, agree on the rule "No one is to blame, or we are all to blame!"

1. Which category produced the highest score?
   a. Why do you believe you scored well in this category?

b. What specific behavior contributed to this score?

_____
_____
_____
_____

1. Which category produced the lowest score?
    a. Why do you believe you scored low in this category?
    b. What specific behavior contributed to this low score?

_____
_____
_____
_____

2. Review the individual items and the scores for each item in the other categories.
    a. These scores suggest that we could improve what behavior to improve the inter-personal dynamics within our team?

_____
_____
_____
_____

## IMPROVING THE INTER-PERSONAL DYNAMICS OF YOUR TEAM

Perhaps the first and most important thing any team can do to improve the dynamics within the team is to periodically "process" their own functioning as a team. Stop and think, reflect, and then discuss how your team is functioning. Doing this periodically, in an open and honest way is the most essential step in improving the inter-personal dynamics of any team.

Over the past years many exercises have been developed to improve the dynamics of teams. Some are done within the normal team setting, and others are experiential exercises that require going off-site for outdoor, more physical experiences.

One of the most effective exercises I have experienced was when a company leadership team decided to take on a service project as a team. This company was in a construction related business. They knew how to build things. They found that the local YWCA/YMCA needed to reconstruct the building that had been donated to them. Over a six month period this management team worked together to reconstruct the building. After doing this, the team reported that they learned more about each other, came to trust each other, and had better feelings toward each other than ever before. This was a true "action-learning" experience that both improved the performance and "spirit" of the team, and also improved the company's relations in the community.

# TRUST BUILDING EXERCISES

## 3. TWO TRUTHS AND A LIE

This is an easy and effective first exercise. It is an "ice-breaker" and a simple get-to-know each other game. The purpose of the game is to learn something about each team member that you would not learn through the routine of team meetings focused on work.

**Directions:** Ask each member of the team to write down three things. Two of them are true things that other members of the group are not likely to know. The third one is a lie.

Then go around the room and have each person read their three things. Ask everyone to guess which one is the lie. After everyone guesses, then ask the person to share which are true and which was a lie.

**Debrief:** Make it simple. Ask the group what was the most surprising thing they learned about a team member.

## 4. IF I MADE A MOVIE...

This exercise is somewhat similar to the above, but it gets to a more serious level of knowing other members of the group. To share hopes, dreams and fears requires trust in other members. This is another practice session in building trust.

**Facilitator:** It is important that group members share their stories voluntarily. Some may not be comfortable sharing and they should be invited, but not pressured to share.

**Directions:** If I made a movie and it was about my life, what scene would be a defining moment in the movie? It can be tragic or heroic. Describe the scene and why it would be a defining moment of my life. This can be an actual scene or one that you make up to illustrate a key event or transition in your life. If you were casting an actor to play you in this movie, who would you cast in your role?

Ask each member of the group to spend ten to fifteen minutes defining the scene and which actor would play them in the movie.

Then, ask members to volunteer to share their scene and the actor. Ask them what this scene tells us that is important about their life.

**Debrief:** After each person has shared their story, ask the group "What have we learned about another team member that helps us understand them better?"

## STRAIGHT TALK EXERCISES

Trust and honesty are two sides of the same coin. The more honest we are, the more we will be trusted by others. The kind of honesty that we are concerned with on the team is not honesty about telling lies. It is more about "straight-talk," the honesty that is sharing what you really feel, saying what is on your mind. Group cohesion and group decision-making are often hindered by members of the group simply not "honestly" sharing what they think and feel. This type of honesty may also be called "being open" or willing to share what is inside of you.

### 5. THE TRUTHS I DENY MYSELF

One of the ways that we are not entirely honest is not being honest with ourselves. We all (at least most of us) tell ourselves little falsehoods to avoid confronting something we may want to avoid confronting. The purpose of this exercise is to initiate openness and sharing among team members.

**Directions:** Ask each team member to write down two different ways that "I fool myself" or "I am not completely honest with myself." It is important that the facilitator model, give examples, him or herself. So start by sharing two things you, the facilitator, do to fool yourself. For example:

I tell myself I am trying to lose weight and then I sneak ice cream with pure maple syrup on top, late at night before I go to bed.

I am trying to save money by spending less, yet I cannot resist buying some latest gadget because it is the newest, best whatever, even though I know I don't really need it.

Give the group five or ten minutes to write down their little falsehoods that they tell themselves. Then ask the members of the group to share. It is best not to go around the room, but just ask for volunteers so members who are uncomfortable don't feel pressured.

When others are sharing, no one else should make any disapproving comment ("Oh my God! I can't believe you do that!") Remember that the purpose of this exercise is to confront the common habit of denial within all of us.

**Debrief**: The facilitator should point out that we all have things in common. What are the common habits that we shared?

Ask the group, what does this tendency to not confront things, even to ourselves, tell us about how we communicate or work together?

Do we fail to be open and honest with others for the same reasons we may fail to be honest with ourselves?

## Unity of Purpose

Teams are most successful when the members of the team share common goals and common purpose. Your team developed a charter that included a purpose statement, and this should be your shared purpose. But we all have our own purpose, our own goals or concerns, and sometimes these personal issues are more dominant than our collective purpose.

### 6. The Purpose Diagram

This exercise is intended to elicit personal reflection on the part of team members and develop understanding of the goals we have in common.

**Directions:** This exercise has three parts: first, private reflection; second, developing an "affinity diagram"; third, debrief. This exercise can be used as practice in developing an affinity diagram, a skill that will be useful in other activities.

Explain to the group that we will use an "affinity diagram" to share our understanding of our own purpose and goals and how they are common or different.

Explain what an affinity diagram is: *A brainstorming and decision technique designed to generate and then sort a large number of ideas into related groups in a visual display.* Ask the group to follow the following steps to generate this diagram.

**Step 1: Describe the Problem or Issue:** The issue in this case is "why are we here?" What is our goal or purpose that brings us together as a team? What do I hope to gain, achieve or experience by participating on this team?

**Step 2: Generate ideas:** Distribute small pads of post-it-notes to each member of the team. Ask them to write down, each on a separate note, as many ideas that answer the question as they can think of. The ideas can be big ones or small ones. Give the group ten minutes to think about and write down their ideas.

**Step 3: Display the ideas.** Post the ideas on a wall, or a table in a *random* manner. Just get them up so they can all be seen. Then ask them to start studying all of the ideas that have been posted. IMPORTANT: ask them to do this and the next step in SILENCE. This is hard for most teams. Explain that this may be a new experience, but we will learn that sometimes the team can learn and decide without talking at all.

**Step 4: Sort the ideas into related groups.** Ask the team members physically sort the cards into groupings, **without talking**, using the following process:

- Start by looking for two ideas that seem related in some way. Place them together in a column off to one side.
- Look for ideas that are related to those you've already set aside and add them to that group.
- Look for other ideas that are related to each other and establish new groups. This process is repeated until the team has placed all of the ideas in groups.

**NOTE:** Ideally, all of the ideas can be sorted into related groups. If there are some "loners" that don't fit any of the groups, don't force them into groupings where they don't belong. Let them stand alone under their own headers or under a "miscellaneous" heading.

**Step 5: Create header cards for the groups.** A header is an idea that captures the essential link among the ideas contained in a group of cards. This idea is written on a single card or post-it-note and must consist of a phrase or sentence that clearly conveys the meaning, even to people who are not on the team. The team develops headers for the groups by...

- Finding already existing cards within the groups that will serve well as headers and placing them at the top of the group of related cards.
- Alternatively, discussing and agreeing on the wording of cards created specifically to be headers.
- Once you have completed the affinity diagram ask the group to discuss what they learned from doing this. Ask the following questions:

What does this tell us about the goals and purpose that we share?

What does this tell us about how we are different in our goals and purpose?

Does this tell us anything about how we function as a team, or how we should function as a team?

Summarize by pointing out the importance of common purpose and how this is present or how it needs to be developed by the team.

## Appreciation of Diversity:

The subject of diversity in the workplace is one that has been addressed by many forms of training. Most of this has focused on two issues: race and gender. Over the past fifty years our workplace has changed dramatically in the increased number of women and African-Americans, Hispanics and Asians in the workplace. There are many specialized workshops to address how we respond to these changes.

You may think of the following exercise as merely an introduction to this subject, and an opportunity to recognize, understand and appreciate all of the different forms of diversity that are present on our team.

### 7. We Are All Different – We Are All the Same

Among the members of any team there are similarities and differences that affect the way we view problems and solutions. These differences also affect our manner of speech, our emotions, and how we interpret events. The purpose of this exercise is to share some of those differences among team members and how they influence our behavior.

**Directions:** Explain that the purpose of this exercise is to recognize some of the differences -- the unique qualities and experience -- of each member of our team.

- Ask the team members to spend ten to fifteen minutes alone, reflecting on how they may be different from all or the majority of other team members. These differences may be ethnic, age, gender, religion, work experience, education, personality or other life experience. Ask them to write down three ways that they are unique or different.
- The facilitator will then ask that each member share his or her three differences.
- The facilitator will instruct all the team members to listen well and think about how the differences being described present the team with an asset, some value or virtue that can be appreciated and contribute to the team.
- Immediately after an individual shares his or her differences, the facilitator will ask the group "How do you feel those qualities or experiences can be an asset to our team?" Let the group share their thoughts for a few moments and then go on to the next person.

**Debrief:** After everyone has shared and received this appreciation from the group, ask the team to spend three minutes just thinking about and reflecting on what they heard. Then ask the group the following questions:

- How did the group's response to your diversity cause you to feel?
- How did it make you feel about the team in general?
- How may what you learned affect the future behavior of the team?

## TEAM COMMITMENT

The purpose of this exercise is to help the team explore the meaning of "commitment" to the team and each other and to practice giving and receiving feedback on their commitment.

There are four stages of this exercise: first, brainstorming indicators of commitment; second, private assessment of each individual's demonstration of those indicators; third, sharing and processing that feedback; and fourth, reflection and sharing commitments to future behavior. The exercise is structured to provide confidential feedback and minimize the possibility of painful confrontations that sometimes occur over this issue.

You will need a large number of post-it-notes, preferably of the same color so as not to indicate which member is providing which feedback.

**Directions:**

1. **Identifying Indicators:** Brainstorm what "commitment" means in a team setting. Ask the group, "How do you know it when you see it?" Or, "What pinpointed behaviors demonstrate that a member is committed to the success of the team?" Also, ask "What behavior indicates personal commitment to each other?"

- Generate a list of as many ideas as come to mind within ten minutes. This will probably be ten to twenty indicators such as "attends meetings regularly;" "participates in problem-solving and discussion;" or, "follows through on action items."
- Combine similar indicators. Your goal is to get down to only five indicators. Be sure that they are still pinpointed, observable behavior.
- Vote on the five that are most important and most reliable indicators of commitment to the team.

2. **Assessing Fellow Team Members:** On the following page is a sheet to record each person's evaluation of the other members of the team.

- Place the five indicators across the five columns titled "Indicators of Commitment." Each member should have a sheet like that on the following page. This sheet should be kept private by that member.
- Place the names of the other team members down the left hand column.
- Ask each member to rate each other member on each of these qualities using a ten point scale. You can give the team fifteen minutes to do this in the meeting, or (and this is preferable) give them time between meetings to think about their assessment and complete the ratings during the time between this and the next meeting.

3. **Sharing Feedback:** The purpose of the following is to allow for each team member to receive absolutely frank and honest feedback without public discussion that could be painful or humiliating. The facilitator should keep in mind that it is often difficult for members to give public feedback and this leads to individuals receiving little or no feedback on their behavior.

- On a wall, the facilitator should make a table, somewhat like that on the following page, with the team member's names to the left in a column, and column headings for each of the indicators.
- Pass out post-it-notes to the team members. Ask them to write their ratings on the adhesive side of the post-it-note. It will help if they write the indicator on the visible side, such as "Attendance." This way, when they are placed on the wall, the side with the indicator will be visible and the rating will not be visible.
- For each other team member, each participant will write their rating on five notes, one for each indicator. They will then place them on the wall in the appropriate column and row.

- When all the notes have been placed on the wall, ask each individual to gather up their notes, keeping track of which indicator they represent. Returning to their seat, they should then average their scores for each item.

4. **Reflection and Commitment:** Give the team fifteen or twenty minutes to read and average their scores. Ask them to consider sharing the following based on the feedback they have received:

- What is one thing you will do in the future to strengthen your commitment to the success of the team?
- What help would you like to receive from other team members in the future?

# Team Commitment Assessment

| Team Member | Indicators of Commitment | | | | |
|---|---|---|---|---|---|
| | | | | | |
| | | | | | |
| | | | | | |
| | | | | | |
| | | | | | |
| | | | | | |
| | | | | | |
| | | | | | |
| | | | | | |
| | | | | | |
| | | | | | |
| | | | | | |
| | | | | | |
| | Score each team member on each indicator on a 1 to 10 scale. 1 would indicate that the team member never demonstrates this behavior; 5 that they demonstrate this sometimes; and 10 that they demonstrate this to a very high degree. | | | | |

# Glossary

- **5S:** 5S is a common tool and component of a lean workplace. The Five S program focuses on having visual order, organization, cleanliness and standardization. The results you can expect from a Five S program are: improved profitability, efficiency, service and safety. The 5S's are Sort, Set in order, Shine, Standardize, and Sustain
- **5 Why's:** The 5 Why's is a simple problem-solving technique that helps you to get to the root of a problem quickly. Made popular in the 1970s by the Toyota Production System, the 5 Whys strategy involves looking at any problem and asking: "Why?" and "What caused this problem?"
- **7 Forms of Waste:** Waste is the use of any material or resource beyond what the customer requires and is willing to pay for. Shigeo Shingo identified "Seven" forms of waste (Plus one – The eighth waste, under-utilization of people) These 7 forms of waste are 1) Over production, 2) Inventory, 3) Motion, 4) Waiting, 5) Transportation, 6) Over-processing, 7) Scrap or rework.
- **A3:** An A3 is literally a size of paper (297 × 420 mm). However, it has become popular in lean management as a simple and structured form of problem-solving that can fit on or be displayed on one A3 sized paper.
- **A4:** An A4 is again a size of paper. However, it has become known for an even simpler problem-solving process than an A3. It is a one sheet PDCA cycle problem-solving tool. (see PDCA)
- **ABC Model:** This is a model for changing behavior, whether at work or in any setting. It stands for Antecedents, Behavior and Consequences. Doing an ABC analysis is a way of analyzing why someone may be behaving in a given way and what can be done to change that behavior.
- **Action Planning:** After deciding on a solution to a problem, a team should develop an action plan that clearly states what steps are going to be taken to implement a solution; who is going to do them; and, when are they going to be done by. Action plans are generally reviewed at each team meeting.
- **Affinity Diagram:** An affinity diagram is a component of brainstorming in which participants write ideas down on Post-it-Notes, then put them on a wall, and then silently organize them into like blocks of notes.
- **Antecedents:** A stimulus that precedes a behavior and acts as a stimulus or cue for that behavior to occur.
- **Balanced Scorecard:** A team or management scorecard that includes four types of measures: Financial, learning and development, customer satisfaction and process measures. This concept was developed and promoted in a book by Kaplan and Norton.
- **Behavior Analysis:** The application of behavioral psychology to behavior in a natural setting. Also referred to as *behavior management* or *performance management*.

# Glossary

- **Behavior Management:** A term used to describe the application of behavior analysis or behavior modification in the work place. It generally involves seeking to employ positive reinforcement to increase the strength and learning of desired behavior.
- **Behavioral psychology:** That school of psychology developed by B.F. Skinner and others that states that behavior is learned a function of the contingencies of reinforcement in the environment. Behavioral psychology is based on scientific or the experimental analysis of behavior in which antecedent stimuli and consequences to behavior are controlled and modified and the resulting changes in rate of behavior are monitored.
- **Brainstorming:** Brainstorming is one component of both problem-solving and group decision-making. It is a way to bring out the creativity of the group by focusing on generating ideas while not judging them. There are many methods of brainstorming but they all include the element of suspending judgment, allowing, even encouraging, wild and crazy ideas so that each idea may stimulate another.
- **Cause and Effect:** A cause and effect diagram is also known as a fishbone diagram because it looks something like the skeleton of a fish. At the backbone of the diagram is the definition of a problem. Then each of the major parts of the skeleton are labeled (and this is only one way of many) People, Process, Materials, Equipment, Information. Then you use this to brainstorm possible causes under each of these categories.
- **CEDAC:** Cause and Effect Diagrams with the Addition of Cards. This is simply a very large cause and effect diagram placed on a wall in a prominent place, such as a hallway where employees pass by, and there are two color cards, one for problems and the other for solutions. Employees are encouraged to add problem or solution cards as they think of them. This creates an on-going brainstorming process.
- **Command Decisions:** Command decisions are those made by one individual. This is generally considered most efficient when time is a priority and/or the one individual has superior expertise. Command decision is considered the traditional military model of decision-making and battlefield conditions are the environment where this is most appropriate.
- **Consensus Decisions:** Consensus decisions are those decisions that are owned by an entire group and the entire group agrees on a decision after giving everyone an opportunity to speak and be heard respectfully. Consensus decision-making assumes that the formal leader is willing to delegate the decision authority to the group. Consensus decisions are more time consuming but result in greater commitment from the group.
- **Consultative Decisions:** Consultative decisions are those in which one individual owns and controls the decision, but does not make it alone. Rather the individual consults with those who have knowledge, who care, or who must act to implement the decision.
- **Continuous Improvement:** Continuous improvement is one of the fundamental ideas of lean management. It is based on the simple idea that every process can always be improved in some increment. It is a process in which all employees engaged in the work are encouraged to participate in thinking about better ways to do things, conducting experiments, and agreeing on improved standard work.

- **Cycle Time:** A cycle time is the time from the beginning to the end of a work process. There are generally two types of cycle time: CT = The actual Cycle Time from beginning to end, and VCT=Value Adding Cycle Time. In other words, if you look at your daily work process, that may be eight hours, how much of that time is actually adding value to your customers? It is usually a fraction of the actual time. In lean terms, the remaining time is considered "waste."
- **Debate:** Debate is a form of conversation in which two or more parties have predetermined positions on a matter and are attempting to convince others that they are correct and the others are wrong. The participants are not willing to learn from each other or change their positions.
- **Dialogue:** Dialogue is the art of thinking together rather than thinking alone. It is often considered the opposite of debate, a conversation in which all parties are seeking to learn, to discover truth together.
- **DIMPABAC:** This is an acronym representing one problem-solving model. *Define* the problem to be solved; *Inquire* with all those who have facts regarding the problem to gain different understanding and insight; *Measure* actual performance on the problem; *Principles* should be defined that are important to understanding this problem and its solution; *Analyze* the data and causes of the problem; *Brainstorm* solutions to the problem; Agree to *Act* on a solution; *Control* and standardize the process and evaluate results.
- **Empathy:** Empathy is the capacity to recognize and, to some extent, share feelings (such as sadness or happiness) that are being experienced by another. Empathy is one of the effective listening skills that enables another person to express their thoughts and feelings.
- **Facilitation:** Facilitation is the skill or art of helping others participate in group problem-solving or decision-making. There are a set of skills that are components of effective facilitation and these include clarifying topics, active listening, conflict resolution, and helping a group reach and clarify a decision.
- **Feedback:** Feedback is information on performance that is "fed back" to the group or individual in control of that performance. Feedback is not necessarily positive or negative, but may simply be information on performance. Feedback is the most essential element of all systems of human performance.
- **Fishbone Diagrams:** See cause and effect diagrams.
- **Gemba:** Gemba is a Japanese word meaning "the real place where work gets done." It refers to the place where value is created in a work system. Being "on-the-spot" is another term meaning being where the work gets done. This is an important concept in lean management and it expresses the value of managers "going and seeing" what is really happening where the work is being done.
- **Gemba Walk:** The Gemba walk is simply that act of managers talking a walk around the work place and observing, learning, from those doing the work. In manufacturing it is recommended that plant managers take frequent Gemba walks to be in touch with the real work.

- **Kaizen:** Kaizen is the Japanese word for continuous improvement. It is one of the core philosophies and practices of lean management. Kaizen is intended to be practiced by all employees, at every level, engaged in every work process in the organization.
- **Kaizen Event:** A kaizen event is an intensified and short effort to make a major improvement in a process. It generally involves a cross-functional team of employees who work for a period, such as a week, studying a process to solve a problem and make a recommendation at the end of that period.
- **Leader Standard Work:** Leader standard work (LSW) is a process by which standard work, activities that are to be done daily, weekly or monthly, are defined by or for a manager. LSW involves the regular review of the completion and lessons learned from these activities by the manager at the next level above.
- **Lean Management:** Lean management is the set of management and work practices derived from the Toyota Production System (TPS). These include the elimination of waste, continuous improvement, and involvement of all employees in improvement activities. Lean and TPS are not a static set of practices, but are continually evolving as lessons are learned from application in different settings such as health care.
- **Healthcare Lean:** Healthcare Lean (LTM) is the merger of the lessons from lean management and those learned from the implementation of self-directed teams and the socio-technical system (STS) design of high performance work systems.
- **Magnet Healthcare:** A term used to describe high performing health care organizations that demonstrate both a superior environment for staff and superior health care outcomes. The first magnet hospitals were found to be places where nurses had autonomy and control over their practice settings; good relationships with their colleagues; adequate support services; enough staff to provide high quality care; time to discuss patient problems with their colleagues; the opportunity to participate in policy decisions; a powerful nursing leader; and an environment that recognized the value of their work. Hospitals with these characteristics had significantly lower staff turnover and attracted well-qualified and committed staff
- **PDCA Cycle:** The PDCA (Plan, Do, Check and Act) cycle of problem-solving is also known as the Schewhart Cycle after Walter Schewhart a pioneer in the quality field. During the quality movement it was adopted as a common problem-solving model at many companies. The PDCA cycle is best used for relatively simple problems, although you can place many different methods or steps within these four major steps.
- **PDSA:** This is essentially the same as the PDCA cycle of problem-solving: Plan, Do, Study, Act. This is the term used at ThedaCare.
- **Performance Analysis:** A model of problem-solving human behavior. It is based on the work of Robert Mager who suggested that we ask "Is the problem a can't do, or a won't do problem." In other words, does the individual have the required skill or knowledge, or is it a motivation problem.
- **Performance Management:** This term has two different usages. One is another term to describe behavior management or applied behavior analysis in the work setting. A second describes the process of individual performance appraisal and the development of periodic personal improvement plans, generally negotiated between an employee and his or her manager.

- **Positive Reinforcement:** In behavioral psychology or applied behavior analysis positive reinforcement is the presentation of a stimulus following a behavior that results in a subsequent increase in the rate of that behavior.
- **Population Based Holistic Care:** Population-based health care is based on health promotion and disease prevention. Population based nursing care is holistic in nature, with nurses and their clients developing care plans that address the client's needs from a variety of perspectives, including socio-economic, cultural, racial, religious, gender, abilities, and sexual affiliation. The application of the nursing process greatly assists the nurse in providing holistic care on the community, health system, and population levels
- **Process:** A process is a set of related activities that together produce a desired outcome. All processes have both input and output. The process transforms input to a value adding output. Teams are generally organized around, and take responsibility for, a defined process.
- **Process Management Teams:** A team that owns and takes responsibility for the continuous improvement of a defined process.
- **Process Maps:** A visual display of a process that illustrates each step in a process and their chronological relationship to one another. It describes the flow of the process. Process mapping allows a team to define cycle times, identify waste and variances in the process.
- **Process Measures:** Measures of process performance. These measures may be derived from within the process or at the end of a process. For example, if you are cooking a turkey dinner (a process) you may take a measure of the temperature of the meat while it is cooking (a measure within the process), and you may measure the satisfaction of the guests when they are finished eating the turkey (end of process measure).
- **Reflective Listening:** Also known as rephrasing or active listening. Reflective listening is somewhat like holding up a mirror, a reflection, of what you think another person meant to say. For example, "In other words I hear you saying that you enjoy doing that job." This gives the other person the opportunity to say "Well, no, that isn't really what I meant." Or, "Yes, that's right." The other person may clarify and will feel that he or she has genuinely been heard.
- **Scorecards**: A score card is an agreed upon set of metrics that reflect the performance of a team. See "balanced scorecard." Scorecards are best visually displayed and reviewed regularly.
- **Self-Directed Teams:** Also known as autonomous or semi-autonomous teams, self-directed teams take responsibility for managing a process and continuously improving that process. While no team is ultimately "self-managed", the process of self-directed teams seeks to maximize the responsibility and maturity of a team to manage performance. Healthcare Lean is a self-directed team process.
- **Shaping Behavior:** Shaping is a concept of behavior analysis. Shaping is the successive reinforcement of approximations to a terminal goal set of responses or skill. In other words, when your child is first learning to play the piano, you praise (reinforce) small improvements and effort, rather than waiting for the ultimate performance.

# Glossary

- **SIPOC:** An acronym that stands for Supplier, Input, Process, Output and Customer. This describes the process flow through a team or organization and is a fundamental tool of lean and process improvement.
- **Six Sigma:** An improvement process first developed at Motorola and an extension of the total quality movement. It relies heavily on statistical methods and has been used predominantly in manufacturing. A six sigma process is one in which 99.99966% of the products manufactured are statistically expected to be free of defects (3.4 defects per million).
- **SMED:** Single Minute Exchange of Dies. This is a component of lean manufacturing and was one of the early efforts to eliminate waste from the a core work process in automotive or other metal manufacturing.
- **Socio-Technical Systems (STS):** A process developed, originally at the Tavistock Institute in Great Britain by Fred Emery and Eric Trist to improve both the productivity of the work system while at the same time improving the social system. The theory of STS is that there is one whole-system, comprised of both social and technical components that are interdependent. Failing to change one element sub-optimizes any change effort.
- **Special Cause:** Dr. W. Edwards Deming described the statistical evidence of a process *in control* in which all of the causes of variation are within three standard deviations of the mean. The cause of variation is common to the system and can only be improved by changing the system itself.
- **Standard Work:** A set of activities that have been agreed to be the best way to perform any work activity. Standard work is the best way we know now to perform a work process. However, continuous improvement will find better ways that will then become standard work.
- **Statistical Variation:** A set of statistical recording of performance that define a mean of that set and the variations around that mean.
- **Subject Matter Experts**: (SME's) May be permanent or temporary members of a team who are assigned or recognized to possess expertise in some function or knowledge area that contributes to the performance of the team.
- **Team Charter:** A document that defines a team's purpose, its processes, its customers and the principles by which it will function.
- **TQM:** Total Quality Management, a set of practices that involves a focus on the requirements of customers (or clients), the use of statistical measures of quality performance, teams improving quality and customer service at every level of the organization.
- **Value Stream Mapping:** Mapping the work flow, or processes, in a manner that identifies the points where value is added and non-value adding activities, or waste.
- **Variances or Variation:** A variance may be described statistically, or it may simply be something that deviates or varies from how things should be done in order to meet customer or client requirements. A variance is a problem.
- **Waste:** Any activity that does not directly add value to the customer or client.

- **Whole System Architecture:** A variation of socio-technical systems design in which all elements of an organization's systems are examined together to assess how they enhance or reduce the quality of product or service to customers or clients.

# INDEX

| | |
|---|---|
| A3 | 126 |
| A4 | 126 |
| A-B-C" Model | 146 |
| Action Planning | 139 |
| Action Plans | 210 |
| Action-Learning | 21 |
| Adult learning | 21 |
| Affinity diagram | 134 |
| Agenda | 208 |
| American Hospitals Study | 11 |
| Analysis of Variances | 181 |
| Antecedents | 146 |
| Attitudes of Process Improvement | 168 |
| Balanced scorecard | 112, 113 |
| Behavior analysis | 146 |
| Behavioral psychology | 146 |
| Berry, Leanard L | 7 |
| Blake and Mouton's Managerial Grid | 40 |
| Bodek, Norman | 196 |
| Brainstorming | 131 |
| Cause-and-effect | 132 |
| CEDAC | 132 |
| Coach | 68 |
| Command decisions | 81 |
| Common cause | 182 |
| Consensus | 135 |
| Consensus decisions | 82 |
| Consultative decisions | 82 |
| Conversation | 247 |
| Csikszentmihalyi, Mihaly | 164 |
| Cycle time | 171 |
| Cycle time analysis | 172 |
| Debate | 247 |
| Deming | 107 |
| Deming, W. Edwards | 41, 42, 120 |
| Deming. Dr. | 182 |
| Design team | 166, 167 |
| Dialogue | 245 |
| Dialogue | 247 |
| DIMPABAC | 126 |
| Discussion | 247 |
| DIVERSITY | 262, 269 |
| Eastman Chemicals | 106 |
| Effective listening skills | 226 |
| Empathy | 230, 261 |
| Enron | 252 |
| Facilitating | 214 |
| Facilitation | 65 |
| Facilitator | 63, 214 |
| Family farm | 37 |
| Feedback | 103 |
| Feedback, Giving and Receiving | 239 |
| Feedback, Guidelines for Giving | 240 |
| Feedback, Guidelines for Receiving | 240 |
| Fishbone\ | 132 |
| Flow | 164 |
| Frederick Taylor | 39 |
| Gemba | 128 |
| Gemba Walk | 128 |
| Harvey, Jerry | 238 |
| Healthcare provider | 166 |
| Healthgrades | 11 |
| Herzberg | 40 |
| Hierarchy of purpose | 47 |
| Honda | 8 |
| HONEST STRAIGHT-TALK | 260 |
| Institute of Medicine | 11 |
| Kaplan, Robert S | 112 |
| Kingsport, Tennessee | 106 |
| Knowles, Malcom | 21 |
| Leader standard work | 87 |
| Leadership Teams | 61 |
| Lean | 8 |
| Lean management | 20 |
| Lean Management | 32 |
| Lean Team Management | 59 |
| Lewin, Kurt | 39 |
| Mager, Robert F | 160 |
| Magnet healthcare concept | 9 |
| Maslow, Abraham | 40 |
| Mayo Clinic | 7, 34 |
| Mcgregor | 40 |

Page 281

| | |
|---|---|
| Meyer, M. Scott | 40 |
| MIT Lean Study | 42 |
| Motivation | 144 |
| Norton, David P | 112 |
| Ohno, Taichii | 42, 195 |
| Open-Ended Questions | 226 |
| Pareto Analysis | 135 |
| PDCA | 123, 126, 277 |
| PDCA cycle | 22, 123, 277 |
| PDSA | 7 |
| Performance analysis | 160 |
| Pipe, Peter | 160 |
| Population based holistic care | 10 |
| Population-based health care | 10 |
| Positive reinforcement | 154 |
| Process Management Teams | 59 |
| Processes | 165 |
| Processes Maps | 168 |
| Project Improvement Teams | 62 |
| Punishment | 154 |
| Purpose Diagram | 267 |
| Purpose, | 47 |
| Quality Circles | 40 |
| Recognition | 210 |
| Reflecting | 216 |
| Reflective listening | 232 |
| Rephrasing | 232 |
| Rogers, Carl | 39 |
| Scorecard | 213 |
| Self-managing teams | 60 |
| Sergeant Friday | 122 |
| Shaping | 157 |
| Shaping behavior | 157 |
| Shewhart | 41 |
| Shewhart, W.A | 41 |
| Shingo, Shigeo | 42, 195 |
| SIPOC | 94, 103 |
| Situational motivations | 146 |
| SMED (Single Minute Exchange of Dies) | 42 |
| Social motivations | 145 |
| Social psychology | 39 |
| Socio-technical systems (STS) design | 41 |
| Sonnenfeld, Jeffrey A. | 252 |
| Spear, Steven J. | 25 |
| Special cause | 182 |
| Spiritual capital | 47 |
| Spiritual level of motivation | 144 |
| Straight-Talk Exercises | 266 |
| STS | 42 |
| Subject Matter Experts | 67 |
| Tavistock Institute | 41 |
| Team Charter | 46 |
| Team Commitment | 270 |
| Team Development | 73 |
| TEAM DYNAMICS ASSESSMENT | 260 |
| Team Feedback Exercise | 242 |
| Team Scorecard | 105 |
| Teams | 59 |
| Teamwork | 7 |
| The Honda Way | 32 |
| Thedacare | 7, 34 |
| Theory X and Theory Y | 40 |
| To Err Is Human | 11 |
| Total Quality Management | 123 |
| Toussaint, John, | 8 |
| Toyota | 8, 13, 21, 42, 43, 194 |
| Toyota Production System | 11, 13, 32 |
| Toyota's Georgetown, KY plant | 24 |
| TQM | 42, 120 |
| Training Within Industry (TWI) | 21 |
| Trist, E., | 41 |
| TRUST | 260 |
| Trust Building | 265 |
| Tuckman, Bruce | 74 |
| UNITY OF PURPOSE | 261 |
| Value adding time | 172 |
| Value stream | 163 |
| Value stream mapping | 171 |
| Variances | 178 |
| Variation | 182 |
| Variation within Human Performance | 189 |
| VON Canada | 18, 34 |
| Waste | 171, 194, 195 |
| Whole-System Architecture | 14, 16, 18, 42 |
| Womack, James P | 8, 42 |
| Work Process Maps | 170 |

# About the Author

For the past thirty-five years Lawrence M. Miller has worked to improve the performance of organizations and the skills of their leaders. His expertise is derived from hands on experience creating change in the culture of hundreds of organizations.

He began his work in North Carolina prisons after recognizing that the system in the organization had exactly the opposite of its intended effect – increasing, rather than decreasing, dysfunctional behavior. For four years he worked to redesign the prison system by establishing the first free-economy behind prison walls, where each inmate had to pay rent, maintain a checking account, and pay for everything he desired. This was one of the first applications of *behavior analysis* in the correctional setting.

He has been consulting, writing and speaking about business organization and culture since 1973. He and his firm were one of the early proponents of team-based management and worked with many clients from the senior executive team to include every level and every employee in the organization. Mr. Miller personally coaches the senior management team of many of his clients.

Among his consulting clients have been Allina Health Systems, VON Canada, 3M, Corning, Shell Oil Company, Amoco and Texaco, Shell Chemicals, Air Canada, Eastman Chemicals, Xerox, Harris Corporation, McDonald's and Chick-fil-A, Merck and Upjohn Pharmaceuticals, United Technologies, American Express, and Metropolitan Life.

His website is www.LMMiller.com and His blog is www.ManagementMeditations.com. His email is LMMiller@lmmiller.com.

## Previous Publications

- *Behavior Management: The New Science of Managing People at Work,* John Wiley & Sons, Inc., 1978.
- *American Spirit: Visions of a New Corporate Culture;* William Morrow & Company, Inc., 1984.
- *Barbarians to Bureaucrats: Corporate Life Cycle Strategies;* Clarkson Potter (Crown Books), 1989.
- *From Management to Leadership;* Productivity Press, 1995.
- *Team Management: Creating Systems and Skills for a Team Based Organization;* Miller Howard Consulting Group, (with Jennifer Howard), 1994.
- *Change Management: Creating the Dynamic Organization through Whole System Architecture,* Miller Howard Consulting Group, 1997.
- *Spiritual Enterprise: Building Your Business in the Spirit of Service;* George Ronald Publishers, 2007.
- *Lean Team, Management: How to Build Lean Organizations & High Performing Teams – The Process and the Skills.* L.M. Miller Consulting, 2009.
- *Lean Culture – The Leader's Guide;* L. M. Miller Consulting, 2011

# Services

## Surveys

Lean Culture Survey: Survey your employees to determine your degree of conformance to the ten cultural principles of lean culture. This survey can be the basis for planning improvement and engaging employees.

Lean Leadership Survey: Do your leaders support lean culture through their own behavior, modeling the behavior that supports lean culture? This confidential survey is intended to provide private and personal feedback to leaders and serves as a foundation for leadership coaching.

## Consulting

Mr. Miller works with clients on long term culture change and lean implementation. He assists with both more revolutionary change, Whole-System Architecture, and with continuous improvement. He works with internal coaches or change agents to prepare and assist them as they coach teams throughout the organization. He also directly coaches the senior leadership teams of his clients.

## Executive Coaching

Senior managers often can benefit most from one-on-one private coaching and feedback. Mr. Miller has coached senior executives at major corporations such as Honeywell, American Express, Shell and others. This coaching is most often a component of a larger effort to improve the culture of the organization.

## Training and Training Materials

Mr. Miller provides training to internal coaches and senior managers in the process of *Healthcare Lean* and Lean Culture. His Healthcare Lean workbook is accompanied by a complete set of PowerPoint presentation and teaching notes.

## Speaking Engagements

Mr. Miller has been a popular speaker at hundreds of company and association conferences. He speaks both on lean culture and corporate life-cycles and leadership based on his Barbarians to Bureaucrats book. He also leads leadership workshops to initiate lean culture change.

CPSIA information can be obtained at www.ICGtesting.com
Printed in the USA
BVOW051311200812

298162BV00001B/5/P

9 780578 107783